Grace and Assurance

THE MESSAGE OF THE CANONS OF DORDT

MARTYN McGEOWN

Second printing 2019

Printed in the United States of America

Scripture cited is taken from the King James (Authorized) Version

Reformed Free Publishing Association
1894 Georgetown Center Drive
Jenison, Michigan 49428
616-457-5970
www.rfpa.org
mail@rfpa.org

Cover design by Christopher Tobias/tobiasdesign.com
Interior design by Katherine Lloyd/theDESKonline.com

ISBN: 978-1-944555-39-9 (hardcover)
ISBN: 978-1-944555-40-5 (ebook)
LCCN: 2018948762

To the saints of the Limerick Reformed Fellowship,
Limerick, Ireland, who first partook of the fruit of my
study of the Canons and whose zeal for the truth makes my
ministry among them a joy and a privilege.

Contents

Preface

In 1980 the Reformed Free Publishing Association published a commentary on the Canons of Dordt entitled *The Voice of Our Fathers* by Homer C. Hoeksema. This book, an invaluable exposition of the Canons, was revised and republished in 2013. Given that the Reformed Free Publishing Association already has a commentary on the Canons, the question might be asked, "Why a second commentary on the same subject?"

First, the timing is appropriate. Four hundred years ago (1618) the great Synod of Dordt met to counter the Arminian error that was threatening the peace and welfare of the Reformed churches in the Netherlands. Therefore, it is fitting, if not imperative, for the Reformed churches that subscribe to the Canons of Dordt to mark this important anniversary with speeches, conferences, and even a book.

Second, this new commentary is not intended to replace *The Voice of Our Fathers,* which is unquestionably a classic, especially in Protestant Reformed circles. This commentary is designed to be shorter and therefore more accessible to younger readers, and hopefully more attractive to those who find the size of Hoeksema's commentary to be somewhat daunting. Indeed, I hope that non-Reformed people will read the book, so that they can see that much of what they have heard about the Reformed faith is based on caricature not the truth. In fact, unbelievers ought to read the book because they will find in it a clear explanation of the gospel and a clear call to believe in Jesus Christ, the only savior of sinners. Therefore, I aimed for simplicity and clarity while avoiding a superficial treatment of the subject.

Third, my approach to the Canons is not primarily that of a

scholar, but of a pastor. The basis of the book is a class that I taught to the Limerick Reformed Fellowship between January and September 2013. The reader will therefore find few references to the original Latin text of the Canons or extensive discussions on translation issues, except where this is absolutely necessary to clarify the meaning. Instead, the aim of the commentary is to explain from the text of the Canons the wonderful gospel of God's grace and the assurance, peace, and comfort that come to the believer through faith in that gospel. That, too, explains the title: *Grace and Assurance*. The theology of the Synod of Dordt defends the grace of God and promotes the personal assurance of believers, so that they enjoy assurance of their own eternal and unchangeable election, as well as assurance of their own personal perseverance in salvation by the grace of God. The theology of doubt is not the theology of the Canons—and therefore not the theology of this book.

Perhaps the reading of this shorter volume will whet your appetite so that you will pick up and read other books on the same subject, including Hoeksema's masterful work *The Voice of Our Fathers*. May God bless the author and reader with a greater appreciation of his grace and a deeper assurance of the same.

A Historical Introduction to the Synod of Dordt

Four hundred years ago in 1618, the Synod of Dordt, a synod of Reformed theologians, began to meet in the Dutch city of Dordrecht. The fruit of that great synod, which concluded in 1619, is the Reformed creed or confession, the Canons of Dordt.

The history behind the great Synod of Dordt begins with a Dutch orphan called Jakob Hermanszoon (James Arminius) (1560–1609). Having been orphaned in his childhood, Arminius was given a soundly Reformed education in Leiden, the Netherlands, and in Geneva, Switzerland, where he studied under John Calvin's successor, Theodore Beza (1519–1605). In 1588 Arminius was ordained as a pastor in Amsterdam, where Pieter (Peter) Plancius (1552–1622) was also a pastor. In the 1590s when Arminius began a series of sermons on Romans, his theology began to alarm Plancius, the consistory in Amsterdam, and many of the members of the congregation. For example, Arminius taught contrary to Romans 5–6 that Adam would have died even without sin. Moreover, he taught that in Romans 7:19, where Paul wrote, "For the good that I would I do not: but the evil which I would not, that I do," the apostle is describing an *unregenerate* person. By teaching such doctrines Arminius implied—and even taught—that the unregenerate person has the will to do good and has a real, spiritual hatred of evil. Such a teaching contradicts the scriptures and the

James Arminius

creeds, which teach that the unregenerate sinner *cannot* desire to do good but is totally depraved. In his sermons on Romans 9, where the apostle clearly teaches sovereign predestination, Arminius undermined the teaching of unconditional predestination, proposing instead conditional predestination.

Arminius was given the task of refuting the writings of a Dutch heretic called Dirck Volckertszoon Coornhert (1522–90), who had attacked predestination. However, as Arminius studied the writings he found himself in agreement with Coornhert. Nevertheless, instead of admitting that he disagreed with the Reformed creeds on predestination, Arminius stalled by repeatedly delaying his promised refutation of Coornhert, a task that Arminius never accomplished.

Arminius' behavior became increasingly troublesome for the orthodox consistory and membership in Amsterdam, as well as for his Reformed colleague Plancius. Nevertheless, Arminius was evasive—he refused to be frank about his true beliefs. In addition, Arminius had friends in high places, which made censuring him difficult. One of his close friends, who had been a fellow student in Geneva, was Jan Uytenbogaert (1557–1644), shared the heterodox convictions of Arminius. Uytenbogaert was the chaplain of Johan van Oldenbarneveld (1547–1619), who was the governor in the Netherlands. During that time in the Netherlands, the civil government wielded an inordinate amount of power over the church. For example, the state even interfered with discipline and funded the churches, paying for the buildings and the salaries of pastors. Therefore, although the church in Amsterdam greatly desired an official examination of Arminius' doctrine—and his suspension and deposition from office, if he should be condemned for his false

Jan Uytenbogaert

teachings—political conditions made it impossible to accomplish that. Arminius and his followers enjoyed the protection of the state.

The situation worsened further when in 1602 the theological professor at Leiden University, Franciscus Junius (1545–1602), died, leaving the chair of theology open. To the horror of the consistory of Amsterdam, but with the urgent recommendation of his good friend, Uytenbogaert, and with the approval of the civil magistrate, Arminius was appointed to the theological chair. If Arminius could disturb the sheep in the Amsterdam congregation, how much more havoc could he not cause in the theological school, where he would train future pastors for the Reformed churches in the Netherlands? (Unfortunately, the meddling of the state allowed such a wolf access to the theological students, for the appointment of professors to theological chairs was not under the authority of the church alone but required governmental approval.) The other professor of theology in Leiden was Franciscus Gomarus (1563–1641), a staunchly Reformed theologian who resisted Arminius' appointment to the faculty. Gomarus only reluctantly agreed to the appointment after a meeting with Arminius in which Arminius claimed to be orthodox and promised to be faithful to the Reformed confessions.

Franciscus Gomarus

Arminius lied!

Soon Arminius began to undermine the Reformed faith in the theological school. He had to be careful, however, because Gomarus did not trust him and kept a careful eye on him. Arminius gathered a following among the students, teaching them one form of doctrine privately and in secret, while appearing orthodox in his public lectures. Gomarus and others tried multiple times to expose him, but Arminius responded with lies, equivocation, or delaying tactics. When put under pressure, Arminius would appeal to his friends,

Johan van Oldenbarneveld and Jan Uytenbogaert, in the Dutch government. Arminius' heresy spread through the churches like leaven. As his views spread, those who loved the Reformed faith began to ask for a national synod to examine the teachings of Arminius, but the government repeatedly refused to permit the convening of such a synod.

Arminius was like many heretics: sophisticated, likeable, friendly, and debonair. He was a brilliant scholar and a gifted preacher, but he was dishonest and manipulative. Gomarus, his opponent in the theological school, was the opposite: blunt, bad tempered, and unsociable, but a fierce defender of the truth.

Suddenly, Arminius died of tuberculosis on October 19, 1609, but his heresy did not die with him. In fact, after Arminius' death his followers, confident of the state's protection and even approval, became more outspoken in their views. On January 14, 1610, some forty-six Arminian preachers presented their Remonstrance in The Hague in the Netherlands. The Remonstrance, written by Jan Uytenbogaert, outlined five points of doctrine that the Arminian preachers, known as Remonstrants, wished to protest against the Reformed faith. It was in response to those five points of the Remonstrance that the great Synod of Dordt was assembled and against which the synod formulated five points, which have become known as the five points of Calvinism.

The five points of the Remonstrance are, briefly, as follows: conditional election; universal atonement; partial depravity; resistible grace; and conditional perseverance. I will examine these ideas in considerable detail as I explain the articles of the Canons of Dordt.

Theologians in the Netherlands continued to debate the doctrines presented in the Remonstrance for some time. What was needed—what was *urgently* needed—was a national synod. At such a synod the Arminian doctrine could be thoroughly examined. At such a synod doctrinal controversy could be settled from the word of God. Nevertheless, the Arminians, whose numbers and political influence were growing, resisted the convening of a synod. The only kind of synod to which the Arminians would consent was a synod at which the creeds (the Heidelberg Catechism and the Belgic Confession) would be revised and at which they, the Arminians, would be fellow-delegates, not defendants whose theological views would be examined. Enjoying growing political influence, the Arminians succeeded in shielding their party from ecclesiastical discipline, and even in orchestrating the suspension and deposition from office of orthodox and Reformed pastors. Some believers began to meet separately to hear the pure preaching of God's word in what were called the *doleerende Kerken* or mourning churches. Those in attendance at such unauthorized worship services were subject to persecution.

With the death of Arminius in 1610, the theological chair in Leiden again became vacant. The Arminians pushed for the appointment of Conrad Vorstius (1569–1622) as Arminius' replacement. In that the Arminians overplayed their hand, for Vorstius was a worse heretic than Arminius had been—Vorstius was a Socinian. Socinianism denies fundamental doctrines of Christianity such as the Trinity, the substitutionary atonement of Christ, and justification by faith alone. In disgust Gomarus resigned from the theological faculty in 1611. The appointment of Vorstius also caused international unrest, for King James I of England protested his appointment, so that Vorstius was dismissed in 1612.

Calls for a national synod increased, but Johan van Oldenbarneveld and Jan Uytenbogaert still refused to authorize such a gathering of the church. With a change in direction in the blowing of the political winds in the Netherlands, the situation in the church suddenly took a turn for the better when in 1617 Prince Mauritz (Maurice) of Orange (1567–1625) openly sided with the *doleerende Kerken* against the Arminians. From 1618 Maurice ruled the Netherlands, while his rival, Johan van Oldenbarneveld, was arrested, imprisoned, tried, and finally beheaded on May 13, 1619, supposedly for treason. Whether Van Oldenbarneveld was guilty or was fairly tried or not is hard to determine, but God used the political situation for the welfare of his church. Finally, a national synod could be called to examine the Arminian question and bring peace to the church.

The great Synod of Dordt (1618–19) saw the gathering together of delegates from the Netherlands and from Reformed churches throughout Europe, making it a truly international synod. Present at the synod were thirty-eight ministers, twenty-one elders and five professors (from the Dutch churches), eighteen representatives of the state, and twenty-eight foreign delegates from the Palatinate, Hesse, Nassau, Emden, Bremen, Switzerland, and Great Britain. The French Reformed Church appointed delegates, but the king of France refused to let them attend the synod, so the French delegates submitted their opinions to the synod in writing. The Brandenburg delegates declined to come because of the opposition of the Lutherans.

Johannes Bogerman

Simon Episcopius

The opening of the synod took place on November 13, 1618, with Johannes Bogerman (1576–1637) appointed as the president. On December 6, 1618, the Arminian party appeared at synod, represented by their leader, Simon Episcopius (1583–1643). Immediately, the Arminians attempted to disrupt the synod, refusing to recognize its authority, attempting to delay its proceedings, engaging in procedural wrangling, and seeking to curry favor with the foreign delegates, who, of course, were not as familiar with the duplicity of the Arminians as the Dutch were. The Arminians wanted the synod to recognize them as delegates instead of defendants in a theological trial. The Arminians were required to explain and defend their views from the scriptures, something they refused to do. Episcopius, for example, in his speech before the synod on December 7, 1618, strongly condemned the Reformed teaching of predestination, seeking to prejudice the minds of the delegates, especially the foreign delegates, against reprobation in particular.

After enduring months of wrangling by the Arminians, the president, Bogerman, exasperated by the Arminians' behavior, rose to his feet, and dismissed the Arminians with a fiery speech.

> The foreign delegates are now of the opinion that you are unworthy to appear before the Synod. You have refused to acknowledge her as your lawful judge and have maintained that she is your counter-party; you have done everything according to your own whim; you have despised the decisions of the Synod and of the Political Commissioners; you have refused to answer; you have unjustly interpreted the indictments. The Synod has treated you mildly; but you have—as one of the foreign delegates expressed it—"begun and ended with lies." With that eulogy we shall let you go. God shall preserve His Word and shall bless the Synod. In order that she be no longer obstructed, you are sent away![1]

"Thereupon the undeniably wrathful president thundered: ...'You are dismissed, get out!'"[2]

With the departure of the Arminians, the synod could begin its work. Its procedure was simple. First, the delegates studied the writings of the Arminians, including the Opinions of the Arminians that they had submitted to the synod. Then, various articles were written

---

1 Homer Hoeksema, *The Voice of Our Fathers: An Exposition of the Canons of Dordrecht* (Grandville, MI: Reformed Free Publishing Association, 1980), 27.

2 Ibid.

in response to the Arminians, these being crafted in committees and then openly debated on the floor of synod. Finally, the wording of the articles was finalized and approved. The result was the Canons of Dordt, which consist of fifty-nine positive articles setting forth the truth from the word of God, alongside thirty-three negative articles, or errors and rejections, arranged under five heads of doctrine.

The five heads of doctrine are a direct response to the five points of the Remonstrance of 1610. Against conditional election the synod set forth unconditional election and reprobation; against universal atonement the synod expounded the truth of limited, effectual, or particular atonement or redemption; against partial depravity and the heresy of free will the synod defended the truth of total depravity; against resistible grace the synod taught irresistible grace; and against conditional perseverance of the saints the synod insisted on the truth of unconditional perseverance of the saints.

The synod completed its examination of Arminianism when the Canons were officially adopted and signed on April 23, 1619. On May 29, 1619, after the synod dealt with other ecclesiastical issues of interest to the Dutch churches, the great Synod of Dordt came to a close, having defended the Reformed faith to the glory of God and the comfort of pious souls.

I thank God for preserving the truth of the gospel through the work of the Synod of Dordt. In this book, I will explain the individual articles of the Canons of Dordt.

The Importance of Creeds

THE IDEA OF CREEDS

Before beginning an exposition of the Canons of Dordt, I will examine the matter of creeds in general, for the Canons of Dordt, like the Heidelberg Catechism and the Belgic Confession that preceded them, are a *creed* or a *confession*. Why do churches, especially Reformed churches, adopt creeds, and why would anyone want to study a creed such as the Canons of Dordt? In this introductory essay, I will explore some of these questions to prove to the reader the value of the creeds and of the Canons of Dordt in particular.

I will begin with some definitions. The word *creed* comes from the Latin word *credo,* which means I believe. Therefore, a creed is a statement of faith. For example, one of the earliest Christian creeds, the Apostles' Creed, begins with these words: "*I believe* in God the Father, Almighty, Maker of heaven and earth."[1] The Belgic Confession begins this way: "*We all believe with the heart,* and confess with the mouth, that there is one only simple and spiritual Being, which we call God."[2] Since every Christian believes, every Christian is creedal, and if a Christian is creedal, he must speak what he believes: "I believed, therefore have I spoken" (Ps. 116:10).

A creed answers the questions: *What* exactly do you believe? What do you believe about the many important doctrines revealed in

1 Apostles' Creed, in *The Confessions and the Church Order of the Protestant Reformed Churches* (Grandville, MI: Protestant Reformed Churches in America, 2005), 9 (emphasis added).

2 Belgic Confession 1, in ibid., 23 (emphasis added).

scripture? A creed explains the details of a person's faith. Thus a creed is a kind of identifying mark, a banner, or a flag that declares something about the one carrying it and about the church displaying it. But a creed is more than that, for it is not merely a personal statement of faith; it is also an official, ecclesiastical statement of faith. Therefore, a creed is committed to writing so that others can read and study it. Moreover, a creed is the fruit of the deliberation of the church, for an individual does not write a creed by himself in isolation from other believers, but believers study the word of God together and record it in a formal statement of faith, which, when the church officially adopts it, becomes a creed. Such was the Nicene Creed on the deity of Christ adopted by the Council of Nicea (AD 325/381); such was the Creed of Chalcedon on the two natures in the one person of Christ adopted by the Council of Chalcedon (AD 451); and such are the Canons of Dordt adopted by the Synod of Dordt (1618–19).

A confession is like a creed. If the Latin word *credo* means I believe, the word *confession* comes from a Latin word that means to say with or to speak with, while the Greek word *homologeoo*, translated as confess, means I say the same thing.

To confess means, first, to say the same thing as, or to say with, God. For example, when a believer confesses his sins, he says the same thing as God with respect to his sins. When God declares, "You are a sinner," the confessing believer does not retort, "No, I am not a sinner," but he says, "Yes, Lord, I agree with your assessment: I *am* a sinner. Forgive me in the blood of Christ." This principle is then applied to every other truth of the Bible, for to confess is to say the same thing as God, or to say with God, on any subject. God says in his word, "In the beginning, God created the heaven and the earth" (Gen. 1:1). Therefore, the confessing Christian says, "I believe that God is the creator." God says in his word, "The Word was made flesh" (John 1:14). Thus the confessing Christian says, "I believe in the incarnation of Christ." God says in his word, "Christ died for our sins according to the scriptures" (1 Cor. 15:3), to which the confessing Christian responds, "I believe in the substitutionary atonement of Christ." A confession, therefore, could be understood as a kind of echo—God speaks, and believers echo what God has said, even employing their own words and adopting their own theological terminology, confessing the truth in opposition to the world and the false church that refuse to confess the truth.

Second, a confession is corporate, for in making a confession all those who believe the confession say the same thing together. Remember the idea of a banner or a flag: you might wave a flag alone, but it is much more meaningful and effective when you wave it with your fellow citizens, perhaps on a public holiday, for example. The citizens of a country *together* hold aloft the flag; the soldiers of an army march *together* under a banner; Christians *together* hold up the truth as their confession in the world; the members of the church *together* constitute the pillar and ground of the truth (1 Tim. 3:15). "Who is she that looketh forth as the morning, fair as the moon, clear as the sun, and terrible as an army with banners" (Song of Sol. 6:10)? When a church adopts a confession, such as the Heidelberg Catechism, the Belgic Confession, or the Canons of Dordt, she says, "We say this about God, Christ, salvation, and we confess this truth *with* God and *with* other saints, and *with* other churches." We are not alone in our confession. We share the Nicene Creed with others; we share the Creed of Chalcedon with others; and we share the Heidelberg Catechism, the Belgic Confession, and the Canons of Dordt with others. Such a shared confession is part of what it means to enjoy the communion of the saints. Thus a creed or confession has a unifying effect—it is not for nothing that the Reformed creeds (the Heidelberg Catechism, the Belgic Confession, and the Canons of Dordt) are called the three forms of unity!

Third, there is a historical aspect to the confessions, for in adopting a confession believers are confessing, "We say the same thing as" or "we say with" saints and churches *of the past*. We do not ignore the work of the Spirit of Christ in his church: for some two thousand years he has been leading the church into all truth. Wisdom, therefore, does not begin and end with us or in our generations. It would be foolish and terribly prideful to say, "I will ignore what the church of the past has discovered from the word of God. I will ignore her struggles and I will disregard her battles. With my Bible alone, I will begin from scratch, and I will reinvent the wheel." That is what non-creedal Christians do when they reject creeds and confessions.

OBJECTIONS TO CREEDS

The objection of many to creeds is the sufficiency of the Bible—is the Bible not enough to define doctrine and to define what a Christian or a church believes? Of course, the Bible is sufficient, and those who compiled and adopted the Reformed creeds believed in the sufficiency of scripture (Belgic Confession 3–7). The creeds are never a replacement for scripture, nor are they above the scriptures, nor are they even of equal authority with the Bible. The Bible alone is the word of God—the supreme judge of all the writings of men, including the judge of creeds and confessions, is the Bible, which alone is the word of God. We believe the creeds *because* they are faithful summaries of the teaching of the Bible.

Nevertheless, those who are anti-creedal and who cry (often sincerely), "No creed, but Christ!" have missed something. The Bible itself requires the writing of creeds, for it is written in such a way as to compel the church to compose creedal statements. The word of God does not come to us in the form of a theological dictionary, or a textbook of systematic theology, or dogmatics, with a glossary and indices. Instead, we might use the illustration of a seed—everything necessary to be believed is contained in the holy scriptures, but the truth must be developed, arranged, organized, and systematized. As we dig into the scriptures, we discover the riches of the truth of God, which we must place in opposition to the lies that the devil ceaselessly attempts to introduce into the church. As the church has dug into the scriptures, she has developed creedal statements in order to define what the scriptures teach.

When Jesus promised the Holy Spirit in John 16:13, "Howbeit when he, the Spirit of truth is come, he will guide you into all truth," he taught the disciples to expect such a development of the truth. This promise of "all truth" is not a promise of omniscience—the Spirit will not cause us to know everything, not even everything religious and theological, and not even everything in the Bible, for the Bible is inexhaustibly rich. You might study the Bible for a lifetime, and you will not understand everything in it. The church has reflected on the Bible for thousands of years, but she has not mined all its riches. The promise of "all truth" is not a promise of infallibility—the Bible is infallible, but the church, the vain pretensions of the popes notwithstanding, is not infallible. The church has been led into all truth stumbling, struggling, and making numerous mistakes along the way, the result of which has been greater clarity in her understanding of the truth. The promise of "all truth" is not even a promise of all truth *at once*—the church was given the truth gradually, as the canon of scripture, first the Old Testament, and then the New Testament, was committed to her. Over two millennia the church has gradually come to see the many rich implications of the truth given to her. This process of development has been long, slow, and even painful at times. And what the church has discovered through careful study and development she has written down and confessed, "I believe; I confess."

Nevertheless, despite the great importance of creeds and confessions, many reject them in our day. Some reject them because they want to be free to believe and teach whatever they desire, including error. The Arminians desired to revise the creeds because they detested the Reformed faith taught therein. While they pretended to believe the Heidelberg Catechism and the Belgic Confession, they objected to many statements in the creeds. Today theologians cry academic freedom in order to be liberated from the creeds and confessions so that they can teach contrary to the confessions without fear of ecclesiastical discipline. Some denominations have creeds and confessions, but they are little more than relics of a more faithful, bygone age, for they are never used, never mentioned, and never taught. If a church member asks about the creeds, the mention of such documents is an occasion for embarrassment: "We *used to* believe those creeds. Our ministers *once* subscribed to those confessions. Some of the ministers might still believe them, but we have modified the formula of subscription, so that we do not *really* have to subscribe to the letter of the creeds. We respect the creeds, of course, but only as venerable documents of the past, dusty with age."

A faithful Reformed church must not view her creeds, the Heidelberg Catechism, the Belgic Confession, and the Canons of Dordt, in that way. A faithful Presbyterian church must not view her creeds, the Westminster Confession and catechisms, in that way. Faithful Reformed believers love the creeds; they preach the creeds, especially the Heidelberg Catechism; and they teach the creeds to their children, lest a generation should arise that is ignorant of the creeds and thus ignorant of the faith of their fathers.

Nevertheless, some have genuine difficulties with the idea of creeds, especially if they come from churches where creeds are not used. When they encounter the Reformed faith, they are puzzled—why do these churches use creeds? Such people should be instructed about the value and importance of creeds, the desire of which instruction is that they also come to love the creeds.

Imagine that you enter a place of worship where creeds are rejected. Out of curiosity about the beliefs of the church, you ask one of the members or the pastor, "What do you believe in this church?" The answer comes back, "We believe the Bible." What have you learned from that answer? Precisely nothing. Every Christian group (and even the cults) will give the same answer, but if the questioner now reads through the sixty-six books of holy scripture, he will not discover what that church believes. Therefore, it is insufficient to say,

"We believe the Bible." Mark well—it is not insufficient to believe the Bible, but it is insufficient to *say* that you believe the Bible. The issue is not whether you claim to believe the Bible, but what do you believe the Bible teaches?

The questioner might persist in his pursuit for truth by making some further queries: "Do you believe that God is triune and that Jesus Christ is the eternal Son of God, true God and true man, one divine person in two distinct natures?" If he receives honest answers, he will discover something about the church's theology and Christology, but it would have been easier if the church had simply adopted the Creeds of Nicea and Chalcedon, for these questions have already been answered in the church's historic creeds. I challenge the reader—explain your (I hope, orthodox) theology and Christology without using the theological and creedal (extra-biblical) terms of *essence/being*, *person*, and *nature*. You will discover why the early church felt compelled to define the relationships between the Father, the Son, and Holy Spirit using precise, albeit extra-biblical, theological terminology. If "I believe the Bible" is the only criterion for the church's doctrine, for church office, or for church membership, anyone could join, anyone could believe whatever he wants, and anyone could teach anything he desires, even someone espousing the worst of heresies, for the only thing he needs to claim is that he believes the Bible. "I believe the Bible" is no guard against heresy.

Moreover, such an anti-creedal position is rarely implemented with consistency. If a person tries to promote the Reformed faith, requests baptism for his child, or denies the rapture of the church, he will often discover that the Reformed faith and infant baptism are not part of the anti-creedal church's creed, while premillennial dispensationalism with its belief in the rapture is zealously promoted as part of the church's creed. Such churches—indeed, all churches—have a creed: the issue is simply whether they are honest enough to publish their creed so that others can see what they believe and teach.

Besides, such an attitude against the creeds ignores the history of the church. Given the development of both the truth and the lie, and given Satan's many attacks on the church, the church needs creeds to identify orthodoxy and to ward off heresy. In Acts 8:37 the Ethiopian eunuch is baptized on confession of his faith, which consisted in a simple declaration, "I believe that Jesus Christ is the Son of God." That beautiful confession is absolutely true, but it is surely insufficient for church membership today. A church does not baptize a person and receive him as a member today based merely on that confession.

Therefore, as the truth developed, so did the confession required of the believer. The early church after the death of the apostles required members to confess the twelve articles of the Apostles' Creed. For a while, that confession was sufficient, but soon the church required a more detailed confession. Some historical examples will make this point clear.

In AD 325 controversy was swelling in the church, for Arius (c. AD 250–336) taught that Jesus Christ is the Son of God, which certainly *sounds* orthodox. However, Arius meant by the term *Son of God* the *created* son of God, or the first and highest of all God's creatures, a heresy espoused by the cult of the Jehovah's Witnesses today. The church in Arius' day understood that the simple confession "Jesus is the Son of God" was insufficient because Arius could confess it while maintaining his heresy. Therefore, the church adopted a confession called the Nicene Creed in order to distinguish orthodoxy from heresy and insisted that to be orthodox a church member must also confess that Christ is *homoousion*, of the same essence with the Father. In other words, the church required a more precise definition of the term *Son of God*. Arius and his followers objected to the word *homoousion* on the grounds that it is not a biblical term, but they agreed to confess a similar word: they agreed that the Son is *homoiousion*, of a similar essence to the Father. One word, *homoiousion*, is heresy; the other word, *homoousion*, is orthodoxy, with only one letter, the Greek *iota*, distinguishing between them.

In AD 451 controversy again swirled around the identity of

Christ. Some taught that Christ is not a true man (he only appeared to be human); others denied that he is a complete man (he has human flesh, but he does not have a human soul); still others viewed Christ as two persons (a human and divine person); while others saw Christ as having one nature, a mixture of human and divine. The church did not say, "We have no creed but Christ," for everyone's creed was Christ, but the issue was, who is Christ? The church studied the relationship between the humanity and divinity of Christ and adopted another confession, the Creed of Chalcedon, in which the truth is sharper and even more precisely defined. With the development of the truth it was no longer enough to confess, "I believe that Christ is the Son of God," or even "I believe that the Son is of the same essence with the Father, *homoousion*." Then a member of the church had to confess one eternal Christ, in one divine person, *homoousion*, in two distinct natures, human and divine, and in the words of Chalcedon, "without confusion, without change, without division, without separation."[3] The simple statement, "Jesus is Lord," while absolutely true and biblical, had been unfolded and developed in order to rule out a number of serious heresies, while at the same time the church enjoyed a richer, deeper understanding of the identity of her Savior and Lord.

At the time of the Reformation, additional doctrines such as justification by faith alone and the doctrine of predestination were developed and defined from the scriptures, with the result that a person had to make an orthodox confession of soteriology, the doctrine of salvation, as well as an orthodox confession of theology and Christology, in order to be a member of the church. As truth develops, more, not less, is required of church members.

Therefore, to the objection that creeds are divisive Reformed believers respond that the creeds are designed to be divisive, for they divide orthodox believers from those who refuse to confess what

---

3 Creed of Chalcedon, in ibid., 17.

the word of God teaches. The Nicene Creed deliberately excluded the false confession of Arius; the creed of Chalcedon deliberately excluded various Christological heresies; the Reformed confessions deliberately excluded Roman Catholicism and Anabaptism; and the Canons of Dordt deliberately excluded Arminianism. Creeds are a distinguishing mark, just as an army has a distinguishing banner. Only the soldiers of King Jesus march under his banner. It would be chaos and confusion if all soldiers, both the soldiers of Jesus and the soldiers of the devil, marched under the same banner. It would cause chaos and confusion if all churches marched under the same banner without confessing the same truth.

Therefore, creeds and confessions *must* distinguish Christians and churches from one another, so that a person can know what a church believes before he joins. This can only occur, however, when a church is honest about what she believes. Creeds are divisive because of man's sin: it is not the truth's fault, but the fault of men who do not confess the truth. If all were faithful to God in equal measure, all would have the same confessions and creeds. Nevertheless, the main function of creeds is not to divide but to unite, for the Reformed creeds are called the three forms of unity. They are a rallying cry to call Reformed believers together, not to scatter them. This is why the Belgic Confession begins, "*We all believe* with the heart, and confess with the mouth" (emphasis added).

THE CHARACTERISTICS OF THE CANONS

The Canons of Dordt are a creed with some distinct features.

First, the Canons of Dordt are explicitly *biblical*. This is obvious from the number of direct biblical citations in many of the articles, especially in the sections of errors and rejections. The delegates swore an oath at the beginning of the synod that their deliberations would be strictly biblical. The Canons, therefore, make no direct appeals to any of the earlier confessions, such as the Heidelberg Catechism and the Belgic Confession. Instead, the Reformed fathers worked directly with the scriptures. It is clear from their work that they were faithful to their promise:

> I promise before God, in whom I believe, and whom I worship, as being present in this place, and as being the Searcher of all hearts, that during the course of the proceedings of this Synod, which will examine and decide, not only the five points, and all the differences resulting from them, but also any other doctrine, I will use no human writing, but only the word of God, which is an infallible rule of faith. And during all these discussions, I will only aim at the glory of God, the peace of the Church, and especially the preservation of the purity of doctrine. So help me, my Saviour, Jesus Christ! I beseech him to assist me by his Holy Spirit![4]

Second, the Canons are also beautifully *pastoral*. Those who have never read them, and who perhaps have unfavorable impressions of the Reformed faith, might be surprised when they read them. If they were expecting a cold, academic treatment of the Reformed faith, they will be struck by the warm, pastoral approach of the Canons, as they address not merely theologians, but the ordinary child of God in his doubts, fears, and struggles with sin. Read especially the sections on assurance of election and salvation, the pastoral advice to the doubting saint, and the whole fifth head on perseverance. In this personal, pastoral approach, the Canons follow the experiential emphasis of the Heidelberg Catechism.

Third, the Canons are deliberately *antithetical*, for not only do they clearly set forth the truth, but they also contrast the truth sharply with the Arminian lie. Perhaps no creed does this so clearly, for few creeds have a separate section of errors and rejections of

---

4 Samuel Miller, introductory essay, in Thomas Scott, ed., *The Articles of the Synod of Dort: Translated from the Latin, with Notes* (Philadelphia: Presbyterian Board of Publication, 1841), 37.

errors, every article of which begins with this line: "The true doctrine concerning...having been explained, the Synod *rejects* the errors of those: who teach." The synod not only refuted the Arminian error, but it also explicitly rejected it.

Fourth, the Canons constitute the original five points of Calvinism, as these have been officially defined and adopted by a Reformed synod at which not only delegates from the Dutch Reformed churches, but also delegates from across the then Reformed world were present. The Synod of Dordt was practically a Reformed *ecumenical* synod, where almost all Reformed churches were represented. Therefore, if one wants to define what true Calvinism and the Reformed faith are, one must look to the Synod of Dordt and its authoritative Canons. True Calvinism, for example, includes election and reprobation and insists on limited (or effectual) atonement. Compromise on these issues constitutes a departure from the Reformed faith. Adherence to the Canons is not hyper-Calvinism but genuine Calvinism or the genuinely Reformed faith.

Fifth, the Canons are not, or were not initially designed to be, a third creed. The Formula of Subscription, which all officebearers in Reformed churches must sign, expresses the relationship between the Canons of Dordt, the Belgic Confession, and the Heidelberg Catechism in these words:

> We, the undersigned...do hereby sincerely and in good conscience before the Lord declare by this, our subscription, that we heartily believe and are persuaded that all the articles and points of doctrine contained in the Confession and Catechism of the Reformed Churches, together *with the explanation of some points of the aforesaid doctrine made by the National Synod of Dordrecht, 1618-'19*, do fully agree with the Word of God.[5]

---

5 Formula of Subscription, in *Confessions and Church Order*, 326 (emphasis added).

Notice these words, which are binding upon all officebearers in Reformed churches. We declare that everything in the creeds "fully agree[s] with the Word of God." The Formula, therefore, binds officebearers "diligently to teach and faithfully to defend the aforesaid doctrine," and especially to keep the churches free from the errors condemned by the Synod of Dordt. In the officebearer's preaching, teaching, and writing, he must especially refute Arminianism.

Some Reformed churches today are revising the wording of the Formula of Subscription to provide wriggle room for those who do not believe the confessions and who do not wish to be bound to them. (The Arminians wanted wriggle room to deny the truth too, something the Synod of Dordt refused to grant.) They do so by having signatories of the Formula declare that they believe all the articles and points of doctrine contained in the Confession *insofar as they agree with the word of God*. While that might sound pious, it is really a form of subterfuge—they subscribe to the confessions, pretending to believe them, while allowing themselves to entertain reservations about them and even to hide disagreements with them. Such an officebearer, who subscribes to the Confession only *insofar as it agrees with the word of God*, is not required to explain where he believes the confession does not agree with the word of God.

The original Formula of Subscription addresses such reservations and differences in a forthright manner and requires honesty from all officebearers:

> And if hereafter any difficulties or different sentiments respecting the aforesaid doctrines should arise in our minds, we promise that we will neither publicly nor privately propose, teach, or defend the same, either by preaching or writing, until we have first revealed such sentiments to the consistory, classis, and synod, that the same may be there examined, being ready always cheerfully to submit to the judgment of the consistory, classis, and

> synod, under the penalty in case of refusal to be, by that very fact, suspended from our office.[6]

This is exactly what Arminius had refused to do. He had difficulties with the doctrines of the confessions, but when asked about those difficulties he equivocated and lied. He had taught, especially in private, contrary to the confessions, and when challenged, he equivocated and lied. He refused to submit to the judgment of the ecclesiastical authorities, and when challenged he appealed to his influential friends in the civil sphere. Officebearers today must not be guilty of such duplicitous behavior in the churches. If they have difficulties with the confessions, they must make that plain, and they may not hide behind the word "insofar."

In other words, the Canons of Dordt constitute the authoritative interpretation and explanation of the Belgic Confession and the Heidelberg Catechism. When, for example, the Heidelberg Catechism states, "[Christ] sustained in body and soul the wrath of God against the sins of all mankind,"[7] this must be interpreted in light of the entire second head of doctrine of the Canons of Dordt, which teaches that Christ died *only for the elect* "out of every people, tribe, nation, and language."[8] Far from revising the creeds, the fathers at Dordt strengthened the churches' adherence to the precious truths found in the creeds, further defined the truth contained in them, and countered the Arminianism that attacked them.

It is with thankful hearts that in 2018 the Reformed churches commemorate the four hundredth anniversary of God's preserving of his truth through the great Synod of Dordt. It is the prayer of the author and the publisher that this commentary on the Canons might cause us to appreciate even more deeply the sovereign grace of God in our salvation.

---

6 Formula of Subscription, in ibid.

7 Heidelberg Catechism A 37, in ibid., 98.

8 Canons of Dordt 2.8, in ibid., 163.

Discussion questions on the introduction and the importance of creeds

1. What lessons about false teachers can be learned from the behavior of Arminius and his followers? Can you think of any biblical examples of this?

2. Read through the Canons of Dordt, preferably in one sitting. What strikes you about them? Do they make a favorable or unfavorable impression on you? Explain.

3. What do the Canons of Dordt add to your understanding of the truths contained in the Belgic Confession and the Heidelberg Catechism?

4. Which objections have you heard from Christians, both in your own church and from other churches, against the creeds? How would you respond to them?

5. Before you started reading this book, how would you have described your attitude toward the creeds in general and toward the Canons of Dordt in particular? (a) I have never heard of them; (b) I am opposed to them; (c) They are a mere historical curiosity to me; (d) I accept them as authoritative in the church, but they mean nothing to me personally; (e) I find them a useful summary of the teachings of my church; (f) They express what I believe; (g) I love the creeds and I strive to know them more, preserve them in the church, and teach them to my children.

6. How could you promote the use of creeds in your own life and in your church; and how could you instill in your children an appreciation for the creeds?

7. Are creeds only important for the officebearers of the church? Explain.

8. Could the church have preserved the truth without the creeds? Explain.

9. Why is the insertion of the word *insofar* into the Formula of Subscription a dangerous and deceptive subterfuge?

10. The Canons are biblical, pastoral, and antithetical. Produce examples to prove this assertion. Why are these important features of the Canons?

11. Which statements from the Canons comfort your heart? Why do you think this is so?

The First Head of Doctrine on Divine Predestination

INTRODUCTION

The Canons of Dordt begin with predestination. Therefore, the traditional acronym TULIP (total depravity, unconditional election, limited atonement, irresistible grace, and preservation of the saints) is actually ULTIP with the *U* being a reference to unconditional election. The TULIP acronym is good, however, for memorization purposes, and because it is a Dutch flower, a tribute to the fact that the location of the great Synod of Dordt was the Netherlands.

Dordt began with predestination because that was the focal point of the Arminian assault on the truth. However, the Reformed fathers wisely did not permit the Arminians to determine the approach. The Arminians wanted to begin with reprobation in order to portray the Reformed faith in as negative a light as possible. Dordt refused to begin there because that is not where the Bible begins. Reprobation is always subservient to election in the Bible (Isa. 43:3–4). To begin with reprobation is, therefore, unwise because it gives occasion to the enemy to blaspheme. It is foolish, for example, to begin a discussion with an Arminian today by telling him that God has made some men vessels of wrath fitted to destruction. We are never ashamed of the truth, but the truth must be presented wisely.

To understand the approach of the Canons, we need to know what the Arminians taught about predestination. The Arminians taught an impersonal and conditional election. They taught that God has decided to save all those who will believe and persevere in faith. However, the wily heretics refused to confess that God has elected specific persons or that God has elected those persons unconditionally. There is one non-negotiable issue in Arminian election: election in Arminianism must depend upon man, for salvation must depend upon man. The idea that election, and therefore salvation, depends upon God alone is anathema to the Arminians, a truth that they fight against tooth and nail.

But before Dordt even addressed that subject, the synod addressed the justice of election. This is necessary because the primary objection to election in all ages is the allegation that it is not fair or that it is unjust for God to elect only some. We also should remember the pastoral concern of the Canons: this creed is not designed to be the presentation of cold, abstract dogma, but to be a clear defense of the truth, the truth of the gospel of God's grace. Many in the Reformed churches were confused and troubled by the doctrine of election because of the Arminian attack on it. The Reformed fathers took the time to address some of those concerns in order positively to set forth the truth in order to direct it "to the glory of the divine name, to holiness of life, and to the consolation of afflicted souls."[1] Therefore, the Canons take an apologetic approach. By "apology," I do not mean that the fathers were sorry to teach election, or that they did so reluctantly or ashamedly. An apology or apologetic is a reasoned defense, in this case a reasoned biblical defense.

One other remark about the approach of head one is in order. The Canons do not begin their approach to predestination from the viewpoint of eternity, but from the viewpoint of time. Certainly,

---

1 Canons of Dordt conclusion, in *Confessions and Church Order*, 180.

the Canons teach *eternal* predestination, but the fathers deliberately approached the subject from the viewpoint of God's purpose *in history*. In fact, God's eternal decree does not become prominent until head one, article 6. This is also the approach of the Belgic Confession, article 16, which the Arminians rejected and wanted to revise:

> We believe that, all the posterity of Adam being thus fallen into perdition and ruin by the sin of our first parents, God then did manifest Himself such as He is; that is to say, merciful and just: merciful, since He delivers and preserves from this perdition all whom He in His eternal and unchangeable counsel, of mere goodness, hath elected in Christ Jesus our Lord, without any respect to their works: just, in leaving others in the fall and perdition wherein they have involved themselves.[2]

Instead of treating the articles of the Canons of Dordt in order and the errors and rejections separately, I intend to study the errors and rejections in conjunction with the positive articles, which will make the contrast between the Reformed faith and Arminianism even sharper. It is to the articles of the Canons that I now turn.

ARTICLE 1: UNIVERSAL GUILT

> As all men have sinned in Adam, lie under the curse, and are deserving of eternal death, God would have done no injustice by leaving them all to perish, and delivering them over to condemnation on account of sin, according to the words of the apostle, Rom. 3:19, *that every mouth may be stopped, and all the world may become guilty before God.* And verse 23: *for all have sinned, and come short of the glory of God.* And Rom. 6:23: *for the wages of sin is death.*[3]

---

2 Belgic Confession 16, in ibid., 41.

3 This article and all subsequent articles, errors, rejections, and the conclusion to the Canons are quoted from the Canons of Dordrecht, in ibid., 155–80.

This first article teaches two very basic truths. First, all men are guilty before God. Second, God is obligated to save no one.

Guilt is, first, a feeling or sense of having done something wrong, which we call subjective guilt. All men are subjectively guilty to various degrees, depending on the sensitivity of their consciences. That, however, is not the meaning of guilt in this article. Guilt is, second, an objective status before a moral standard. The moral standard is God's standard, which means that such a guilty person does not conform to God's law. A criminal is objectively guilty as soon as the judge pronounces him guilty, whether he feels guilty or not. Guilt includes the liability to punishment. All men stand before God as objectively guilty and worthy of punishment. They are guilty in Adam, their first father, a truth called original guilt, which will be explored in more depth in the third and fourth heads of doctrine.

Although Arminians pay lip service to the truth of universal guilt, in practice they often deny it, especially with respect to children and to those who are not evangelized. If one teaches, as many Arminians do, an age of accountability before which one is supposedly innocent, or if one teaches that those who have never heard the gospel will not be punished for their unbelief and other sins, one does not really believe in universal, objective guilt.

The consequence of this guilt is that all men "lie under the curse." This does not mean that all men are cursed, for God never curses his elect. However, God does curse the reprobate wicked (Ps. 37:22; Prov. 3:33; Matt. 25:41). God's fearful but just curse is the word of his wrath, a word that pursues the wicked through this life and into eternity where it destroys them forever. All men are liable to that curse. All men are "deserving of eternal death." Death is separation from God or everlasting punishment in hell. If you or I stood before God and he sentenced us to everlasting death, he would do us no injustice.

Do you believe that? Do you believe that about yourself? Do you believe that about everybody?

The Arminians did not believe that, for Arminianism has an objection. Arminians believe that it would be unjust for God to damn anyone who never had a chance of salvation. Arminians really believe that God should save everyone, or (at the very least) should make it possible for everyone to be saved.

But the Canons have a different answer. God could have saved no one. God could have determined not to send Jesus Christ. God could have condemned everyone to hell. God could have left everyone to perish. God's act in sending Christ was an act of free, sovereign mercy. It was not something that he was obligated to do.

Arminianism does not believe this. We know this because of the Arminian's objection of injustice. If you teach from scripture that God saves only some, the response is to complain, "That is not fair!" If it is only fair for God to save all, then it follows that it is not fair for God *not* to save all, and that God is really obligated to save all. But man does not determine what is fair. He has neither the right nor the competency to determine what is just. To accuse God of injustice is terrible wickedness, for it places man and not God on the judgment seat. God is just, whether man recognizes God's justice or accuses him of injustice: "What shall we say then? Is there unrighteousness with God? God forbid" (Rom. 9:14).

Consider this illustration. Ten guilty murderers await execution in prison on death row. The governor of the state exercises his prerogative of clemency to spare one of the ten murderers. One guilty man is pardoned, while nine guilty men are hanged. The governor was not obligated to pardon any of the criminals, but he freely chose to show mercy to one. The other nine have no reason for complaint, while the pardoned man has every reason for gratitude. Of course, the illustration is limited, for God does not arbitrarily pardon people, but he has a just basis for doing so in the cross of Christ, as will become plain in head two of the Canons.

The Canons prove man's guilt and God's justice by referring to three texts (Rom. 3:19, 23; 6:23). The conclusion of article 1 is simple:

there are no innocent people, but only guilty people. Therefore, God is not obligated to save any, and he could justly condemn all.

ARTICLE 2: THE MANIFESTATION OF GOD'S LOVE

> But in this the love of God was manifested, that He sent his only begotten Son into the world, that whosoever believeth on him should not perish, but have everlasting life (1 John 4:9; John 3:16).

The Canons began somewhat hypothetically by stating what God *could have* done. The second article begins to teach what God has actually done.

It is striking that the Canons' treatment of salvation begins with the love of God. Perhaps if you are new to the Reformed faith or if you have only encountered caricatures of it, you are surprised because you have heard that the Reformed faith makes little of the love of God. But the Reformed faith actually extols and highly celebrates the love of God.

God's love in the Bible is a beautiful concept. It is not a soppy, sentimental emotion, but it is the purpose of God's will. From the main Hebrew and Greek words for love in scripture, we learn that love includes several important ideas. First, to love is to breathe after with desire and ardent affection. Second, love is to cling to or to cleave to in order to establish a bond of fellowship with the object of one's love. Third, love is to take pleasure in, to prize, and to treasure the object of one's love as precious and dear. Fourth, love is to seek the welfare, and ultimately the salvation, of the beloved.

God's love for himself within his own triune being includes these aspects. (The Father breathes after, cleaves to, and treasures the Son in the Holy Spirit, while the Son perfectly reciprocates this love in the Holy Spirit.) That love is natural or essential to God's being, for he must love himself as the sum of all perfection and "the overflowing fountain of all good."[4] But God also loves objects outside of his being, for he loves creatures. This love for the creature is not necessary, however, but it is deliberate: God chooses, purposes, or determines to love. God chooses to love his own people, while he chooses not to love the reprobate wicked. Thus God's love for the creature is perfectly free and sovereign.

According to article 2, God's love was "manifested." God's love cannot remain hidden eternally within the mind of God, but it must display itself. The chief display of God's love, declare the Canons, is in the sending of his Son, our Lord Jesus Christ, into the world to save sinners.

Therefore, the incarnation of the Son of God and the cross of Christ are the fruit of God's love. That must be clearly understood, because some confusedly imagine a vengeful deity whose wrath had to be appeased to cause him to love his people. Nothing could be further from the truth. It is not the work of Christ to convince a hateful God to love his people. Instead, God's love is first, and out of that immense, immeasurable love God sent his Son.

As proof of this the Canons cite 1 John 4:9 and John 3:16. "In this was manifested the love of God toward us, because that God sent his only begotten Son into the world, that we might live through him." "For God so loved the world, that he gave his only begotten Son, that whosoever believeth in him should not perish, but have everlasting life."

The Synod of Dordt, to the surprise of many Arminians today, did not fear to use John 3:16 as a proof text. Contrary to popular opinion, this text does not teach a love of God for all men. The word *world* in scripture does not mean the entire human race head for head. One example should suffice: "Behold the world is gone after him" (John 12:19). The Pharisees in that text were not concerned

---

4 Belgic Confession 1, in ibid., 23.

that *every single person on earth* was following Jesus, but they were concerned about his increasing popularity. The word *world* should be interpreted according to its context. In John 3 Jesus was speaking to Nicodemus, a Pharisee and leader of the Jews. In that context Jesus wisely employed in verse 16 the most appropriate term, "world," to explain God's saving purposes to Nicodemus. By this term Jesus emphasized to the narrow-minded Nicodemus that salvation was extended to the Jews and Gentiles, which is how Nicodemus understood that term. The word "world" in that context does not include every individual of every nation in the whole of mankind. Moreover, if Jesus had said "the elect," Nicodemus would have understood them to be the Jews, which was not the point Jesus was articulating to Nicodemus.

In addition, the word "whosoever" in verse 16 (although a legitimate translation) must not be stretched beyond its linguistic limits. "Whosoever" does not mean that anyone and everyone *can* believe. "Whosoever believeth" is a loose translation of the Greek for *every believing one*, and it identifies those who are saved as all believers. However, in John 3:16 Jesus did not tell Nicodemus who the believers are, and he did not tell him why or how certain people believe the gospel in distinction from other people who do not believe. We must wait until article 6 before the Canons address that issue.

ARTICLE 3: THE MERCIFUL SENDING OF THE GOSPEL

> And that men may be brought to believe, God mercifully sends the messengers of these most joyful tidings to whom He will and at what time He pleaseth; by whose ministry men are called to repentance and faith in Christ crucified. Rom. 10:14–15: *How then shall they call on him in whom they have not believed? And how shall they believe in him of whom they have not heard? And how shall they hear without a preacher? And how shall they preach except they be sent?*

The main idea of the third article is the truth that God uses means to bring his people to saving faith in Jesus Christ. Thus the Canons take direct aim at one of the main objections of Arminianism to the truth of sovereign, unconditional predestination, namely, that it makes preaching unnecessary. If God has predestinated the elect to salvation, there is no reason to preach, complain the Arminians. But the answer is simple: God uses means.

God does not save without means, which are the instruments that God ordinarily uses to accomplish his purposes. The Canons insist on the sovereignty of God in preaching, for God sends preachers. And in sending preachers God determines who the preachers are, where they shall preach, when they shall preach, and to whom they shall preach. In the Old Testament the gospel was preached almost exclusively to the Jews (Ps. 147:19–20). In the New Testament, while God includes the Gentiles, he continues to direct the preaching as it pleases him (Acts 16:6–10). Never, therefore, is the preaching outside of the sovereign, determinative will of God.

The logic is inescapable: if God has determined who shall hear the gospel, which is the only means of salvation, he has also determined who shall be saved. If God has determined the means or the instrument, surely, he has also determined the end or the goal. We know from the scriptures and from our observation of history that multitudes have lived and died without ever hearing the gospel of salvation. We confess with the Canons that it was no accident that they did not hear, but that it was the will of God who sends the gospel to some and withholds it from others.

The Canons explain this by insisting that the gospel is governed by God's "good pleasure." God's good pleasure is simply that which he is pleased to do, or that which he is pleased to have done. God is pleased to send the gospel to some and not to send it to others. When we seek for causes, we cannot find a deeper reason than God's good pleasure. Jesus recognized this in Matthew 11:26: "Even so, Father: for so it seemed good in thy sight," where the context is God's hiding the truth from some ("the wise and prudent") and revealing it to others ("babes") (v. 25). When we are tempted to rebel against God and to murmur that his ways are unfair, we respond humbly as Eli did, "It is the LORD: let him do what seemeth him good" (1 Sam. 3:18).

The gospel is sent out in God's mercy, which is his tenderhearted compassion for the miserable. Rather than see his miserable people perish, as they deserve, God sends the gospel to them. Article 3 teaches that "God *mercifully* sends the messengers of these most joyful tidings to whom He will and at what time He pleaseth" (emphasis added). Nevertheless, article 3 does not yet define the objects of God's mercy. Clearly, not all who hear the gospel are the objects of God's mercy because not all hearers are saved, and God's mercy is an effectual, saving mercy. Even the preaching of the gospel is in itself not mercy to all the hearers, for God hardens the reprobate wicked by means of the gospel: "Therefore hath he mercy on whom he will have mercy, and whom he will he hardeneth" (Rom. 9:18). "For we are unto God a sweet savour of Christ, in them that are saved, and in them that perish: to the one we are the savour of death unto death; and to the other the savour of life unto life. And who is sufficient for these things?" (2 Cor. 2:15–16).

The content of the preaching of the gospel is "these most joyful tidings." The word *gospel* means good news. The Canons call the gospel "joyful," even "most joyful," tidings. What tidings or news could be more joyful than the truth that God out of his immeasurably great love has sent his Son into the world? What tidings or news could be more joyful than the truth that there is salvation full and free for all who believe in Jesus? That, surely, is the content of preaching: the truth not of what man has done or must do, but the truth of what God has accomplished in Jesus Christ for the salvation of sinners.

With the announcement comes a call, which is the call of the gospel. This call is an authoritative command from God issued through human instruments (preachers). God does not boom loudly from heaven with a terrifying, earth-shattering voice, but his voice in the preaching is just as serious: "Repent!" "Believe!" This is not an offer or an invitation, but a command, a call to repent and believe in Christ crucified. It is by this kind of preaching that sinners are saved (Rom. 10:14–15).

Have you *heard* that gospel? Have you *believed* that gospel?

ERROR AND REJECTION 9: THE SENDING OF THE GOSPEL DETERMINED BY HUMAN WORTHINESS

> Error 9: Who teach that the reason why God sends the gospel to one people rather than to another is not merely and solely the good pleasure of God, but rather the fact that one people is better and worthier than another to whom the gospel is not communicated.
>
> Rejection: For this Moses denies, addressing the people of Israel as follows: *Behold, unto Jehovah thy God belongeth heaven and the heaven of heavens, the earth, with all that is therein. Only Jehovah had a delight in thy fathers to love them, and he chose their seed after them, even you above all peoples, as at this day* (Deut. 10:14–15). And Christ said: *Woe unto thee, Chorazin! woe unto thee, Bethsaida! for if the mighty works, which were done in you, had been done in Tyre and Sidon, they would have repented long ago in sackcloth and ashes* (Matt. 11:21).

The Arminians were so opposed to God's sovereignty that they denied even God's sovereignty in the preaching of the gospel. They did this by denying that God's good pleasure determines the direction of the preaching: "The reason…is not merely and solely the good pleasure of God." Instead, they argued that the worthiness of nations determines where the gospel is preached. If a nation is worthy, the inhabitants of that nation are privileged to hear the gospel, but if a nation is unworthy, the inhabitants of that nation are deprived of the gospel. Perhaps, suggested the Arminians, God sees potentiality for a positive response in certain nations, which is why he sends the gospel to them and withholds it from others: "One people is better and worthier than another to whom the gospel is not communicated."

The fathers at Dordt made short work of such a proud error: "For this Moses denies." Israel, who received marvelous revelation from God while the rest of mankind perished in darkness, was a stiff-necked and unworthy people. This is clear from the texts that the synod quoted (Deut. 7:6–8; 10:14–15; Matt. 11:21–30). Jesus even says that if his miracles had been performed in Sodom and Gomorrah, they would have believed. Yet the gospel was not preached to them!

The conclusion is clear: the only means of salvation is the preaching of the gospel, which preaching God sovereignly directs as it pleases him. Therefore, we know that salvation is under the sovereign good pleasure of God. That is exactly where the child of God wants it to be.

ARTICLE 4: THE TWOFOLD RESPONSE TO THE GOSPEL

> The wrath of God abideth upon those who believe not this gospel. But such as receive it, and embrace Jesus the Savior by a true and living faith, are by Him delivered from the wrath of God and from destruction, and have the gift of eternal life conferred upon them.

When the gospel is preached according to the good pleasure of God, there is always a twofold response from the hearers. The two possible responses to the glad tidings, to these "most joyful tidings," are faith and unbelief. Some of the hearers believe the gospel and trust in the Christ presented therein. Other hearers reject the gospel with scorn, contempt, or indifference. Believers are saved, while unbelievers remain under God's wrath and perish.

We should notice that the Canons have not yet mentioned predestination, for the fathers were wisely building a foundation on which to introduce this doctrine. That basic approach is a good one for us to follow when we present the truth, especially to a hostile hearer. One prejudiced against the truth of predestination will want to frame the parameters of the debate. He will want to jump immediately to predestination, especially to reprobation. The fathers at Dordt wisely refused to allow the Arminians to do that.

God's wrath, declare the Canons, "abideth upon those who believe not this gospel." This is an obvious reference to John 3:36: "He that believeth on the Son hath everlasting life: and he that believeth not the Son shall not see life; but the wrath of God abideth on him." The Canons carefully explain that God's wrath is upon unbelieving sinners even before they hear the gospel. It is not that God loves all men before they hear the gospel, but that he becomes angry with them when they hear and reject the truth. It is not that they were not yet worthy of condemnation before their unbelief was manifested. The truth is rather this: they always lay under, or were liable to, the curse. They always deserved eternal death because they are sinners. When they hear the gospel and reject it, God's wrath abides, or remains, upon them.

God's wrath is a terrifying and fearful reality, for it is his burning anger against sin and against sinners. The greatest expression of God's wrath is everlasting punishment in hell. Sometimes it is asked whether God's wrath is ever on his people. This answer is yes, for God can be, and sometimes is, angry with his people. Godly King Jehoshaphat learned that: "Jehu the son of Hanani the seer went out to meet him, and said to king Jehoshaphat, Shouldest thou help the ungodly, and love them that hate the LORD? Therefore is wrath upon thee from before the LORD" (2 Chron. 19:2). However, although God can be, and sometimes is, angry toward his children, he never hates his people whom he eternally loves.

Moreover, before God's elect people believe, they, too, are under his wrath, for Paul wrote in Ephesians 2:3 that we "were by nature the children of wrath, even as others." Nevertheless, although they were under his wrath, they were never the objects of his hatred, for he loved them with an everlasting love, a love by which he willed and planned their salvation before the foundation of the world. Some theologians have suggested that God hated his elect children before they believed in Jesus Christ, which would mean that his disposition toward them changed. But that cannot be true, for God's disposition—his love for the elect and his hatred for the reprobate—is unchangeable (Ps. 103:17; 136:1; Jer. 31:3).

God's hatred is not the same as his wrath, for God's hatred, which is directed toward the reprobate wicked, is his will to destroy the wicked and to thrust them from himself into everlasting desolation and misery. God hated Esau with such hatred (Rom. 9:13), and God hates the reprobate wicked in every age with such hatred (Ps. 5:5; 11:5). Although we tremble at the idea of God's hatred, we confess that God's hatred is perfectly holy and just. Especially parents should understand the difference between anger and hatred. They are sometimes very angry with their children, but they must never, ever hate them. Even as they discipline them, they must do so in love, just as God disciplines and chastises his children in love (Heb. 12:6).

Believers, however, are "delivered from the wrath of God and from destruction." The wrath and destruction that they deserved do not fall upon them (1 Thess. 1:10). They are delivered, saved, or rescued when they receive this gospel, which means that they hold this gospel for truth. They believe the good news that Jesus is lord, that he was crucified for sinners, and that he was raised from the dead. And by a true and living faith they embrace Jesus the savior who is presented or set forth in the gospel. They trust in Jesus, expecting from him salvation and eternal life.

As a result believers are saved and the gift of eternal life is conferred upon them.

What is your response to the gospel? Have you rejected it in haughty scorn and unbelief, or in cold indifference? If so, you must know that the wrath of God abides on you. Have you received the gospel and Jesus Christ presented therein with a true and living faith? Then rejoice, for you have been delivered from the wrath of God. God has given you the gift of eternal life.

But do not be tempted to boast, as if you made yourself to differ from your unbelieving neighbor, for in the next article the Canons will explain the reasons for this twofold response to the most joyful tidings of the gospel.

ARTICLE 5: THE GUILT OF UNBELIEF AND THE GIFT OF FAITH

> The cause or guilt of this unbelief, as well as of all other sins, is no wise in God, but in man himself; whereas faith in Jesus Christ and salvation through Him is the free gift of God, as it is written: *By grace ye are saved through faith, and that not of yourselves, it is the gift of God* (Eph. 2:8). *And unto you it is given in the behalf of Christ, not only to believe on him,* etc. (Phil. 1:29).

Let me recap what the Canons have taught thus far. First, all men are guilty before God and, therefore, God could have left all of them to perish in their sins. Second, God was pleased not to leave all men to perish in their sins. Instead, out of his immeasurable love, God sent his Son to save sinners. Third, God brings sinners to saving faith by sending preachers to proclaim this gospel, the most joyful and glad tidings, to them. Fourth, people respond in one of two ways to this gospel: some reject it and remain under God's wrath; while some believe it and receive salvation and eternal life.

Article 5 explains this twofold response.

First, unbelievers are to blame for their unbelief. They are guilty or at fault for the great sin of unbelief. Unbelief is sin, for it is wickedness for a person to refuse to believe in Jesus Christ. Since unbelief is sin, we conclude that God commands faith, for sin is the transgression of God's commandments. God commands, "Repent and believe!" The unbeliever responds, "No, I will not repent and believe!" That wicked response is sinful rebellion. To disbelieve is to call God a liar: "He that believeth on the Son of God hath the witness in himself: he that believeth not God hath made him a liar; because he believeth not the record that God gave of his Son" (1 John 5:10).

Unbelievers are also guilty for their other sins. Sinners are guilty for all of their transgressions against God's law, whether idolatry, blasphemy, Sabbath-desecration, rebellion against authority, murder, adultery, theft, lying, or covetousness. Sinners are guilty for all of the sins that proceed from their sinful hearts, whether pride, lust, envy, hatred, malice, or any other form of depravity (Mark 7:20–23).

The Canons are emphatic that the cause or guilt of man's unbelief is "no wise in God." It is not God's fault that sinners do not believe. It is not God's fault that sinners transgress God's commandments. It is not God's fault that sinners are by nature corrupt and depraved. It is not God's fault that sinners, when confronted with the call of the gospel, continue in sin. It is a common ploy of the sinner to seek to blame God, but this is simply a foolish and sinful evasion.

The Arminians argued that God could only charge man with sin for unbelief if man had the ability to believe. Since man refuses to believe (although he could believe, if he so decided), man is guilty and worthy of condemnation. In other words, guilt must be determined according to ability. Man cannot be held accountable for something he cannot do. Man can only be held accountable for something he can do but refuses to do.

Dordt, reflecting question and answer 9 of the Heidelberg Catechism, responded that man's accountability is not based on his ability, but on the fact that he is a creature. The creature, whether able or unable, is accountable to the Creator. Besides, it is the fault of man that he is unable, that he has *become* unable. God created man with the power to obey him, to believe, and to worship him. Man forfeited those powers in the fall, as we shall see especially in the third and fourth heads of doctrine.

Second, the believer receives no credit for his faith, but the glory for faith must be ascribed to God alone. This does not seem to follow, for if the unbeliever is guilty for his unbelief, should we not conclude that the believer receives the credit for his faith?

The answer is that while unbelief is the fault of man, faith is the gift of God: "Faith in Jesus Christ and salvation through Him is the free gift of God." And to prove this the Canons cite two texts. "For by grace are ye saved through faith; and that not of yourselves: it is the gift of God" (Eph. 2:8). "For unto you it is given in the behalf of Christ, not only to believe on him, but also to suffer for his sake" (Phil. 1:29).

Grace, salvation, and faith (the whole salvation package) are a gift of God. Emphatically, declares Paul, the salvation package (including faith) is "not of yourselves," for it does not come from you, and you do not produce it by the power of your supposed free will. Moreover, it is "given" (freely and graciously given) to you to believe in Jesus Christ. That gift comes to you "in the behalf of Christ," that is, on account of Christ's work of atonement on the cross. The synod will have more to say about the relationship between faith and the cross in the second head of doctrine.

Thus even before mentioning the subject of divine predestination, the synod already laid low the proud error of Arminianism. Faith is not in the power of man's free will, but it is the free, gracious gift of God to some. That brings us to the next questions: *To whom* does God give this gift of faith and *why*? To these questions the synod turned in article 6.

ARTICLE 6: THE SOURCE OF FAITH IN GOD'S ETERNAL DECREE

> That some receive the gift of faith from God and others do not receive it proceeds from God's eternal decree, *For known unto God are all his works from the beginning of the world* (Acts 15:18). *Who worketh all things after the counsel of his will* (Eph. 1:11). According to which decree He graciously softens the hearts of the elect, however obstinate, and inclines them to believe, while He leaves the non-elect in His just judgment to their own wickedness and obduracy. And herein is especially displayed the profound, the merciful, and at the same time the righteous discrimination between men equally involved in ruin; or that decree of election and reprobation, revealed in the Word of God, which, though men of perverse, impure, and unstable minds wrest to their own destruction, yet to holy and pious souls affords unspeakable consolation.

The main idea of article 6 is the explanation of why some receive the gift of faith and others do not receive it. Arminianism detests the notion of the gift of faith. In Arminianism salvation *itself* is a gift, while faith is man's contribution to salvation. In other words, faith is the condition that man must fulfill in order to receive the gift of salvation. The standard Arminian presentation is that salvation is available to all men if they are willing to accept it. All men, argues the Arminian, have the ability to accept or reject the freely offered gift of salvation. God really has nothing to do with whether a person accepts salvation or not. On his part God desires to give salvation to all men, but he allows man to make that decision. Thus salvation depends on the sinner's response.

Some Arminians are more refined in their subtlety because they recognize the need to include the Holy Spirit in salvation. Therefore, they will concede that the Holy Spirit helps, or is willing to help, sinners to accept salvation. The Holy Spirit woos or sweetly influences man, he tugs at man's heartstrings, he knocks on man's heart, but the sinner is able to resist the gracious operations of the Spirit and his efforts to give the sinner salvation. In fact, the characteristic doctrine of Arminianism is *resistible grace*, to which the Reformed faith responds with the *I* of TULIP, *irresistible grace*, which is the subject of the third and fourth heads of doctrine. Alas, the sinner cannot respond positively to the preaching of the gospel: "Their poison is like the poison of a serpent: they are like the deaf adder that stoppeth her ear; which will not hearken to the voice of charmers, charming never so wisely" (Ps. 58:4–5; see also John 3:19–21).

Scripture teaches that the whole of salvation is a gift of God's grace, which salvation includes faith. Faith is not something separate from salvation, but faith is *part of salvation*. Faith is the gift of God worked in the hearts of the elect by which they are united to Jesus Christ. Before a person exercises faith (or becomes active in believing), he must have the gift of faith worked into him.[5]

Faith cannot be something offered to man, as if God would say, "I will give you the gift of faith *if you accept it*." That would translate as, "I will give you the gift of faith *if you believe*," which would be absurd. Article 6 answers these questions: To whom does God give the gift of saving faith and why?

The difference is not in man's freewill choice. The difference is in God's decree.

Before I proceed, I need to explain some theological terminology. The Bible speaks of God's decree in different ways and with various expressions. First, the Bible refers to God's *good pleasure*, which is what God is pleased to do or what God is pleased to ordain to be done (Eph. 1:5, 9). Second, the Bible refers to God's *counsel*, which is his eternal plan according to which he has determined all things done in time (v. 11). Third, theologians refer to God's *decree*

5 See Heidelberg Catechism Q&A 20–23, in ibid., 90–91.

or *decrees.* Although God's counsel is one, it can be distinguished into various decrees. (God has one counsel, but many decrees.) In the Bible, the word *decree* usually refers to the edicts of kings (Ezra 6:1), but theologians rightly apply the word to God's purposes. Fourth, the Bible refers to *predestination,* which is God's decree determining the eternal destiny of all rational, moral creatures (men and angels). When the Bible uses the word *predestinate,* it invariably refers to election (Rom. 8:29–30; Eph. 1:5, 11), but the theological use of the word includes both election and reprobation. Finally, theologians refer to *election* and *reprobation,* where election is God's eternal, unconditional *choice* of some, and reprobation is God's eternal, unconditional *rejection* of others.

With respect to this decree of God, the Canons declare, "That some receive the gift of faith from God and others do not receive it *proceeds from God's eternal decree*" (emphasis added). That decree, since it is eternal, is first, for it is neither an afterthought, nor a reaction to unforeseen or unexpected events. God acts in time according to his own eternal counsel, so that all the events in history are the outworking of that counsel. The decree in view here in article 6 is God's decree of election and reprobation. Since God's one decree includes election and reprobation, it is impossible consistently to confess election while denying reprobation. The fathers at Dordt taught double predestination (election *and* reprobation); all true children of the Reformation are faithful to that truth.

God acts "according to [this] decree." It is not that God has a decree, which he then sets aside or ignores. Rather, God does all things according to his decree, some of which acts of God are listed in article 6. This, too, is the teaching of Ephesians 1:11, where God is called the one who "worketh all things after the counsel of his own will." God actually does work after, according to, or in harmony with, his counsel. He never works contrary to it, for to do so would be for God to act contrary to his own mind, or to act contrary to himself.

This decree is not the invention of speculative theologians, but declare the Canons, it is "that decree of election and reprobation, *revealed in the Word of God*" (emphasis added).

According to God's decree of election and reprobation, then, God takes certain steps in time, both with respect to the elect and the reprobate. Because he takes these steps, the elect receive eternal salvation, while the reprobate wicked are eternally condemned.

First, God "graciously softens the hearts of the elect." This shows that the hearts of all men, including the hearts of the elect, are by nature hard. There is no difference between the hearts of the elect and the reprobate in this respect. The Canons use the word "obduracy," which means stubbornly resistant to moral influence, hard, impervious to persuasion, or persistently impenitent. An obdurate heart is incompatible with the notion of free will, for how could an obdurate heart choose to accept salvation? Nevertheless, an obdurate heart, although an impossible obstacle for the most persuasive preacher, is no obstacle for the Holy Spirit. By softening an obdurate heart God opens that heart and works his salvation in it.

This softening of an obdurate heart is gracious, for it is the result of God's favor. God loves the elect and delivers them from this obduracy of heart, no matter how hard their hearts might be. When God opens and softens our hearts, we thank God for his grace. What a wonder it is to receive a softened heart, a new heart! Lydia, the first recorded convert in Europe, was the recipient of a new heart: "A certain woman named Lydia...whose heart the Lord opened, that she attended unto the things which were spoken of Paul" (Acts 16:14). How foolish is the Arminian presentation of Jesus, impotently or helplessly knocking on the sinner's heart, when the truth is that the almighty Lord sovereignly opens the hearts of elect sinners. And this is not a new idea found only in the New Testament, for the prophets, especially Ezekiel, promised it: "A new heart also will I give you, and a new spirit will I put within you: and I will take away the stony heart out of your flesh, and I will give you a heart of flesh. And I will put my spirit within you, and cause you to walk in my statutes, and ye shall keep my judgments, and do them" (Ezek. 36:26–27).

Second, according to the same decree, God "leaves the non-elect in His just judgment to their own wickedness and obduracy." It is no accident that the reprobate wicked are left in their sins, but it is according to the same decree. Election and reprobation constitute one decree. To be left in the bondage and corruption of one's sins is a dreadful judgment of God, but it is a just judgment of God. If God abandons the sinner to the obduracy of his heart, the fault lies with him, not with God. Sinners have no claim on God, as if he owed them a new heart. Since the obduracy of man's heart is the result of his fall into sin, God is perfectly just to leave him in such obduracy if it pleases him to do so.

The Canons call this activity of God, according to which he softens the hearts of some and leaves others in their sins, "discrimination." What an offensive word today is *discrimination*. Above all things, the world insists that we must not discriminate because everyone must be treated in the same way. But God discriminates, which means that he makes a difference or distinction. Man does not make the difference between election and reprobation or between salvation and damnation—God does. "For who maketh thee to differ from another? and what hast thou that thou didst not receive? now if thou didst receive it, why dost thou glory, as if thou hadst not received it" (1 Cor. 4:7)?

Many object to discrimination because, they argue, God is not a respecter of persons (Acts 10:34; Rom. 2:11; Eph. 6:9; Col. 3:25; 1 Pet. 1:17). In the Old Testament especially judges were forbidden to treat people differently because of their social class, their wealth, or some other earthly difference. If God treats people differently by giving a new heart to some and not to others, is he not a respecter of persons? The answer is no because God's choice is free, sovereign, and unconditional. If God chose his people on the basis of something in them, something according to which they differed from others, which moved God to choose them, then he would be a respecter of persons. If God favored his people because they were rich, numerous, powerful or for some other reason, then he would be a respecter of persons. Far be it from the righteous God that he should be a respecter of persons. Ironically, then, it is the Arminian with his conditional election who makes God a respecter of persons.

Listen to Jehovah's word to Israel: "The LORD did not set his love upon you, nor choose you, because ye were more in number than any people; for ye were the fewest of all people: but because the LORD loved you, and because he would keep the oath which he had sworn unto your fathers, hath the Lord brought you out with a mighty hand, and redeemed you out of the house of bondmen, from the hand of Pharaoh king of Egypt" (Deut. 7:7–8).

Listen to Paul's instruction to the saints in Corinth:

26. For ye see your calling, brethren, how that not many wise men after the flesh, not many mighty, not many noble, are called:
27. But God hath chosen the foolish things of the world to confound the wise; and God hath chosen the weak things of the world to confound the things which are mighty;
28. And base things of the world, and things which are despised, hath God chosen, yea, and things which are not, to bring to nought things that are:
29. That no flesh should glory in his presence. (1 Cor. 1:26–29)

About this discrimination of God, the Canons teach three things.

First, this discrimination is "profound," so deep that we cannot plumb the depths of it. We cannot understand the reasons hidden in the mind of God for why he chose one over another. We do not know why God opened Lydia's heart, for example, while he hardened the hearts of others. We are not called to understand, but to believe it, to marvel at it, and to worship God for it.

If God opened your heart, thank him, but do not grumble because he did not open your neighbor's heart. And do not boast that your heart is open, while your neighbor's heart remains closed. Rather, your calling is to beseech God in prayer for the opening of your neighbor's closed heart. Perhaps God will be merciful.

Second, this discrimination is "merciful." Clearly, the reference is to election, for reprobation, the other side of the decree of predestination, is not merciful. It is supreme mercy for God to give to a wicked sinner a new heart so that he can love God and believe in him.

Third, this discrimination is "righteous." It is righteous for God to give this gift of faith to some and to withhold it from others. It is God's prerogative, for he determines what he shall do with his gifts. Since he is not obligated to give this gift to anyone, he is not unjust when he withholds it from some. The Canons view those from whom God withholds faith as "equally involved in ruin." Listen to the Lord in Matthew 20:15: "Is it not lawful for me to do what I will with mine own? Is thine eye evil, because I am good?"

There is a twofold response to this truth.

Some wrest (or twist) it to their own destruction (2 Pet. 3:16). Such are men of "perverse, impure, and unstable minds." They either attack the doctrine, snarling at it like dogs, or they abuse the doctrine to excuse their wicked lives, wallowing in their iniquities like filthy swine, to use the imagery favored by John Calvin: "Hereby are we admonished, that although our salvation proceed from the only grace of God, and that therein it consisteth to the end. Notwithstanding it followeth not, that under the shadow thereof, we can let loose ourselves to evil, and give ourselves over thereto. But there are villains and dogs that bark against God, and there are also hogs, which overthrow this doctrine of election, by their loose and lewd life."[6]

---

6 John Calvin, *Sermons on Election and Reprobation* (Audubon, NJ: Old Paths Publications, 1996), 45.

Such twisters of the truth hate the doctrine of election, and by such hatred of God's word they are justly destroyed.

Others, who are called "holy and pious souls," derive from this truth "unspeakable consolation" (or comfort). The doctrine of election comforts God's children because in it they find salvation that is sure, which depends on God's power, wisdom, and grace alone. Any other doctrine, which depends upon man, makes salvation uncertain, and it makes comfort unattainable.

Thank God for your election, believing reader. It is the only difference between you and those who perish. Your attitude should not be, "Why has God not chosen everyone?" but "Why has God chosen me—even me?"

ARTICLE 7: ELECTION DEFINED AND EXPLAINED

> Election is the unchangeable purpose of God whereby, before the foundation of the world, He hath out of mere grace, according to the sovereign good pleasure of His own will, chosen, from the whole human race, which had fallen through their own fault from their primitive state of rectitude into sin and destruction, a certain number of persons to redemption in Christ, whom He from eternity appointed the Mediator and Head of the elect, and the foundation of salvation.

This elect number, though by nature neither better nor more deserving than others, but with them involved in one common misery, God hath decreed to give to Christ, to be saved by Him, and effectually to call and draw them to His communion by His Word and Spirit, to bestow upon them true faith, justification, and sanctification; and having powerfully preserved them in the fellowship of His Son, finally to glorify them for the demonstration of His mercy and for the praise of His glorious grace; as it is written: *According as he hath chosen us in him before the foundation of the world, that we should be holy and without blame before him in love; having predestinated us unto the adoption of children by Jesus Christ to himself, according to the good pleasure of his will, to the praise of the glory of his grace, wherein he hath made us accepted in the beloved* (Eph. 1:4–6). And elsewhere: *Whom he did predestinate, them he also called, and whom he called, them he also justified, and whom he justified, them he also glorified* (Rom. 8:30).

In this article the synod defined election. The definition might appear long and complicated, but remember that every long sentence can be broken down into its constituent parts for easier comprehension. If we pare down the sentence to its barest bones, we will readily understand the differences between biblical, Reformed election and the counterfeit version of election pedaled by the Arminians.

There really is one main difference: biblical election is God's choice *of persons*, while Arminian election is God's choice *of conditions*. According to Arminianism, God has determined to save all those who will fit themselves into a certain category, but God has not determined who those persons shall be. According to the Bible, God has determined to save definite, specific, individual persons in distinction from others, whom he has determined not to save. This will become clearer as we proceed.

About God's election article 7 teaches a least ten truths.

First, election is God's purpose: "Election is the unchangeable *purpose* of God" (emphasis added). Some have viewed predestination as a kind of divine lottery or the throwing of the cosmic dice: "Heads, you are elected. Tails, you are reprobated." The accusation is that God's election is arbitrary, based on a random, reasonless whim. Such an accusation is unworthy of God, wicked, and false. Take note of the fact that the Reformed fathers began their definition with the word "purpose." There is nothing random or arbitrary in God's counsel, for everything serves the one purpose of God's glory. God chose certain men and angels and rejected others so that the full display of his glory could be given (Rom. 9:22–23). In Ephesians 1:11, where the context is election, Paul declares that God "worketh all things after the counsel of his own will." There is nothing arbitrary in this.

Second, election is the "*unchangeable* purpose of God" (emphasis added). Election is unchangeable or immutable because it is eternal, and it is unchangeable because it is the purpose of God. Men change their purposes either because of powerlessness or ignorance, for they cannot overcome a difficulty or they do not foresee difficulties before they arise. In contrast to weak, ignorant men and women, God is almighty, omniscient, and immutable. Therefore, his purpose is unchangeable. Who or what could ever induce God to change his mind?

Third, election is the *eternal* purpose of God, which the Canons express with the biblical phrase "before the foundation of the world." If God determined to do something (to choose some and to reject others) before the foundation of the world, he did so in eternity before the beginning of time itself (Eph. 1:4; Matt. 25:34). God did not, therefore, make his choice after man had fallen into sin. Instead, before God created man, he chose to save certain persons out of the mass of mankind. Before God declared, "Let there be light" (Gen. 1:3), God had already chosen his elect people in Jesus Christ. What a wonder!

Fourth, election is *unconditional*, for God's choice does not depend on any quality, real or potential, in the ones chosen. The reason for election is "the sovereign good pleasure of His own will." Perhaps an illustration will help. If someone offered you a plate of cookies, you would choose a cookie based on some quality in it. You might choose based on the size, the shape, the color, the smell, or the flavor. Perhaps you prefer chocolate to coconut cream. Perhaps you dislike raisins or marzipan. That is an example of conditional election. However, unconditional election is a choice based on the elector (the one choosing) instead of the elected (the one being chosen). Arminianism teaches conditional election, for God supposedly chooses according to some quality that he sees, or rather foresees, in the elect. God chooses those who, according to his foreknowledge, shall believe and persevere to the end, while God rejects those who, again according to his foreknowledge, shall not believe or who shall believe for a time but not persevere. The Canons will address the subject of God's foreknowledge in article 9.

Fifth, election is *gracious*: "Out of mere grace." God's grace is his beautiful attitude of favor, and when it is shown to sinners, God's grace is undeserved, unmerited, and even forfeited favor. In choosing to elect and save sinners, God displays his grace, which excludes all works, worth, or merit as the cause or ground of salvation and election (Rom. 11:5–6). Arminianism, for all its talk of grace, is a system of salvation based on the worth of men. The word or concept *grace* in the writings of Arminians is merely a smokescreen to confuse the unwary.

Sixth, election is *personal*. This is a key difference between the Arminian error and the truth of the scriptures. It is not merely that God has chosen to save believers, but also that God has determined who those believers shall be. Read the following passages, taking note of the personal pronouns ("we," "us," "you"): Romans 8:29–30; Ephesians 1:3, 5; 1 Thessalonians 1:4; 2 Thessalonians 2:13; 2 Timothy 1:9; and 2 Timothy 2:10.

Seventh, election is *in Christ*. Jesus Christ is the elect one, and the elect are chosen in connection with him. The Canons call Christ "the Mediator and Head of the elect, and the foundation of salvation." A mediator is one who brings together two or more who are at variance with one another and between whom there is enmity (1 Tim. 2:5; Heb. 8:6; 9:15; 12:24). Jesus Christ is "the Mediator… of the elect." It is the work of Christ to reconcile the elect (and them only) to God by removing the enmity between them and God. Jesus does this by removing the sins of the elect, which are the cause of the enmity. Jesus Christ is "[the] Head of the elect." Therefore, he represents the elect (and them only) legally before God, and he is the source of life for them (and them only) who are his members. The elect are chosen to be the members of Christ and are, therefore, given to him (John 6:37, 39; 17:2, 9, 24).

This is significant language, for the Arminians will concede that Christ is the head of the church, but they will not confess that he is the head *of the elect*. If Christ is the head of the elect, God determines who the elect are, which Arminianism denies and even detests. In Arminianism *man* determines who the elect are, for anyone could, by the exercise of his free will, make himself elect or place himself into the category of the elect. Anyone could, by failing to believe or by failing to persevere in faith, make himself reprobate or place himself into the category of the reprobate, even, as will be discussed in the fifth head of doctrine, if he was previously elect.

The truth of Christ's headship of the elect means that the elect were given to Christ in the decree of election. Therefore, Christ and the elect stand or fall together. The only way in which the elect could perish—or any individual elect person could perish—is if Christ the head should perish, which, of course, is impossible and unthinkable.

Consider this citation from the first point of the Remonstrance of the Arminians:

> That God, by an eternal, unchangeable purpose in Jesus Christ his Son, before the foundation of the world, hath determined, out of the fallen, sinful race of men, to save in Christ, for Christ's sake, and through Christ, those who, through the grace of the Holy Ghost, shall believe on this his Son Jesus, and shall persevere in this faith and obedience of faith, through this grace, even to the end.[7]

---

7 Five Arminian Articles 1, in Philip Schaff, ed., *The Creeds of Christendom with a History and Critical Notes*, 6th ed., 3 vols. (New York: Harper and Row, 1931; repr., Grand Rapids, MI: Baker Books, 2007), 3:545.

The astute reader will notice that the Arminians pretend to make much of Christ: "That God, by...*Jesus Christ* his Son, before the foundation of the world, hath determined...to save *in Christ, for Christ's sake*, and *through Christ*" (emphasis added). The name Christ is repeated, but the use of his name is a clever ruse, a kind of misdirection. Arminianism denies that Christ is the head of a definite elect people. Instead, Christ is the potential head of a potential elect people. Indeed, Christ is the potential head of everyone—or of no one. By "in Christ" Arminianism means that God will save those who by their own free will shall believe in Christ, or that God will save those who choose to be in Christ, or that God foresees who shall choose Christ and elects them accordingly. If you pare down the sentence, you will see this: "God...hath determined...to save... those who...shall believe...and shall persevere."

But in the Arminian scheme, anyone might believe and persevere or no one might believe and persevere. God has nothing to do with it. Arminian election is therefore impersonal.

Eighth, election is *unto salvation*, and God's decree *includes all the blessings of salvation*: "To be saved by Him, and effectually to call and draw them to His communion by His Word and Spirit." A common way in which Arminians deny election is by insisting that election is only unto external privileges or positions of service. The nation of Israel was elected, or Saul was elected to be king, for example. Those examples of election were not salvific (unto salvation). While there is some truth to this, for "they are not all Israel, which are of Israel" (Rom. 9:6), there is more to election than external, national, temporal privileges. "God hath from the beginning *chosen you to salvation* through sanctification of the Spirit and belief of the truth" (2 Thess. 2:13, emphasis added).

In addition, election is not only to final salvation, but it also includes all the blessings of salvation in the *Ordo salutis* (order of salvation)—effectual calling, being drawn into communion with God by the word and Holy Spirit, bestowal of true faith, justification, sanctification, powerful preservation, and final glorification.

Ninth, election is *of the undeserving.* This is a further development of the point made earlier that election is gracious. Since the elect are viewed as involved in common misery with the reprobate, they are "by nature neither better nor more deserving than others." It is, therefore, a matter of God's gracious sovereignty that he chooses one over another, the result of which is that no one can boast. In Arminianism it is the worthy who are chosen and ultimately saved. God's grace might help along the way, but in the final analysis, the sinner makes the decisive contribution to salvation by his freewill choice, his faith, his good works, and his final perseverance.

Finally, tenth, the *ultimate goal of election* is "the demonstration of His [God's] mercy and for the praise of His glorious grace." That is the fundamental quarrel the Reformed faith has with Arminianism: it is a proud heresy that robs God of his glory in salvation. Any other election than the one set forth here from the holy scriptures is an election that glorifies man and is really no election at all.

Believing reader, this subject is not merely academic. Take a moment to thank and praise God from the bottom of your heart that he has chosen you. For who are we that we should be chosen by God in distinction from others? "Blessed is the man whom thou choosest, and causest to approach unto thee, that he may dwell in thy courts: we shall be satisfied with the goodness of thy house, even of thy holy temple" (Ps. 65:4).

26. For ye see your calling, brethren, how that not many wise men after the flesh, not many mighty, not many noble, are called:
27. But God hath chosen the foolish things of the world to confound the wise; and God hath chosen the weak things of the world to confound the things which are mighty;

28. And base things of the world, and things which are despised, hath God chosen, yea, and things which are not, to bring to nought things that are:
29. That no flesh should glory in his presence. (1 Cor. 1:26–29)

ERROR AND REJECTION 1: NO ETERNAL DECREE OF ELECTION

> Error 1: Who teach that the will of God to save those who would believe and would persevere in faith and in the obedience of faith is the whole and entire decree of election unto salvation, and that nothing else concerning this decree has been revealed in God's Word.
>
> Rejection: For these deceive the simple and plainly contradict the Scriptures, which declare that God will not only save those who will believe, but that He has also from eternity chosen certain particular persons to whom above others He in time will grant both faith in Christ and perseverance, as it is written: *I manifested thy name unto the men whom thou gavest me out of the world* (John 17:6). *And as many as were ordained to eternal life believed* (Acts 13:48). And: *Even as he chose us in him before the foundation of the world, that we should be holy and without blemish before him in love* (Eph. 1:4).

The Arminians gutted election of any essential meaning. For the Arminians, God's decree did not concern persons but conditions: God has determined to save all those who fulfill certain conditions, namely, God has determined to save "those who would believe and would persevere in faith and in the obedience of faith." Apart from that, claimed the Arminians, "nothing else concerning this decree has been revealed in God's Word." That is, insisted the Arminians, "the whole and entire decree of election unto salvation."

The answer of the Canons is clear, for God has "from eternity chosen certain particular persons." Election is personal. To those persons (and to them only), God will "grant both faith in Christ and perseverance." The Arminian teaching, charged the fathers at Dordt, serves only to "deceive the simple," who are easily fooled by pious-sounding words. Moreover, Arminians "plainly contradict the Scriptures" in John 17:6, Acts 13:48, Ephesians 1:4, and many other places.

The Arminians said, "Faith and obedience determine who are elected." The Reformed fathers said, "Election determines who will believe and obey." Arminianism proclaims an election in which God elects nobody. The Bible teaches an election in which God chooses a particular people for himself. Those two positions are poles apart.

ARTICLE 8: ONLY ONE DECREE OF ELECTION

> There are not various decrees of election, but one and the same decree respecting all those who shall be saved, both under the Old and New Testament; since the Scripture declares the good pleasure, purpose, and counsel of the divine will to be one, according to which He hath chosen us from eternity, both to grace and glory, to salvation and the way of salvation, which He hath ordained that we should walk therein.

If you have ever wondered why theology is so complicated, blame the heretics. They make it complicated. The main idea of this article is the unity of election. In this article, and especially in error and rejection 2, we see the duplicity of the Arminians. The truth is simple, but the lie is complicated and convoluted, perhaps nowhere so much as here.

The Arminians, in an attempt to appear orthodox, proposed several different kinds of decrees of election, none of which was unconditional election. The Reformed fathers responded to the Arminians with a clear confession of the unity of election.

Article 8 states: "There are not various decrees of election, but one and the same decree respecting all those who shall be saved." This one decree of election includes all of the elect; the elect from both the Old Testament and the New Testament; and the end (salvation and grace and glory) and the means to the end (the way of salvation and our walking in that way). The unity of election depends on the unity of God's will, for "the good pleasure, purpose, and counsel of the divine will" is "one."

The oneness of God's will rules out various modern theological errors in which God supposedly wills or desires contradictory outcomes at the same time. The best known of these theological views is the idea that God in predestination decrees to save only some (the elect), but that in the preaching of the gospel he desires to save all men (including the reprobate), which is the error of the well-meant or free offer of the gospel. This leads to a contradiction in God's will: he supposedly wills to save and he wills not to save the reprobate. For proof of the oneness of God's will, see Job 23:13, Psalm 115:3, Psalm 135:6, Isaiah 46:10, Daniel 4:35, and Ephesians 1:11.

This article also rules out the modern heresy of dispensationalism, for there is only one people of God, chosen in Christ, redeemed in the cross, called by the Spirit, saved by grace, and destined for grace and glory. Dispensationalism teaches that there are two peoples of God with different origins and different destinies: the Jews and the church. Dispensationalism is incompatible with the Reformed faith.

The truth is simple—God chooses his elect and saves them to the end according to *one* decree. Arminianism, unsurprisingly, is much more complicated than that. That complexity is exposed and refuted in head one, error and rejection 2, to which we now turn.

ERROR AND REJECTION 2: VARIOUS DECREES OF ELECTION

> Error 2: Who teach that there are various kinds of election of God unto eternal life: the one general and indefinite, the other particular and definite; and that the latter in turn is either incomplete, revocable, non-decisive, and conditional, or complete, irrevocable, decisive, and absolute. Likewise: that there is one election unto faith and another unto salvation, so that election can be unto justifying faith without being a decisive election unto salvation.
>
> Rejection: For this is a fancy of men's minds, invented regardless of the Scriptures, whereby the doctrine of election is corrupted, and this golden chain of our salvation is broken: *And whom he foreordained, them he also called; and whom he called, them he also justified; and whom he justified, them he also glorified* (Rom. 8:30).

The Arminians, when asked about election, were masters of deception. They claimed to believe in election, but they had different kinds of election in mind. It was, therefore, difficult to determine what they meant when they used the word "election."

The subject of error and rejection 2 is emphatically "election of God unto eternal life." About *that* election, the Arminians distinguished different kinds. I say "*that* election" because there are different kinds of election in scripture. First, there is the election of national Israel in distinction from the rejection of nations such as Moab, Edom, and Babylon. Within the elect nation of Israel were elect and reprobate individuals, for "they are not all Israel, which are of Israel" (Rom. 9:6). Second, there is the election of men to different offices—Saul was chosen to be a king; Cyrus was chosen to be a shepherd; Judas Iscariot was chosen to be a disciple (1 Sam. 9:16; Isa. 44:28; 45:1–5; John 6:70–71), but they were not chosen to everlasting salvation, grace, and glory, for it is clear from scripture that those men were reprobate ungodly who perished in their sins.

The Canons are not concerned with these legitimate distinctions, and the Arminians did not have those kinds of distinctions in mind. The Arminians had in mind the election of God unto eternal life—they sought to corrupt *that*.

Arminianism is complicated. Especially the Arminianism of James Arminius and the teachings of the Remonstrants who followed Arminius were complicated. Modern Arminians are much less convoluted in their theology. Therefore, most modern Arminians would not recognize these distinctions. They are satisfied to teach conditional election based on God's foreknowledge, which error is addressed in article 9. Much of what follows, therefore, is a historical curiosity. Let me warn the reader before you proceed—you will find the views of the Arminians very complicated. Perhaps you will not understand them at all. Do not be overly concerned about that. The writer shares your perplexity. Instead, bear in mind that there is one decree of predestination, the ravings of the Arminians notwithstanding.

First, the Arminians posited a *general* decree, which is God's choice of the whole of humanity. In a certain sense, God chose the whole of humanity to be saved, for the Arminians taught that God desires the salvation of all men without exception. This general decree is *indefinite*, which means that it does not define or determine whether a person shall be saved or not. It comprises all men, but no man in particular. Many Arminians today believe that God has chosen all men in a certain sense.

Second, the Arminians posited a *particular* decree, which includes only particular people. You might call this decree an election within an election. This particular decree was also *definite*, because it defined or determined who the people within it should be. Perhaps the particular, definite decree sounds orthodox, but the Arminians were not finished making distinctions.

They further subdivided the particular, definite decree in four ways.

First, the particular, definite decree could be *incomplete*, which means that it might be an open-ended decree, or a decree that must be completed by man. An individual person may "complete" the decree by faith and perseverance in faith. However, God in his decree has not determined who shall believe and persevere to the end in faith. God does not complete that decree, but the sinner does.

Second, the particular, definite decree could be *revocable*, which means that it might be canceled or annulled. Someone might be "elect" in a revocable sense for a time, but he could forfeit his election by his unbelief or lack of perseverance in faith.

Third, the particular, definite decree could be *non-decisive*, which means that God, although he has "chosen" the persons in that decree, has not decided whether the ones "elected" in that decree shall actually believe or persevere to the end in faith. God does not decide that, but allows that to be determined by the free will of the individual.

Fourth, the particular, definite decree could be *conditional*, which means that God's decree depends on the fulfillment of certain conditions. Thus within that decree, someone might be chosen conditionally unto salvation on the condition that he believes and perseveres to the end in faith.

To recap, Arminianism taught a general, indefinite decree of all men; and a particular, definite decree of some men, which in turn could be incomplete, revocable, non-decisive or conditional.

But the Arminians were still not finished spinning their web of deceit. The particular, definite decree they subdivided four additional ways.

First, the particular, definite decree could be *complete*, which means that God completes the decree. Because God knows that a certain individual will believe and persevere in faith, he determines that person's salvation, thus completing the decree.

Second, the particular, definite decree could be *irrevocable* because God will not cancel or annul his decree. He will not change the number or the identity of the elect because he foresees that certain individuals will choose to believe and persevere in faith.

Third, the particular, definite decree could be *decisive*, because God, having determined to save those who will believe and persevere in faith, decisively determines to include them in his decree of election.

Fourth, the particular, definite decree could be *absolute*, which means that God certainly and absolutely knows that those whom he foresees as believing and persevering will be elected.

To recap once again, Arminianism taught a general, indefinite decree of all men; and a particular, definite decree of some, which could be incomplete, revocable, non-decisive, or conditional, or which could be complete, irrevocable, decisive, or absolute. If your mind is reeling after trying to decipher that, do not worry. That should be your reaction. And do not be overly concerned because, thankfully, the truth is much simpler than Arminianism.

One word, however, is missing, and that word is *unconditional.* Election, for all its supposed completeness, irrevocability, decisiveness, and absoluteness, still depends on man, whose faith and perseverance God foresees, and to which God essentially reacts or responds.

Additionally, the Arminians taught that a person could be elected "unto justifying faith," that is, chosen for a time to believe (and justified by that faith, which election and justification are reversible and losable). This "election" is not the same as "decisive election unto salvation," which, of course, still depends on the sinner's faith and perseverance.

The fathers at Dordt rejected the subtleties of the Arminians: "This is a fancy of men's minds, invented regardless of the Scriptures." The source of this labyrinth of distinctions is not the scriptures, but the depraved minds of men. Arminianism is not an explanation of election, but a corruption of election. Moreover, it breaks the golden chain of salvation. "When the Gentiles heard this [that Christ was set to be a light of the Gentiles], they were glad, and glorified the word of the Lord: and as many as were ordained to eternal life believed" (Acts 13:48). "Whom he did predestinate, them he also called: and whom he called, them he also justified: and whom he justified, them he also glorified" (Rom. 8:30).

So did the Arminians believe in election? The answer is yes and no. Yes, they posited a kind of election; but, no, they did not believe what the Bible teaches about election. Therefore, they used the word *election*, while they poured into it their own fanciful interpretations regardless of the scriptures. When the Arminian uses the word *election*, beware—all that glitters is not gold.

ARTICLE 9: ELECTION THE FOUNTAIN OF EVERY SAVING GOOD

> This election was not founded upon foreseen faith, and the obedience of faith, holiness, or any other good quality or disposition in man, as the prerequisite, cause, or condition on which it depended; but men are chosen to faith and to the obedience of faith, holiness, etc. Therefore election is the fountain of every saving good, from which proceed faith, holiness, and the other gifts of salvation, and finally eternal life itself, as its fruits and effects, according to that of the apostle: *He hath chosen us* (not because we were, but) *that we should be holy and without blame before him in love* (Eph. 1:4).

The main point of this article is that election unto salvation is *unconditional*. This is a very important article because it condemns the concept and the word *condition*. The Arminians used that word and championed that concept, but the fathers at Dordt refused to use it. We would be wise to avoid it also.

Arminianism is at its heart *conditional salvation*—God will save sinners if they do something, that is, if they fulfill certain conditions demanded or required by God. The conditions in Arminianism on which salvation depends are faith and obedience, and perseverance in such faith and obedience to the end of life. "This election," declare the Canons in opposition to Arminianism, "was not founded upon foreseen faith." This brings us to the biblical concept of foreknowledge.

Modern Arminians present election with the following illustration: God looks down the corridor of time and sees, or foresees, that Bob will, if he hears the gospel, choose to accept Jesus by the power of his free will. Therefore, God seeing that, or foreseeing that, elects Bob. However, God sees, or foresees, that Lucy, if she hears the gospel, will not choose to accept Jesus by the power of her free will. Therefore, God seeing that, or foreseeing that, does not elect Lucy. Therefore, election depends on what Bob or Lucy will do if left to the use of their free wills, and God will not interfere, one way or another, except that he will try to persuade both Bob and Lucy to accept Jesus in the gospel.

But what do the scriptures say?

Obviously, the verb *foreknow* is related to the simpler verb *know*. To know in scripture is the intimate knowledge of love. In that sense God knows his people. Consider God's word in Amos 3:2: "You only have I known of all the families of the earth." Clearly, the prophet does not mean that God did not have any knowledge of the other nations of the world. He was well aware of Edom, Philistia, Babylon, and the other heathen nations. The idea is that God disregarded, did not care about, and did not love any other nation. He left them in the darkness of sin and unbelief (Ps. 147:20; Acts 14:16). In that sense he did not know them. Jesus will say to the unbelieving hypocrites on the day of judgment, "I never knew you: depart from me, ye that work iniquity" (Matt. 7:23). This does not mean that Jesus did not know that these men existed or was ignorant of their deeds (he calls them workers of iniquity and he will be their judge), but that he did not know them with the intimate knowledge of love. In that sense, in that awful sense, he never knew them.

Foreknowledge is a similar concept. Sometimes to foreknow means to know beforehand (Acts 26:5; 2 Pet. 3:17). Our foreknowledge is, at best, uncertain. If you say to a friend, "I knew you would come," you simply mean, "Based on your word and on my knowledge of current events, and assuming that nothing would happen to prevent it, I had a very good idea, without infallible foreknowledge, that you were likely to come." God's foreknowledge is infinitely greater than that.

First, God foreknows events because he has determined them: "Him, being delivered by the determinate counsel and foreknowledge of God" (Acts 2:23). We do not deny that God foreknows that the elect will believe, but he foreknows or foresees it because he has predetermined it. God's foreknowledge is not an educated guess, nor does he have a crystal ball in which he divines the future. Rather, God's foreknowledge is causative.

Second, the passages that speak of God's foreknowledge teach that God foreknows persons. There are no passages in the Bible that teach that God foreknows only the faith of certain people. The classic passage is Romans 8:29–30. Notice what the passage does not say: "Whose faith he did foreknow," "whose obedience he did foreknow," or "whose perseverance he did foreknow." Rather, the passage says, "*Whom* he did foreknow" (emphasis added). This is true of the other passages that refer to God's foreknowledge of his people. "God hath not cast away his people which [whom] he foreknew" (Rom. 11:2); "Peter, an apostle of Jesus Christ, to the strangers scattered throughout Pontus, Galatia, Cappadocia, Asia, and Bithynia, elect according to the foreknowledge of God the Father" (1 Pet. 1:1–2).

This is not to deny that faith is the necessary means of salvation, nor is it to deny that unbelievers perish (article 4 has already explained that). But this is to deny that faith is the condition that the sinner must fulfill in order to receive salvation or even to be elected.

Article 9 explains further what the fathers at Dordt meant when they opposed the idea of *conditions*. They used three words to explain: "prerequisite," "cause," and "condition." A prerequisite is something required beforehand. This is the definition of a condition in the Canons, which word is immediately condemned. A prerequisite for entrance into the USA, for example, is a valid passport and a visa. Without these prerequisite documents, a traveler from another country will be denied access to the USA. The Arminians taught that the prerequisite to election is foreseen faith, without which no one shall be elected: "[The] condition on which it depended." The Arminians taught that God elected people *only if* they fulfilled the condition of faith, which he foresaw that they would fulfill. Therefore, God foresaw that certain people would choose to believe and would persevere in faith. On the basis of that foreknowledge, or on the basis of what God foresees man will do, God elects a person to eternal life. Thus in Arminianism election to eternal life is *conditional*.

All of this the Canons emphatically deny.

Election does not depend on any "good quality or disposition in man, as the prerequisite, cause, or condition." Instead of faith being the condition of election, "election is the fountain of every saving good."

A fountain is the source of something. The fountain, which is election, is the source of faith; holiness; the other gifts of salvation; and eternal life itself: "When the Gentiles heard this, they were glad, and glorified the word of the Lord: and as many as were ordained to eternal life believed" (Acts 13:48). "Ye believe not, because ye are not of my sheep, as I said unto you" (John 10:26). "According as he hath chosen us in him before the foundation of the world, that we should be holy and without blame before him in love" (Eph. 1:4). "Moreover whom he did predestinate, them he also called: and whom he called, them he also justified: and whom he justified, them he also glorified" (Rom. 8:30). "The children being not yet born, neither having done any good or evil, that the purpose of God according to election might stand, not of works, but of him that calleth" (9:11). "All that the Father giveth me shall come to me; and him that cometh to me I will in no wise cast out" (John 6:37).

Faith, holiness, and the other gifts of salvation, and finally eternal life itself "proceed" from election. Faith, holiness, and the other gifts of salvation, and finally eternal life itself are the "fruits and effects of salvation." Therefore, if election is the fountain of faith and of all the other gifts of salvation, faith *cannot* be the condition, prerequisite, or cause of salvation. Faith cannot be man's part in salvation, or his contribution to salvation, or the condition that he fulfills to receive salvation.

Faith is the gift of God, which God gives to his people as part of their salvation, which he gives to his elect according to his eternal decree (Canons 1.6). Thus we see two radically different views concerning the relationship of election and faith: the Arminian view is that faith is the "prerequisite, cause, or condition on which it [election] depend[s]," while the Reformed view is that election is "the fountain of every saving good," so that faith is the fruit and effect of election, not its condition. These two positions (condition and fountain) are irreconcilable.

Do you believe that your election and salvation depend on something that you have done or would do? Cast away such a proud error and believe the God-glorifying truth that election is the fountain of every saving good. Such truth will humble you in the dust before your Creator and will fill your heart with gladness.

ERROR AND REJECTION 4: THE CONDITIONS FOR ELECTION UNTO FAITH

> Error 4: Who teach that in the election unto faith this condition is beforehand demanded, namely, that man should use the light of nature aright, be pious, humble, meek, and fit for eternal life, as if on these things election were in any way dependent.

> Rejection: For this savors of the teaching of Pelagius, and is opposed to the doctrine of the apostle, when he writes: *Among whom we also all once lived in the lust of our flesh, doing the desires of the flesh and of the mind, and were by nature children of wrath, even as the rest; but God, being rich in mercy, for his great love wherewith he loved us, even when we were dead through our trespasses, made us alive together with Christ (by grace have ye been saved), and raised us up with him, and made us to sit with him in heavenly places in Christ Jesus; that in the ages to come he might show the exceeding riches of his grace in kindness towards us in Christ Jesus; for by grace have ye been saved through faith; and that not of yourselves, it is the gift of God; not of works, that no man should glory* (Eph. 2:3–9).

The Arminians love conditions, which is why we wisely avoid the word altogether. Reformed theologians have in the past used the word *condition* in the sense of necessary means, and therefore not in the sense of prerequisite, but the Canons simply avoid the word, placing it into the mouths of their Arminian opponents. The Arminians maintained that in order to be elected there were conditions before demanded.

Error and rejection 4 deal with the conditions for election *unto faith*. Remember the distinction made earlier between election unto faith and election unto salvation, a distinction invented by the Arminians but not found in the Bible. Election unto faith and election unto salvation have their own peculiar conditions according to Arminianism, outlined in errors and rejections 4–5 respectively.

The conditions for being elected by God unto faith are to use the light of nature aright; to be pious; to be humble; to be meek; and to be fit for eternal life. Note well: election unto faith *depends upon* these qualities.

The Arminians assume with this assertion that the sinner is not totally corrupt or totally depraved, for by "the light of nature" they understand human reason, free will, and the good inclinations supposedly still remaining in the nature of man. Scripture, however, denies that the sinner can use the light of nature aright because no goodness remains in him. This truth will be explored further in the third and fourth heads of doctrine.

The conditions listed here are impossible for fallen, sinful man to fulfill. They cannot be the conditions for election, for if they were, no one could be elected, and no one could be saved. Instead, these qualities are the fruit of election, which flow from election as water flows from a fountain. We must be very careful to distinguish between conditions and fruit.

To be pious is to be God-fearing, but about sinners God says, "There is no fear of God before their eyes" (Rom. 3:18). To be humble or meek is a fruit of the Spirit, which is not present in natural man (Gal. 5:23), for among the many vices of mankind is pride (Rom. 1:30; 2 Tim. 3:2). To be "fit for eternal life" is impossible, for the natural man is worthy only of death (Rom. 6:23). Therefore, to assert that these qualities (to fear God, to be meek, humble, and fit for eternal life) are the conditions of election to faith is patently absurd and a denial of the truth of God's word.

The fathers at Dordt sharply condemned the teachings of the Arminians. First, Dordt convicted the Arminians of Pelagianism: "This savors of the teaching of Pelagius." Pelagius (c. AD 360–418), a heretic condemned in the early church, taught the free will of man and the ability of man to be saved by his own efforts, while he denied the depravity of man's nature. Indeed, Pelagius denied that grace is necessary for salvation. Second, in response to the error of the Arminians the fathers quoted the following:

> 3. Among whom also we all had our conversation in times past in the lusts of our flesh, fulfilling the desires of the flesh and of the mind; and were by nature the children of wrath, even as others.

4. But God, who is rich in mercy, for his great love wherewith he loved us,
5. Even when we were dead in sins, hath quickened us together with Christ, (by grace ye are saved;).
6. And hath raised us up together, and made us sit together in heavenly places in Christ Jesus:
7. That in the ages to come he might shew the exceeding riches of his grace in his kindness toward us through Christ Jesus.
8. For by grace are ye saved through faith; and that not of yourselves: it is the gift of God:
9. Not of works, lest any man should boast. (Eph. 2:3–9)

What could be clearer? Salvation is the gracious work of God alone for which we cannot fulfill any conditions. Arminianism is closer to Pelagianism than it is to the word of God.

How we should detest and reject the proud error of Arminianism.

ERROR AND REJECTION 5: THE CONDITIONS FOR ELECTION UNTO SALVATION

> Error 5: Who teach that the incomplete and non-decisive election of particular persons to salvation occurred because of a foreseen faith, conversion, holiness, godliness, which either began or continued for some time; but that the complete and decisive election occurred because of foreseen perseverance unto the end in faith, conversion, holiness, and godliness; and that this is the gracious and evangelical worthiness for the sake of which he who is chosen is more worthy than he who is not chosen; and that therefore faith, the obedience of faith, holiness, godliness, and perseverance are not fruits of the unchangeable election unto glory, but are conditions which, being required beforehand, were foreseen as being met by those who will be fully elected,

> and are causes without which the unchangeable election to glory does not occur.
>
> Rejection: This is repugnant to the entire Scripture, which constantly inculcates this and similar declarations: Election is *not* out *of works, but of him that calleth* (Rom. 9:11). *And as many as were ordained to eternal life believed* (Acts 13:48). *He chose us in him before the foundation of the world, that we should be holy* (Eph. 1:4). *Ye did not choose me, but I chose you* (John 15:16). *But if it be of grace, it is no more of work* (Rom. 11:6). *Herein is love, not that we loved God, but that he loved us, and sent his Son* (1 John 4:10).

Error and rejection 4 examined the supposed conditions of election unto faith and found them to savor of Pelagianism. Error and rejection 5 address the supposed conditions of election *unto salvation.*

Again we wade into murky waters because of the convoluted heresy of the Arminians. We are thankful that the Canons serve as a clear guide through the quagmire.

First, the Arminians posited certain conditions for "the incomplete and non-decisive election of particular persons to salvation." These alleged conditions or prerequisites are "foreseen faith, [foreseen] conversion, [foreseen] holiness, [and foreseen] godliness." These foreseen virtues "began or continued for some time."

Because God foresaw that the persons concerned would not persevere to the end in faith, in conversion, in holiness, and in godliness, he included them only in his decree of "incomplete and non-decisive election," but not in his decree of "complete and decisive election," for which there are other conditions or prerequisites.

Second, the Arminians posited certain conditions for "the complete and decisive election." These alleged conditions are "foreseen perseverance unto the end in faith, conversion, holiness, and godliness," which the Arminians called "the gracious and evangelical worthiness for the sake of which he who is chosen is more worthy than he who is not chosen."

You will notice that the main difference between the conditions for "incomplete and non-decisive election" and "complete and decisive election" is that in the former faith, conversion, holiness and godliness are foreseen as merely beginning, while in the latter they are foreseen as continuing to the end. You will also notice the proud error of the Arminians: the person chosen with the latter election is "more worthy" than the person chosen with the former election. Moreover, you will notice the duplicitous language of the Arminians, for this "worthiness" is called "gracious and evangelical." Grace, by definition, excludes worthiness, for grace is God's free favor, not the response to some supposed worthiness in the creature. A gracious worthiness makes as much sense as dry water or cold fire.

Notwithstanding the pious-sounding rhetoric, the prerequisite or condition for any kind of election unto salvation in Arminianism is foreseen faith, or foreseen perseverance, or both. The Bible, however, never speaks of foreseen faith or foreseen perseverance, but only of foreknown persons, as noted in the explanation of article 9. And the reason certain people are foreknown is that God eternally set his love upon them and elected them unconditionally to salvation and glory.

The conclusion of the Arminians is clear. First, faith, the obedience of faith, holiness, godliness, and perseverance are *not* "fruits of the unchangeable election unto glory." In article 9 the Reformed fathers had already stated that "election is the fountain of every saving good." Arminianism abhors and denies that truth, for according to Arminianism election is not the fountain of faith, and faith is not the fruit of election. Second, faith, the obedience of faith, holiness, godliness, and perseverance are "conditions...being required beforehand." Third, these conditions (faith, the obedience of faith, holiness, godliness, and perseverance) are "foreseen as being met by those who will be fully elected." Fourth, these conditions "are causes without which the unchangeable election to glory does not occur."

To recap: these conditions must be met. God foresees that certain people will meet these conditions. Because he foresees that certain people will meet these conditions, he elects them "fully" to salvation. If he foresees that certain people will meet these conditions only for a time (that is, he foresees that they will not persevere in them), God elects them only incompletely and non-decisively to salvation.

The answer of the Canons is brief and sharp: "This is repugnant to the entire Scripture." Repugnant means repulsive, offensive, and disgusting. This whole scheme of twisted reasoning is offensive to the word of God. The Bible "constantly inculcates" the opposite, where the word "inculcate" means to teach persistently, to hammer or to drive home, or to insist upon something. There follows a list of texts proving that election is the fountain of every saving good: "When the Gentiles heard this, they were glad, and glorified the word of the Lord: and as many as were ordained to eternal life believed" (Acts 13:48). "According as he hath chosen us in him before the foundation of the world, that we should be holy and without blame before him in love" (Eph. 1:4). "Ye have not chosen me, but I have chosen you, and ordained you, that ye should go and bring forth fruit, and that your fruit should remain: that whatsoever ye shall ask of the Father in my name, he may give it you" (John 15:16). "If by grace, then is it no more of works: otherwise grace is no more grace. But if it be of works, then it is no more grace: otherwise work is no more work" (Rom. 11:6). "Herein is love, not that we loved God, but that he loved us, and sent his Son to be the propitiation for our sins" (1 John 4:10).

Believing reader, you were chosen not because you were worthy, but because God is gracious. Do not be tempted even to contemplate robbing God of his glory.

ARTICLE 10: GOD'S GOOD PLEASURE THE SOLE CAUSE OF ELECTION

> The good pleasure of God is the sole cause of this gracious election, which doth not consist herein, that out of all possible qualities and actions of men God has chosen some as a condition of salvation; but that He was pleased out of the common mass of sinners to adopt some certain persons as a peculiar people to Himself, as it is written, *For the children being not yet born, neither having done any good or evil,* etc., *it was said* (namely to Rebecca): *the elder shall serve the younger; as it is written, Jacob have I loved, but Esau have I hated* (Rom. 9:11–13). *And as many as were ordained to eternal life believed* (Acts 13:48).

The subject of this article is that election is *personal*, for God "was pleased out of the common mass of sinners to adopt some certain persons as a peculiar people to Himself." Therefore, God has determined to save some (not all), in distinction from others whom God has determined not to save. God views all people as "the common mass of sinners." Therefore, God views them all as deserving only damnation and not as deserving salvation. Salvation is gracious, not based on the merits of people. Yet God is pleased to set his love on some, to have mercy on some, and to show grace to some. The Canons call this blessing, to which we are predestined, adoption.

Adoption is one of the blessings of salvation. It is really an aspect of justification, for adoption like justification is a legal act of God. Adoption is that act by which God makes us legally his children and bestows upon us the privileges of sonship: "Having predestinated us unto the adoption of children by Jesus Christ to himself, according to the good pleasure of his will" (Eph. 1:5).

14. For as many as are led by the Spirit of God, they are the sons of God.

15. For ye have not received the spirit of bondage again to fear; but ye have received the Spirit of adoption, whereby we cry, Abba, Father.
16. The Spirit itself beareth witness with our spirit, that we are the children of God:
17. And if children, then heirs; heirs of God, and joint-heirs with Christ; if so be that we suffer with him, that we may be also glorified together. (Rom. 8:14–17)

4. But when the fulness of the time was come, God sent forth his Son, made of a woman, made under the law,
5. To redeem them that were under the law, that we might receive the adoption of sons.
6. And because ye are sons, God hath sent forth the Spirit of his Son into your hearts, crying, Abba, Father.
7. Wherefore thou art no more a servant, but a son; and if a son, then an heir of God through Christ. (Gal. 4:4–7)

12. But as many as received him, to them gave he power to become the sons of God, *even* to them that believe on his name:
13. Which were born, not of blood, nor of the will of the flesh, nor of the will of man, but of God. (John 1:12–13)

Before the foundation of the world, God determined to adopt his children for himself. He determined whom he would adopt. The reason he chose one in distinction from another is the good pleasure of his will. God determined to make the elect "a peculiar people to Himself." The word "peculiar" does not mean odd or weird, but it refers to something that belongs to God as his special property. It is something on which God has set his heart, something in which God delights, and something which God prizes or treasures as valuable or dear to him. Therefore, those who are God's "peculiar people" are the objects of his sovereign, discriminating love. The term "peculiar people" is derived from the Old Testament and applied to the church in the New Testament. This is significant because it identifies Old Testament Israel and the New Testament church as one people of God: "If ye will obey my voice indeed, and keep my covenant, then ye shall be a peculiar treasure unto me above all people: for all the earth is mine" (Ex. 19:5). "Thou art a holy people unto the LORD thy God: the LORD thy God hath chosen thee to be a special people unto himself, above all people that are upon the face of the earth" (Deut. 7:6). "Thou art a holy people unto the LORD thy God, and the LORD hath chosen thee to be a peculiar people unto himself, above all the nations that are upon the earth" (14:2). "The LORD hath chosen Jacob unto himself, and Israel for his peculiar treasure" (Ps. 135:4). "[Christ] gave himself for us, that he might redeem us from all iniquity, and purify unto himself a peculiar people, zealous of good works" (Titus 2:14). "Ye are a chosen generation, a royal priesthood, a holy nation, a peculiar people; that ye should shew forth the praises of him who hath called you out of darkness into his marvellous light" (1 Pet. 2:9).

The article sets forth a contrast between God's good pleasure and certain qualities and actions of men as the cause of election: "The good pleasure of God is the sole cause of this gracious election." We cannot seek a cause deeper than the good pleasure of God, which is that which God is pleased to do or that which God is pleased to decree to be done. Since election, the sole cause of which is the good pleasure of God, is the fountain of salvation and of every saving good, there are no conditions on which it depends that man has to fulfill.

To summarize: the Arminians taught an impersonal election in which God did not choose *persons* in his decree of election, but God chose *conditions* that men must fulfill in order to be elected and saved. The Arminians declared that God could have chosen many different conditions of salvation, but that God's election consists in this: *he chose faith as the condition of salvation and election*. To that issue, the Reformed fathers turned in head one, error and rejection 3.

ERROR AND REJECTION 3: THE ELECTION OF CERTAIN CONDITIONS

> Error 3: Who teach that the good pleasure and purpose of God, of which Scripture makes mention in the doctrine of election, does not consist in this, that God chose certain persons rather than others, but in this, that He chose out of all possible conditions (among which are also the works of the law), or out of the whole order of things, the act of faith, which from its very nature is undeserving, as well as its incomplete obedience, as a condition of salvation, and that He would graciously consider this in itself as a complete obedience and count it worthy of the reward of eternal life.
>
> Rejection: For by this injurious error the pleasure of God and the merits of Christ are made of none effect, and men are drawn away by useless questions from the truth of gracious justification and from the simplicity of Scripture, and this declaration of the apostle is charged as untrue: *Who saved us, and called us with a holy calling, not according to our works, but according to his own purpose and grace, which was given us in Christ Jesus before times eternal* (2 Tim. 1:9).

Article 10, which we have just considered, taught that God's good pleasure does not consist in this: "That out of all possible qualities and actions of men God has chosen some [qualities and actions of men] as a condition of salvation," but that God's good pleasure consists in his choice of certain *persons* in distinction from other persons.

The Arminians attempted to overthrow the truth that God's good pleasure is the sole cause of gracious election. God, argued the Arminians, could have chosen the works of the law as the condition of salvation. God could have chosen anything at all as the condition of salvation. God had before him in his eternal counsel "all possible conditions" or "the whole order of things" from which to choose.

(Notice, again: God is not choosing persons, but conditions. That cannot be emphasized enough.) Out of all possible conditions, God chose "the act of faith" with "its incomplete obedience" as a condition of salvation.

Arminianism perversely attempted to find God's grace here: God *graciously* considers faith and the imperfect obedience of faith as "worthy of the reward of eternal life." God is gracious because he supposedly lowers the bar to make it easier for man to attain to salvation. God is gracious because he supposedly makes it possible for man to contribute to his salvation, or to fulfill the conditions for salvation, and ultimately because God makes it possible for man to save himself. And if you ask how God can make salvation possible on such "gracious" terms, the answer will be found in head two. The answer can be stated briefly here: in the imagination of the Arminians, Christ died to make it possible for God to offer salvation on the basis of faith and on the basis of the imperfect obedience of faith.

Notice the Arminian subterfuge. First, faith "from its very nature is undeserving." But this is only true *if faith is the gift of God*, for if faith is the work of man, which he performs as a condition for salvation, faith is *not* undeserving. Faith has become a meritorious activity or a work. If faith is the way in which one sinner makes himself to differ from another sinner, faith has become a meritorious work.

Second, Arminianism expects God "graciously [to] consider [faith and incomplete obedience] as a complete obedience." But God cannot do that, for that would be unjust. That would be for God to entertain a falsehood. Incomplete obedience is not, and cannot be considered to be, complete obedience. God cannot pretend that it is, for God is the God of truth and righteousness.

Third, Arminianism expects God to "count [faith and incomplete obedience] worthy of the reward of eternal life." But the reward of eternal life is not given on the basis of worthiness; it is given by grace alone. This is also the teaching of the Heidelberg Catechism,

"The reward is not of merit, but of grace,"[8] and of the Belgic Confession, "We do not deny that God rewards our good works, but it is through His grace that He crowns His gifts."[9]

The Canons respond to this heresy of Arminianism by labeling it "this injurious error." By "injurious" the Reformed fathers meant that Arminianism is harmful and insulting, indeed blasphemous. This error is injurious because it attacks three important truths of God.

First, it is an assault on the "pleasure of God." God is robbed of his sovereignty for the sake of man's supposed freedom. In the Arminian scheme God is not at liberty to choose persons, but merely conditions, qualities, and activities of men. Second, it is an assault on the merits of Christ, for if salvation can be attained on condition of faith and the imperfect obedience of faith, Christ's death on the cross really accomplishes nothing and is not necessary. Third, it is an assault on the justice of God, for how can God accept imperfect obedience in the place of perfect obedience to his law? And finally it draws men away from gracious justification and from the simplicity of scripture and entangles them in "useless questions" about conditions.

In conclusion, the fathers at Dordt quoted 2 Timothy 1:9: "[God] who hath saved us, and called us with a holy calling, not according to our works, but according to his own purpose and grace, which was given us in Christ Jesus before the world began."

Beware of Arminian deceivers who would draw you away from the grace of God.

ARTICLE 11: THE CERTAINTY AND IMMUTABILITY OF ELECTION

> And as God Himself is most wise, unchangeable, omniscient, and omnipotent, so the election made by Him can neither be interrupted nor changed, recalled or annulled;

---

8 Heidelberg Catechism A 63, in *Confessions and Church Order*, 107.

9 Belgic Confessions 24, in ibid., 54.

> neither can the elect be cast away, nor their number diminished.

This article is about the certainty of election. Those who are elected shall certainly be saved. To prove the certainty of election, the fathers at Dordt appealed to God's attributes, for all true theology begins with God. If election were a work of man or if it depended on man, it could not be certain because man is not certain.

Woe to him who places his confidence in man.

The reason so many people in the church world have a low view of election is their low view of God (they are not taught his holiness, righteousness, power, and sovereignty) and their correspondingly high view of man (they conceive of man as essentially good, albeit somewhat flawed, but certainly not totally depraved through sin). Therefore, proud man boasts in God's presence, when he ought to be humbled in the dust before his almighty Creator (1 Cor. 1:31).

The Canons mention four attributes of God as proof for the certainty of election.

First, God is "most wise." Wisdom is the right application of knowledge. God's wisdom is the marvelous adaptation of the riches of his infinite knowledge in order to reach the highest possible goal, which is God's own glory. God displays his wisdom in Jesus Christ through the salvation of his elect church. "To God only wise, be glory through Jesus Christ for ever. Amen" (Rom. 16:27). "Now unto the King eternal, immortal, invisible, the only wise God, be honour and glory for ever and ever. Amen" (1 Tim. 1:17). "To the only wise God our Savior, be glory and majesty, dominion and power, both now and ever. Amen" (Jude 25).

Second, God is "unchangeable." God does not and cannot change in his being, attributes, purpose, or will. God's decree of election does not change, for God does not choose his people, and then regret his choice due to unforeseen sin in his people. Therefore, election never becomes reprobation. "I am the LORD, I change not; therefore ye sons of Jacob are not consumed" (Mal. 3:6). "Every good gift and every perfect gift is from above, and cometh down from the Father of lights, with whom is no variableness, neither shadow of turning" (James 1:17). "The gifts and calling of God are without repentance" (Rom. 11:29).

Third, God is "omniscient." Omniscience is similar to wisdom, for omniscience is God's knowledge by which he possesses infinite knowledge of all things, past, present, and future. Therefore, nothing unforeseen can occur that would cause God to change his purpose in election. "Known unto God are all his works from the beginning of the world" (Acts 15:18). "The children being not yet born, neither having done any good or evil, that the purpose of God according to election might stand, not of works, but of him that calleth" (Rom. 9:11).

Fourth, God is "omnipotent," which does not mean merely that God is more powerful than all creatures, but also that God possesses all power. All power in the creature, by contrast, is derived power, for God gives power to the creature without which no creature could even move:

> We place our firm trust in our faithful God and Father, that nothing shall separate us from His love; since all creatures are so in His hand, that without His will they cannot so much as move.[10]

> This doctrine affords us unspeakable consolation, since we are taught thereby that nothing can befall us by chance, but by the direction of our most gracious and heavenly Father, who watches over us with a paternal care, keeping all creatures so under His power, that not a hair of our head (for they are all numbered), nor a sparrow, can fall to the ground without the will of our Father, in whom we do entirely trust; being persuaded that He so restrains the

10 Heidelberg Catechism A 28, in ibid., 94.

> devil and all our enemies, that without His will and permission, they cannot hurt us.[11]

Such a wise, unchangeable, omniscient, and almighty God cannot fail in his purposes. Such a wise, unchangeable, omniscient, and almighty God cannot make his election depend on man. "I am Alpha and Omega, the beginning and the ending, saith the Lord, which is, and which was, and which is to come, the Almighty" (Rev. 1:8).

The conclusion is clear: God's election cannot be interrupted, changed, recalled, or annulled. Who can interrupt, change, recall, or annul the election of the most wise, unchangeable, omniscient, omnipotent God? Furthermore, the elect cannot be "cast away," and their number cannot be "diminished." None of the elect can be lost, for they are chosen in the decree of the most wise, unchangeable, omniscient, almighty God.

What a solid foundation for our faith!

ERROR AND REJECTION 6: THE UNCERTAINTY OF ELECTION AND THE PERISHABILITY OF THE ELECT

> Error 6: Who teach that not every election unto salvation is unchangeable, but that some of the elect, any decree of God notwithstanding, can yet perish and do indeed perish.

> Rejection: By which gross error they make God to be changeable, and destroy the comfort which the godly obtain out of the firmness of their election, and contradict the Holy Scripture, which teaches that the elect cannot be led astray (Matt. 24:24); that Christ does not lose those whom the Father gave Him (John 6:39); and that God hath also glorified those whom He foreordained, called, and justified (Rom. 8:30).

Arminianism denies the unchangeableness and, therefore, the certainty, of election. "Not every election unto salvation is unchange-

11 Belgic Confession 13, in ibid., 37.

able," the Arminians said. Some election unto salvation is, in fact, changeable. Some of the elect can perish, and some of the elect do perish. And the Arminians added, "any decree of God notwithstanding." In other words, despite God's decree, which expresses the will of the Almighty, some of the elect can—and do—perish.

The fathers at Dordt responded with holy indignation by labeling the Arminian doctrine a "gross error." It is gross, first, because it makes God to be changeable: a changeable election is the decree of a changeable god. You cannot deny God's works without denying God himself. The error is gross, second, because it destroys the comfort of God's people. The doctrine of election is designed to comfort God's people, but a changeable election obliterates the comfort.

If any of the elect can perish, *you*, believing reader, can perish. Let us not view this merely as academic curiosity, for if election is not firm and steadfast in God's eternal, unchangeable decree, the only thing preserving the believer in his election is the power of free will. Woe to the believer if his or her salvation hangs on so uncertain a thread.

Additionally, Arminianism contradicts a host of scriptures, from which the fathers at Dordt quoted a sample: "There shall arise false Christs, and false prophets, and shall shew great signs and wonders; insomuch that, if it were possible, they shall deceive the very elect" (Matt. 24:24). "This is the Father's will which hath sent me, that of all which he hath given me I should lose nothing, but should raise it up again at the last day" (John 6:39). "Moreover whom he did predestinate, them he also called: and whom he called, them he also justified: and whom he justified, them he also glorified" (Rom. 8:30).

ARTICLE 12: THE ASSURANCE OF ETERNAL AND UNCHANGEABLE ELECTION

> The elect in due time, though in various degrees and in different measures, attain the assurance of this their eternal and unchangeable election, not by inquisitively prying into the secret and deep things of God, but by observing in

> themselves, with a spiritual joy and holy pleasure, the infallible fruits of election pointed out in the Word of God—such as a true faith in Christ, filial fear, a godly sorrow for sin, a hungering and thirsting after righteousness, etc.

The Canons of Dordt are beautifully pastoral, for not only do they teach the doctrines of grace and refute the errors of the Arminians, but they also apply these precious doctrines to the hearts of God's children for their edification, comfort, and assurance.

It is one thing to be eternally, unconditionally, and unchangeably chosen to everlasting life. It is quite another thing to be assured of it, to know it, and to be convinced of it. Article 12 deals with the assurance of election.

Article 12 does not merely deal with the assurance *of salvation*. The Arminians taught an assurance of salvation. They believed that a person could know that he is a Christian who possesses salvation today. What he could *not* know was that God had *eternally and unchangeably elected* him and that he would persevere to the end in true faith. This article, then, addresses the assurance of one's "eternal and unchangeable election." In other words, the question is, can you know with certainty not only that you are saved now, but that you will also be saved forever, and therefore that God elected you in eternity? To that question the Reformed fathers at Dordt answered with a resounding yes. Believers can know, they must know, and they do know. To that question, the Arminians answered with a contradictory no. They cannot know, they may not know, and they do not know, for assurance of election is unnecessary and impossible.

But the Canons go further, for assurance of election is not merely possible, but it is also a reality, for "the elect...*attain* the assurance of this their eternal and unchangeable election" (emphasis added). All of God's children are, can be, and must be assured of their eternal election. The issue in the Canons is not the fact—the elect *do* attain assurance—but the manner—*how* do the elect attain this assurance?

Therefore, the Canons teach that it is normal for God's people to be assured of their election. It is abnormal and unhealthy for God's people to doubt their election. This article is a rebuke to many professedly Reformed pastors who teach, encourage, and foster doubt, some of whom even claim to believe the Canons of Dordt. A child of God who doubts or struggles with doubt should be pitied, encouraged, instructed, and gently admonished; but doubt should *never* be encouraged, for doubt is basically unbelief, which is sin. The elders of the church should see to it that the preacher preaches assurance and does not foster doubt in the congregation.

Assurance is, therefore, not something for a select few in the congregation, while the majority of God's children languish in the despondency of doubt. The whole church should enjoy the assurance of their election, for without assurance there is no comfort. Where the gospel is faithfully explained and applied, the whole congregation should, can, must, and shall enjoy the comfort of the assurance of their election.

Consider the following passages concerning assurance: "Being confident of this very thing, that he which hath begun a good work in you will perform it until the day of Jesus Christ" (Phil. 1:6). "For the which cause I also suffer these things: nevertheless I am not ashamed: for I know whom I have believed, and am persuaded that he is able to keep that which I have committed unto him against that day" (2 Tim. 1:12). "Beloved, now are we the sons of God, and it doth not yet appear what we shall be: but we know that, when he shall appear, we shall be like him; for we shall see him as he is" (1 John 3:2). "These things have I written unto you that believe on the name of the Son of God; that ye may know that ye have eternal life, and that ye may believe on the name of the Son of God" (5:13).

> 31. What shall we then say to these things? If God be for us, who can be against us?

35. Who shall separate us from the love of Christ? shall tribulation, or distress, or persecution, or famine, or nakedness, or peril, or sword?
36. As it is written, For thy sake we are killed all the day long; we are accounted as sheep for the slaughter.
37. Nay, in all these things we are more than conquerors through him that loved us.
38. For I am persuaded, that neither death, nor life, nor angels, nor principalities, nor powers, nor things present, nor things to come,
39. Nor height, nor depth, nor any other creature, shall be able to separate us from the love of God, which is in Christ Jesus our Lord. (Rom. 8:31, 35–39)

23. And that he might make known the riches of his glory on the vessels of mercy, which he had afore prepared unto glory,
24. Even us, whom he hath called, not of the Jews only, but also of the Gentiles? (Rom. 9:23–24)

4. For whatsoever things were written aforetime were written for our learning, that we through patience and comfort of the scriptures might have hope.
5. Now the God of patience and consolation grant you to be likeminded one toward another according to Christ Jesus. (Rom. 15:4–5)

4. Knowing, brethren beloved, your election of God.
5. For our gospel came not unto you in word only, but also in power, and in the Holy Ghost, and in much assurance; as ye know what manner of men we were among you for your sake. (1 Thess. 1:4–5)

13. But we are bound to give thanks alway to God for you, brethren beloved of the Lord, because God hath from

the beginning chosen you to salvation through sanctification of the Spirit and belief of the truth:

14. Whereunto he called you by our gospel, to the obtaining of the glory of our Lord Jesus Christ. (2 Thess. 2:13–14)

1. Paul, a servant of God, and an apostle of Jesus Christ, according to the faith of God's elect, and the acknowledging of the truth which is after godliness;
2. In hope of eternal life, which God, that cannot lie, promised before the world began. (Titus 1:1–2)

2. Elect according to the foreknowledge of God the Father, through sanctification of the Spirit, unto obedience and sprinkling of the blood of Jesus Christ: Grace unto you, and peace, be multiplied.
3. Blessed be the God and Father of our Lord Jesus Christ, which according to his abundant mercy hath begotten us again unto a lively hope by the resurrection of Jesus Christ from the dead,
4. To an inheritance incorruptible, and undefiled, and that fadeth not away, reserved in heaven for you,
5. Who are kept by the power of God through faith unto salvation ready to be revealed in the last time. (1 Pet. 1:2–5)

Take note of the personal pronouns—us, you, me, and we. They indicate that the apostles had specific people in mind, and that they enjoyed assurance of their personal election and encouraged their readers to have such assurance: "Knowing, brethren beloved, *your* election of God" (1 Thess. 1:4, emphasis added).

Having made that plain, I examine the qualifying clause in article 12: "in due time, though in various degrees and in different measures." Although all believers are assured of their election, not all believers have *the same degree* of assurance. In addition, in the lifetime of a believer, there can be highs and lows in the believer's *experience* of assurance. Since assurance is of the essence of faith, it will be as strong or as weak as a believer's faith. The Heidelberg Catechism defines faith this way:

> True faith is not only a certain knowledge, whereby I hold for truth all that God has revealed to us in His Word, but also an assured confidence, which the Holy Ghost works by the gospel in my heart; that not only to others, but to me also, remission of sin, everlasting righteousness, and salvation are, freely given by God, merely of grace, only for the sake of Christ's merits.[12]

Assurance of election is affected by various factors, affliction and sin being the most common. This in no way negates what the Canons have just affirmed—the elect *do* have assurance, but they have it "in various degrees and in different measures."

The elect do not attain to assurance of election by "inquisitively prying into the secret and deep things of God." This does not mean that we should not study the doctrine of election, but that we should not seek to go beyond what God has revealed about it in his word. God has revealed that there is an election, and he has revealed what kind of election it is (eternal, unchangeable, sovereign, unconditional), but he has not disclosed to us a list of the persons whose names are written in the book of life. Therefore, it would be presumptuous folly for us to attempt to pry into God's holy decrees.

Calvin wrote,

> Even though discussion about predestination is likened to a dangerous sea, still, in traversing it, one finds safe and calm—I also add pleasant—sailing unless he willfully desire to endanger himself. For just as those engulf themselves in a deadly abyss who, to make their election more certain, investigate God's eternal plan apart from his Word,

12 Heidelberg Catechism A 21, in ibid., 90–91.

> so those who rightly and duly examine it as it is contained in his Word reap the inestimable fruit of comfort.[13]

The elect do not attain to assurance of election by seeking or receiving special revelation or a mysterious sign from heaven. In some mystical circles this is actively encouraged, for it is taught that only those who have received special revelation can know that they are numbered among the elect. Perhaps a person lights upon a certain text in the Bible. Perhaps a person experiences a strange coincidence, which he then interprets as a sign from God. Perhaps a person receives a message from a loved one, or he has a near-death experience, or a miraculous deliverance. Perhaps he feels something in prayer or in public worship. Perhaps he is moved during a sermon or is emotionally stirred during a song. None of these experiences brings assurance of salvation and election. We must not build our assurance on such flimsy foundations.

The way in which the elect attain assurance of their election is not spectacular or sensational, but it is really quite ordinary. Assurance of election comes from an observation of the "infallible fruits of election pointed out in the Word of God." Assurance comes by faith; assurance comes by a use of the ordinary means of grace: "the infallible fruits of election *pointed out in the Word of God*" (emphasis added). One with weak assurance must hear sound preaching and he must avoid preaching that fosters doubt: "So then faith cometh by hearing, and hearing by the word of God" (Rom. 10:17). "Our gospel came not unto you in word only, but also in power, and in the Holy Ghost, and in much assurance; as ye know what manner of men we were among you for your sake" (1 Thess. 1:5). Assurance of election comes through the observing of fruit, which the Canons call "infallible fruit" because it is the fruit produced *only* by the elect.

---

13 John Calvin, *Institutes of the Christian Religion*, ed. John T. McNeill, trans. Ford Lewis Battles, 2 vols., Library of Christian Classics 20–21 (Philadelphia: Westminster Press, 1960), 3.24.4, 2:969 (emphasis added).

No reprobate person can produce this fruit, for election is the fountain of this fruit (Canons 1.9).

The first infallible fruit of election is *faith in Christ*. This is the primary fruit to which all the other fruits are subordinate. All believers enjoy assurance to one degree or another by faith alone. They enjoy assurance by looking away from themselves in confidence to the cross of their savior Jesus Christ. Without faith, assurance is impossible.

The other fruits flow out of faith. They are filial fear; godly sorrow for sin; and hunger and thirst after righteousness.

Filial fear is the fear that sons have for their father. Believers are not terrified of God, as slaves fear a cruel master. Sons love their father and therefore they fear or reverence him. One who fears God loves his approval and fears his displeasure. One who fears God wants always to please him. Such fear rooted in love for God motivates God's children to obedience. The reprobate wicked never fear God with filial fear, for "there is no fear of God before their eyes" (Rom. 3:18). "If ye call on the Father, who without respect of persons judgeth according to every man's work, pass the time of your sojourning here in fear" (1 Pet. 1:17). "Honour all men. Love the brotherhood. Fear God. Honour the king" (2:17).

Godly sorrow for sin is that true sorrow of heart that we have offended God by our sins. There are two kinds of sorrow mentioned in the Bible. One is the sorrow of the world, which is the sorrow that an ungodly person has over the bitter consequences of his sin. It is the sorrow of a guilty conscience, but without repentance. Judas sorrowed with the sorrow of the world and hanged himself. The other is "godly sorrow," which leads to true repentance, daily humility, and daily conversion and mortifying of the flesh. Peter sorrowed with godly sorrow, wept bitterly, and repented. "For godly sorrow worketh repentance to salvation not to be repented of: but the sorrow of the world worketh death" (2 Cor. 7:10).

A hunger and thirst after righteousness is the desire, the ardent, even desperate, longing for the righteousness of God. The elect have this desire, which Christ promises to satisfy. The reprobate wicked abhor the righteousness of God and never experience such a hunger or thirst. "Blessed are they which do hunger and thirst after righteousness: for they shall be filled" (Matt. 5:6). "This is the condemnation, that light is come into the world, and men loved darkness rather than light, because their deeds were evil. For every one that doeth evil hateth the light, neither cometh to the light, lest his deeds should be reproved" (John 3:19–20).

When the elect observe these fruits in themselves, they have a "spiritual joy" and a "holy pleasure." Happy is the man who observes these fruits in his life, for they are the infallible fruits of his election unto life.

Do you believe in Jesus Christ? Do you view God in confidence as your Father, showing to him a godly fear? Do you sorrow over your sins by which you offend God? Do you hunger and thirst after righteousness, yearning to be holy? Then you have salvation, and you must be assured of your eternal and unchangeable election. Rejoice for your name is written in the book of life!

Do not entertain doubts, but reject them as the suggestions of Satan. If these fruits are present in you, you *must* believe that you possess salvation and that, therefore, you are included in God's eternal, unchangeable decree of election. Assurance is *not* the result of an arduous quest. Assurance is the activity of true faith, of ordinary faith. To believe is to be assured. To be justified by faith alone is to have "peace with God" and to "rejoice in hope of the glory of God" (Rom. 5:1–2). To be a child of God is to *know* that you are a child of God. Otherwise, how can the Christian pray "Our Father which art in heaven"? How can the Christian serve God with a thankful heart if he does not know whether God loves or hates him, whether his sins are forgiven or not, and whether he is headed for heaven or for hell?

However, if you do not believe in Jesus Christ for the salvation of your soul, you have no reason to be assured; in fact, you *must not be assured.* Only believers can be and may be assured. Turn from your sins in repentance and cast yourself on the mercy of God in Jesus Christ. God promises to save all those who come in faith to him. And having saved them, he assures them, "You are mine. You always were mine. You always shall be mine, forever."

ERROR AND REJECTION 7: THE IMPOSSIBILITY OF THE CERTAIN ASSURANCE OF ELECTION

> Error 7: Who teach that there is in this life no fruit and no consciousness of the unchangeable election to glory, nor any certainty, except that which depends on a changeable and uncertain condition.
>
> Rejection: For not only is it absurd to speak of an uncertain certainty, but also contrary to the experience of the saints, who by virtue of the consciousness of their election rejoice with the apostle and praise this favor of God (Eph. 1); who according to Christ's admonition rejoice with His disciples that their names are written in heaven (Luke 10:20); who also place the consciousness of their election over against the fiery darts of the devil, asking: *Who shall lay any thing to the charge of God's elect?* (Rom. 8:33).

Arminianism denies that a believer can enjoy assurance of unchangeable election unto glory in this life. This is because Arminian election depends on a person's faith. Only if a person perseveres to the end can he be assured of final salvation and, therefore, of eternal election.

In Arminianism, therefore, a person can be certain that he is saved now. A person can even be certain that God is ready to supply him with the grace necessary to persevere if he is willing to receive it. Nevertheless, he cannot know with any certainty that he will fulfill the conditions of faith in order to persevere. Thus faith, filial fear, sorrow over sin, and the like are *not* infallible fruits of election, but are conditions that men must fulfill. And the only certainty is one that depends on a "changeable and uncertain condition" (of faith and perseverance).

The Reformed fathers responded by charging Arminianism with absurdity. An "uncertain certainty" or a certainty that depends on an "uncertain condition" is absurd. Furthermore, the error of Arminianism denies the experience of the saints, "who by virtue of the consciousness of their election rejoice with the apostle and praise this favor of God." Moreover, Arminianism robs the child of God of comfort and leaves him in suspense his entire life long about his election and salvation. What misery to be a child of God and not to know it. What misery to imagine your whole life long that you are a miserable orphan with no inheritance in heaven. How could such a child of God pray, worship, or live a thankful life? How could such a child of God live and die happily, since he is robbed of his only comfort? Listen to the testimony of Zacharias Ursinus (1534–83), one of the authors of the Heidelberg Catechism, in a private letter to a doubting friend:

> If you mean that we cannot say with certainty that one will be saved, you are right when speaking of others; but with regard to oneself, or one's own conscience and convictions concerning oneself, such a conception is both shocking and blasphemous, and subverts the very foundation of faith. Whoever has taught you such an idea, has instructed you as would a devil, even though he came from heaven. I will say even more; if you are not certain in this world that you are an heir of eternal life, you will not be one after death. From such a fate the Lord deliver you. For faith itself is that certainty which is the beginning of eternal life, which beginning everyone must possess in this life who would have it hereafter. If you would remember the meaning of the word hope, that it is a certain expectation of eternal life, you would not

> write to me what causes my hair to stand on end. I would not accept a hundred thousand worlds and be so far away from my Lord as not to know certainly whether I am His or not.[14]

From such misery Christ delivers his people. Into such misery Arminianism would bring God's people again.

Against the errors of Arminianism, the fathers at Dordt quoted God's word: "Notwithstanding in this rejoice not, that the spirits are subject unto you; but rather rejoice, because your names are written in heaven" (Luke 10:20). "Who shall lay any thing to the charge of God's elect? It is God that justifieth" (Rom. 8:33).

Believing reader, do not allow the Arminians to rob you of the precious assurance of your election and salvation.

ARTICLE 13: THE FRUIT OF THE ASSURANCE OF ELECTION

> The sense and certainty of this election afford to the children of God additional matter for daily humiliation before Him, for adoring the depth of His mercies, for cleansing themselves, and rendering grateful returns of ardent love to Him, who first manifested so great love towards them. The consideration of this doctrine of election is so far from encouraging remissness in the observance of the divine commands, or from sinking men in carnal security, that these, in the just judgment of God, are the usual effects of rash presumption, or of idle and wanton trifling with the grace of election, in those who refuse to walk in the ways of the elect.

What is the practical effect of assurance of "eternal and unchangeable election"?

---

14 Quoted in Otto Thelemann, *An Aid to the Heidelberg Catechism*, trans. M. Peters (Grand Rapids, MI: Douma Publications, 1959), 452–53.

The Arminians not only denied that such assurance is possible, but they also argued that such personal knowledge is both unnecessary and pernicious, or harmful. If people enjoyed such assured confidence, they would no longer have any motivation to persevere in godliness. This scurrilous charge, which is the same made in every age against gracious election and salvation, receives a Reformed response in article 13.

Actually, "the sense and certainty of this election" have the opposite effect. Never does the Bible teach that, because election is sure and certain, we have liberty to multiply our sins and transgressions. Never does the Bible appeal to gracious election and salvation as reasons for carelessness in the Christian life. Never does the assured believer have any excuse to neglect prayer, attendance at public worship, lively membership in a true church, good works, and obedience to God's commandments. The fruits in the lives of God's assured children are sweet and delightful, not the bitter crabapples of the Arminian imagination.

First, the fruit of assurance of eternal and unchangeable election is *humility*: "daily humiliation." The Reformed faith, rightly believed, understood, and confessed, does not make a person proud. The Reformed faith teaches us that we are sinners, hopelessly lost, depraved, and corrupt. The Reformed faith teaches us that we are saved only because God was pleased in his grace to save us. Where is boasting, then? It is excluded. The child of God sees daily reasons to humble himself before God, for he sees daily how sinful he truly is. And since he attributes the whole of his salvation to the grace of God, there is no room for pride in his theology. There is nothing as odious and as contradictory as a *proud* Reformed person. "For who maketh thee to differ from another? and what hast thou that thou didst not receive? now if thou didst receive it, why dost thou glory, as if thou hadst not received it" (1 Cor. 4:7)?

Second, the fruit of assurance of eternal and unchangeable election is *worship*. The child of God finds additional reasons for "adoring the depth of His [God's] mercies." It is good to meditate on how deep God's mercies are. The deeper you see your sins, the deeper you will see God's mercies toward you. God does not save little sinners, but God saves great sinners, indeed, the chief of sinners (1 Tim. 1:15). To believe in election, as the Bible describes it, is to glorify God (Rom. 11:33–36; Eph. 1:3–11; 2:4–9). The main reason that Christians attend public worship is to worship, adore, and praise God for his great mercy. Do you regularly gather with God's people to adore the depth of his mercies? Do you adore his mercies in your personal and family devotions? You must if you have a sense and certainty of your eternal and unchangeable election. One of the marks of the reprobate is their ingratitude, which is manifested in a life without good works and without prayer. Such is not the case with the assured and thankful elect.

Third, the fruit of assurance of eternal and unchangeable election is *holiness*. Those who are elect and who are assured of their election "cleanse themselves." Holiness is one of the chief goals in one's election (2 Cor. 7:1; Eph. 1:4; 2:10; 5:26–27; 1 Thess. 4:7; 2 Thess. 2:13; 2 Tim. 1:9; 1 John 3:2–3). The Bible never separates election from holiness, and neither should we.

Fourth, the fruit of assurance of eternal and unchangeable election is *love for God*. Those who are God's chosen people and who are conscious of their election will have reason for "rendering grateful returns of ardent love" to God. Do you love God ardently, passionately, and fervently? Those loved by God and who know that they are loved of God always love him in return (John 14:15, 21, 24; 1 John 4:19).

Fifth, the fruit of assurance of eternal and unchangeable election is *gratitude*. The assured elect believer offers to God "grateful returns of ardent love" (Col. 1:12; 2 Thess. 2:13).

These are the five positive fruits. In addition, the fathers at Dordt directly refuted the Arminian accusation that the one who enjoys the assured confidence of his personal election is careless and profane.

The first concern of the Arminians was that assurance would encourage "remissness in the observance of the divine commands." Remissness is carelessness or neglect. The elect are not remiss in their observance of God's commandments. The truth is very far from this. This does not mean that the elect are even close to perfect, but they do obey God from the heart and lead lives of holiness: "with a sincere resolution they begin to live not only according to some, but all the commandments of God."[15] Notice several things in answer 114 of the Heidelberg Catechism: first, Christians are holy (not totally depraved, but holy; indeed, some are described as the "holiest men"); second, Christians have a "sincere resolution" (or desire) to keep God's commandments; third, Christians do "begin to live" according to God's commandments; and fourth, Christians begin to live "not only according to some, but all the commandments of God." Do not let the Catechism's reference to "a small beginning of this obedience" distract you from this truth—the beginning is real; it is small, imperfect, inconsistent, but real; and do not despise that small beginning of obedience. An assured Christian (Q&A 1) begins to live according to all the commandments of God (A 114).

The second concern of the Arminians was "carnal security." Carnal security is the security of the flesh. The truth is very far from this. Assurance of election does not encourage God's children to indulge the flesh, but it compels them to be holy and to crucify or mortify the flesh (Rom. 6:1–2; Titus 2:11–12).

Since assurance of election is very far from encouraging the believer to walk in sin, the opposite is the result: humility, worship, holiness, love for God, and profound gratitude.

What kinds of persons respond to the doctrine of election with remissness and carnal security? The Canons give a stark warning: "these, in the just judgment of God, are the usual effects of rash presumption, or of idle and wanton trifling with the grace of election,

15 Heidelberg Catechism A 114, in *Confessions and Church Order*, 133.

in those who refuse to walk in the ways of the elect." A rashly presumptuous person is a hypocritical unbeliever who, without any warrant from the word of God, claims to be a child of God. Often such a presumptuous hypocrite will latch on to certain doctrines in order to justify his wicked way of life. One guilty of "idle and wanton trifling with the grace of election" treats the precious jewel of election as an intellectual curiosity about which he wants to speculate rather than seeking to live in accordance with the scriptures. Such presumptuous hypocrites and idle and wanton triflers refuse to "walk in the ways of the elect."

Election is God's eternal decree, the fruit of which is God's people *walking* in the ways prepared for them (Eph. 2:10). To refuse to walk in the ways of the elect is to deny the truth of election (Jer. 6:16). Every doctrine can be abused and the doctrine of election is no exception.

Let not our way of life be an occasion for the criticism of this precious truth of God's word.

ARTICLE 14: THE NECESSITY AND MANNER OF THE PREACHING OF ELECTION

> As the doctrine of divine election by the most wise counsel of God was declared by the prophets, by Christ Himself, and by the apostles, and is clearly revealed in the Scriptures, both of the Old and New Testament, so it is still to be published in due time and place in the church of God, for which it was peculiarly designed, provided it be done with reverence, in the spirit of discretion and piety, for the glory of God's most holy name, and for enlivening and comforting His people, without vainly attempting to investigate the secret ways of the Most High (Acts 20:27; Rom. 11:33–34; 12:3; Heb. 6:17–18).

Article 14 addresses three important issues: the necessity of the preaching of election, the manner of such preaching, and the purpose of such preaching.

Arminians do not believe in the biblical doctrine of election. Therefore, they believe that it is harmful to preach it. In fact, Arminius himself first came under suspicion because of his sermons on Romans, where he subverted the truth of election.

Sadly, many who claim to be Reformed are also reluctant to preach this beautiful truth. There are several reasons for this. For some the reason is the fear of man. The people in the pew might find the doctrine of election offensive, for it robs man of his pride, it humbles him in the dust before his Creator, and it glorifies God, by ascribing the whole of the glory for salvation to God alone. Others quail before the objection that election is unfair. Although the Reformed faith has answered this objection numerous times, it is difficult to root it from the hearts and minds of the people. For others the doctrine is too difficult, so that the preacher fears that the people will not understand it. The topic is too profound, too mysterious, or even too intellectual, while the people clamor to hear practical sermons. But the doctrine of election is the simple truth of God's word, which even a child can understand. Compare the simple truth with the convoluted heresy of Arminianism. Others fear that the doctrine of election is easily abused, but this is true of every doctrine of God's word. The people's abuse of a doctrine is not a valid reason for not preaching it. If the unbelieving world and the false church abuse the truth, the truth may not be withheld from God's children. To do so would be to rob them of the precious fruits of this doctrine, such as humility, worship, holiness, love, and gratitude.

The fathers at Dordt insisted on the preaching of this doctrine: "it is still to be published…in the church of God." It is the duty of ministers to preach doctrine (1 Tim. 4:13, 16; 5:17; 6:3–5; 2 Tim. 3:16; 4:1–4; Titus 1:9; 2:1). It is the duty of ministers to preach all doctrines (Acts 20:20–21, 27). Although it is not possible for one minister in the course of his ministry to preach every text of scripture, he can and must preach every doctrine of the Christian faith. Some doctrines tend to be avoided or neglected. This is certainly true of election and even more so of reprobation. The practice of Heidelberg Catechism preaching in Reformed churches is an excellent way to make sure that the minister preaches regularly through all the doctrines of the Bible, including election (Q&A 52 and 54).

The main reason the doctrine of election must be preached is that *God has revealed it in his word.* Just as we have no right to preach what God has *not* revealed, so we have no right to refuse to preach what God *has* revealed. Members and elders must insist that the preachers expound the doctrine of election. It is not true to say that this belongs to the "secret things" (Deut. 29:29). This text is often misused to justify silence on election. It is certainly true that there are certain aspects of the doctrine that belong to the "secret things," such as the identity of the elect and God's deepest purpose in election. Much is deep; much is hidden. Article 14 calls these things "the secret ways of the Most High," into which we are forbidden to pry. Nevertheless, the doctrine *itself* is not hidden or secret.

The doctrine of election was declared by the prophets; by Christ himself; by the apostles; and it is "clearly revealed in the Scriptures, both of the Old and New Testament." Therefore, since this truth is carefully and clearly revealed in scripture, it is to be "published" in the church.

The declaration of election by the prophets, Christ, and the apostles occurred by the "most wise counsel of God." It is good for the church to hear about her election. God has determined everything that the church should know. Everything necessary is recorded in holy scripture. Because all scripture is profitable, there is nothing harmful in the Bible. To hide any doctrine from the people of God on the pretext that it might harm them is to make oneself wiser than God. Ignorance of the truth, not a thorough explanation of the truth, harms the people of God (Hos. 4:6).

Calvin wrote:

> But for those who are so cautious or fearful that they desire to bury predestination in order not to disturb weak souls—with what colour will they cloak their arrogance when they accuse God indirectly of stupid thoughtlessness, as if he had not foreseen the peril that they feel that they have wisely met? Whoever, then, heaps odium, upon the doctrine of predestination openly reproaches God, as if he had unadvisedly let slip something hurtful to the church.[16]

Nevertheless, election should be preached in the proper manner. The Canons insist that this should be done "in due time and place." There is a time and a place to preach election. Sometimes election is explicit in a text, while at other times it is implicit. No congregation must ever say, "I have never heard of election." That would be an indictment on the minister. Election should be preached "in the church of God." Election is the doctrine of God's love, of God's merciful good pleasure. The church must hear it often, but so must the unbelievers of the world. The doctrine of election must also be preached on the mission field to the unconverted. Election glorifies God as God; therefore, all men must hear it.

Election must be preached "in the spirit of discretion and piety." Election must be preached wisely and reverently. The preacher must bear in mind the capacity of the hearers, which will determine not *whether* he preaches election (he must!), but *how* he preaches election. Election must be preached carefully and according to its proper place in the whole counsel of God. The Canons give a good example here: look at how the doctrine of election is presented. For example, the Canons do not begin with reprobation, but they carefully lay the groundwork before they expound the doctrine itself. This doctrine must be preached reverently. God's eternal decrees are not to be discussed flippantly. The preacher and congregation alike must be in

16 Calvin, *Institutes of the Christian Religion*, 2.21.4, 2:926.

awe of God's truth. Election and reprobation must never be the subject of jokes or profane stories.

The preaching of election glorifies God, which must also be the aim in preaching it: "For the glory of God's most holy name." In the doctrine of election, God's sovereignty, power, wisdom, love, grace, and mercy are magnified. Election presents God as enthroned on high with the creature as worshiping before him. The preaching of election is for the "enlivening and comforting [of God's] people." Election is a most wholesome and comforting doctrine if one has assurance of it, as article 12 teaches.

Finally, election must be taught without "vainly attempting to investigate the secret ways of the Most High." The doctrine of election is a dangerous labyrinth *when it is studied apart from the scriptures*. The doctrine of election must never be studied speculatively or abstractly. Our motive in studying election must be the glory of God and the edification of our souls.

Does your pastor preach the glorious truth of election? Let the elders insist on it. Let the people require it. That will increase the edification and comfort of God's people and be to the praise of God in the midst of his church.

ARTICLE 15: SOVEREIGN REPROBATION DEFINED AND EXPLAINED

> What peculiarly tends to illustrate and recommend to us the eternal and unmerited grace of election is the express testimony of sacred Scripture that not all, but some only, are elected, while others are passed by in the eternal election of God; whom God, out of His sovereign, most just, irreprehensible, and unchangeable good pleasure, hath decreed to leave in the common misery into which they have willfully plunged themselves, and not to bestow upon them saving faith and the grace of conversion; but leaving them in His just judgment to follow their own ways, at last for the

> declaration of His justice, to condemn and punish them forever, not only on account of their unbelief, but also for all their other sins. And this is the decree of reprobation which by no means makes God the author of sin (the very thought of which is blasphemy), but declares Him to be an awful, irreprehensible, and righteous judge and avenger thereof.

The wisdom of the Reformed fathers at Dordt is noteworthy. They waited *until this article*, number 15 of 18, to treat the important subject of reprobation. The Arminians poured out their most bitter invective against this truth of God's word, and for this reason they wanted to make the synod focus on this one point. Simon Episcopius, the leader of the Arminian party, delivered a speech against this doctrine before the Arminians were dismissed from the synod. Today Arminians employ the same tactics: "You Reformed are horrible people who believe that God hates people and eternally condemns them to hell! You Reformed believe in a god who tyrannically rejects people from salvation at a whim. Who could believe in such a horrible god?"

The Reformed fathers resisted. They did not back away from the truth of reprobation, nor did they deny it, as many professing Reformed theologians do today. Nevertheless, they wisely understood the proper place of reprobation in the body of the truth. They understood that this doctrine must be presented carefully, reverently, and to the glory of God. They understood that reprobation must be preached always in connection with election, for reprobation serves election. Let us bear that in mind as we proceed.

The word "reprobation" means rejection. While election is the choice of some to salvation and glory, reprobation is the rejection of some *from* salvation and glory. Election implies reprobation, for if you choose something, you necessarily reject all other options. If a man chooses to marry one woman, he rejects all other women. If God chooses a church in Christ, he rejects all those whom he has not chosen to be in the church of Christ. Reprobation, like election, is God's decree, that is, what God has determined to do. Reprobation is as much a part of God's decree as election. Therefore, it is no accident that some are rejected from salvation and glory; and it is no accident that some perish everlastingly. Article 6 has already taught us about "that [one] decree of *election* and *reprobation*" (emphasis added).

Four things are predicated of the decree of reprobation in article 15. First, God does not elect all: "the express testimony of sacred Scripture that not all, but some only, are elected." Second, God has determined to pass by some in the decree of eternal election: "while others are passed by in the eternal election of God." Third, God has decreed not to bestow upon the reprobate saving faith and the grace of conversion: "whom God…hath decreed to leave in the common misery into which they have willingly plunged themselves, and not to bestow upon them saving faith and the grace of conversion." And fourth, God has determined to condemn and punish the reprobate forever: "at last for the declaration of His justice, to condemn and punish them forever, not only on account of their unbelief, but also for all their other sins."

We need to understand some distinctions, namely the differences between damnation and reprobation. Reprobation is God's eternal decree, while damnation is God's sentencing a person to hell. Damnation is the result of reprobation. Damnation is on the basis of sin: "on account of their unbelief and also for their other sins." Reprobation is not on account of sin, but like election it is unconditional. God eternally decreed to damn the reprobate out of his sovereign good pleasure. God did not reprobate any *on the basis of sin*, for that is Arminianism, which teaches that God rejected some because of their foreseen unbelief and sin.

At this point a brief excursus into a rather difficult doctrine, the difference between infralapsarianism and supralapsarianism, is necessary. Although these words do not appear in the Canons, they are presupposed. These two words refer to different ways of understanding the relationship between the decrees in God's eternal counsel. Both infralapsarianism and supralapsarianism are Reformed, for both constitute soundly Reformed doctrine. The Canons are written from an infralapsarian perspective, but they do not condemn supralapsarianism. Strong advocates of supralapsarianism who were present at the Synod of Dordt approved the Canons and the synod did not condemn the position of such men.

Supra and *infra*, which are the two prefixes of these theological terms, are Latin words. *Supra* means "above or over," while *infra* means "below or under." The word *lapsarianism* comes from the Latin word *lapsus*, which refers to the fall of man into sin. Therefore, the difference between the two positions concerns the relationship *in God's counsel* between God's decree of election and God's decree to ordain the fall of man into sin. Supralapsarianism is the teaching that God's decree to elect his people is *above* or *over* his decree to ordain the fall. Infralapsarianism is the teaching that God's decree to elect his people is *below* or *under* his decree to ordain the fall.

We should take note of the similarities. First, both positions teach that God's decrees are eternal. Neither supralapsarianism nor infralapsarianism is the teaching that God's decree of election and reprobation happened after the fall in history. Since God's decrees are eternal, any relationship between them is not temporal, but *logical*. Second, both positions teach that God decreed the fall. Neither position maintains that the fall occurred outside of God's counsel. The difference between the two positions comes down to this: how does God view those whom he decrees to elect or reprobate?

First, in the infralapsarian model, God decrees the creation and the fall of man. Therefore, he views mankind, from which he elects and reprobates, *as fallen*. From that fallen mass of humanity (fallen in God's decree, not yet fallen in time, because, remember, God's counsel is eternal), God decrees to save some (Canons 1.7) and decrees to reprobate others (Canons 1.15). The Canons clearly adopt an infralapsarian perspective. Phrases such as "hath decreed to leave in the common misery" and "leaving them in His just judgment to follow their own ways" are clear indications of infralapsarianism.

Second, in the supralapsarianism model, God decrees to save an elect people and to reject the rest. Therefore, he views humanity as one mass or lump of clay, some of whom he elects and some of whom he rejects. God then decrees the creation and the fall. Therefore, he views mankind, from which he elects and reprobates, *as not yet fallen*. From that not yet fallen mass of humanity (not yet fallen in God's decree, because, remember, God's counsel is eternal), God decrees to save some and decrees to reprobate others. Supralapsarianism does justice to the truth that first in God's counsel is Christ. This view means that God first decrees Christ to be the head of the elect. God then decrees a people as the body and bride of Christ, while he rejects the reprobate wicked by not choosing them in Christ. God then decrees the creation and the fall.

The Canons do not express supralapsarianism, but neither do they condemn it. A believer in supralapsarianism is able to subscribe to the Canons of Dordt in good conscience, for supralapsarianism is *not* hyper-Calvinism. Some of the most prominent theologians at Dordt held to supralapsarianism. Nevertheless, the synod determined to express the truth of sovereign predestination using the language of infralapsarianism.

Let me briefly recap. Reprobation is God's *rejection* of some *from* salvation and glory. Reprobation is God's eternal, unchangeable, and unconditional decree to reject some from salvation and glory. Because reprobation is unconditional, it does not depend on the sins of the reprobate. God does not determine to reprobate some because they are sinners, or on the basis of their sins, or even because he foresaw that they would persist in sin. The reason for reprobation is God's good pleasure. Nevertheless, reprobation is just, for none deserve to be elected. Reprobation issues in damnation, which is the righteous, eternal punishment of the wicked on the basis of their sins.

Reprobation occurs because of God's good pleasure, for God is pleased to reject the reprobate wicked in order to glorify himself in the exercise of his just wrath. Reprobation is, to use the words of article 15, according to God's "sovereign, most just, irreprehensible, and unchangeable good pleasure."

God's good pleasure in reprobation is sovereign, for God has the right to do with his creatures as he wills. God's good pleasure is just, for in reprobating some men and angels God displays his perfect righteousness. The Bible simply does not permit the creature to accuse God of injustice. God's good pleasure is irreprehensible, which means that it may not be reprehended, rebuked, criticized, or reproached. God is blameless and faultless in all of his ways. And God's good pleasure is unchangeable, for God never changes his counsel in response to the actions of man.

The Bible teaches reprobation very clearly in several passages. The most prominent passage is Romans 9, where Paul taught that God loved Jacob but hated Esau (v. 13). God's love and election of Jacob were unconditional, as were God's hatred and reprobation of Esau. To prove this, Paul quoted from Genesis 25:22–23 and Malachi 1:2. It will not do to circumvent the clear teaching of God's word here by arguing that to hate means to love less. God's hatred of Esau led not only to the destruction of the individual man called Esau, but also to God's rejection of Esau's descendants, the Edomites:

> 3. And I hated Esau, and laid his mountains and his heritage waste for the dragons of the wilderness.
> 4. Whereas Edom saith, We are impoverished, but we will return and build the desolate places; thus saith the Lord of hosts, They shall build, but I will throw down; and they shall call them, The border of wickedness, and, The people against whom the Lord hath indignation for ever. (Mal. 1:3–4)

To be a people against whom God has indignation forever is hardly to be the object of a lesser form of love. If so, may the Lord spare us from his lesser love!

After Paul answered an objection that God is unjust (Rom. 9:14), he illustrated reprobation by means of the example of Pharaoh. God hardened Pharaoh's heart, for God "hath mercy on whom he will have mercy, and whom he will he hardeneth" (v. 18). Paul's response to a second objection that God is unjust was to assert God's absolute sovereign prerogative to do with his creatures as he pleases (v. 20). Finally, Paul showed that God is sovereign over the "one lump" of mankind out of which he makes some "vessels of wrath fitted to destruction" and others "vessels of mercy, which he had afore prepared unto glory (vv. 22–24). Paul explained that God's motive was to display his wrath and to make his power known, and to make known the riches of his glory. God's glory is more important than the salvation of men, for even the salvation and damnation of men must serve God's glory.

Other chapters and passages that teach reprobation are Matthew 7:23; 11:25–26; 13:11–17; John 12:37–41; 1 Peter 2:7–9; Jude 4; and Revelation 13:8; 17:8; 20:15. Therefore, although we might not like reprobation, which is a doctrine at which we rightly tremble and a doctrine against which our flesh sinfully rebels, scripture compels us to believe and confess it as part of the truth of God.

The purpose of reprobation according to article 15 is to "illustrate and recommend to us the eternal and unmerited grace of election." First, the grace of God shines more brightly against the backdrop of sin and reprobation. Second, the decree of reprobation teaches that not all men belong to God's chosen people: "Not all, but some only, are elected." Salvation, therefore, is precious to believers, for they see what they deserve in the reprobation and damnation of the ungodly. Third, the decree of reprobation shows that the elect have no reason to boast against the reprobate, for they are equally unworthy and undeserving. Fourth, the decree of reprobation teaches the awesomeness of God, for he is not a God to be trifled with, but a God to be worshiped, adored, and feared. Fifth, reprobation displays the glory of God, his power, his absolute sovereignty, and his terrible wrath.

Reprobation serves election. We must never view reprobation abstractly and separate from election, for election and reprobation constitute one divine decree. The reprobate world is necessary for the salvation of the elect. The reprobate world serves the elect as the chaff serves the wheat. Without the chaff, the wheat cannot be grown and harvested. And yet the farmer has no intention to save the chaff, but to burn it as soon as it has served its purpose. Similarly, the reprobate wicked are necessary in the world in order that the elect church should be saved. Reprobate Saul served the salvation of elect Jonathan and David. (For one thing, without reprobate Saul, elect Jonathan would never have been born.) The reprobate Jews who crucified Christ served the salvation of elect Jews and Gentiles. God did not simply create some people in order to damn them, for his purpose is much greater than that:

> 11. I say then, Have they stumbled that they should fall? God forbid: but rather through their fall salvation is come unto the Gentiles, for to provoke them to jealousy.
> 12. Now if the fall of them be the riches of the world, and the diminishing of them the riches of the Gentiles; how much more their fulness?
> 13. For I speak to you Gentiles, inasmuch as I am the apostle of the Gentiles, I magnify mine office:
> 14. If by any means I may provoke to emulation them which are my flesh, and might save some of them. (Rom. 11:11–14)

Article 15 ends with a response to a common objection: the Arminians alleged that the teaching of reprobation makes God the author of sin. This charge the fathers at Dordt vehemently denied. "The very thought," insisted our Reformed fathers, "is blasphemy." God is not to be blamed for the sin of his creatures.

To explain this, it is necessary briefly to examine the relationship between God's counsel and sin. The Arminian teaches either that sin is entirely outside of God's control, or that God merely passively allows sin, but the Bible does not present sin as a sovereign entity outside of God's sovereign providence.

The Bible is not ashamed to confess that God, who is the absolutely sovereign creator and governor of the universe, decrees sin and directs it in his providence. Joseph's brothers wickedly sold him into slavery, but Joseph later confessed the truth of God's sovereign ordination of his brothers' sin:

> 5. Now therefore be not grieved, nor angry with yourselves, that ye sold me hither: for God did send me before you to preserve life.
>
> 7. And God sent me before you to preserve you a posterity in the earth, and to save your lives by a great deliverance.
> 8. So now it was not you that send me hither, but God…
>
> 20. But as for you, you thought evil against me; but God meant it unto good, to bring to pass, as it is this day, to save much people alive. (Gen. 45:5, 7–8; 50:20)

The crucifixion of Jesus was the most heinous act in the history of mankind, yet the sovereign and holy God ordained it for his own purposes:

> 23. Him, being delivered by the determinate counsel and foreknowledge of God, ye have taken, and by wicked hands have crucified and slain.
>
> 27. For of a truth against thy holy child Jesus, whom thou hast anointed, both Herod, and Pontius Pilate, with the Gentiles, and the people of Israel, were gathered together,
> 28. For to do whatsoever thy hand and thy counsel determined before to be done. (Acts 2:23; 4:27–28)

Nevertheless, God does not perform the act of sin; and God never compels, cajoles, manipulates, or tempts his creatures to sin. When the creature commits sin, he does so willingly and willfully. God does not delight in sin, for when he ordains sin and directs sin in his providence, he does so as something that he hates and something for which he punishes the creature. Instead of being the author of sin, God is the judge of sin. Article 15 describes God as the "awful, irreprehensible, and righteous judge and avenger [of sin]." I explained "irreprehensible" above, but there might be confusion over the word "awful." We often designate something bad as "awful," but the word "awful" here refers to "awesome," "fearful," or something worthy of, or causing, awe. Such a judge is the Almighty: the creature may not criticize him; instead, the creature trembles before him. How dreadful to stand before this Judge in one's sins. How urgent is the call: repent and believe in Jesus Christ.

Believing reader, never discuss the doctrine of reprobation flippantly, but always with a holy trembling and with profound thanksgiving that you do not belong to the number of the reprobate.

ERROR AND REJECTION 8: REPROBATION DENIED

> Error 8: Who teach that God, simply by virtue of His righteous will, did not decide either to leave anyone in the fall of Adam and in the common state of sin and condemnation, or to pass anyone by in the communication of grace which is necessary for faith and conversion.
>
> Rejection: For this is firmly decreed: *He hath mercy on whom he will, and whom he will he hardeneth* (Rom. 9:18). And also this: *Unto you it is given to know the mysteries of the kingdom of heaven, but to them it is not given* (Matt. 13:11). Likewise: *I thank thee, O Father, Lord of heaven and earth, that thou didst hide these things from the wise and understanding, and didst reveal them unto babes; yea, Father, for so it was well-pleasing in thy sight* (Matt. 11:25–26).

Given what has been treated in article 15, I can address the Arminian error briefly. God, says the Arminian, "did not decide either to leave anyone in the fall of Adam," or "to pass anyone by." In other words, the Arminian simply denies reprobation. In Arminianism there is no reprobation. For the Arminian the only reprobation is God's decree to punish all those who will not believe. However, in Arminianism God has not determined whether a person shall believe or not. Therefore, reprobation like election is conditional.

In response to the Arminian error, the Reformed fathers simply quoted scripture, stating that, "this is firmly decreed." It is foolish and wicked to argue against the clear teaching of God's word. If God has decreed, even firmly decreed, who are we that we should attempt to overturn it? Who is the creature of the dust that he dares to reply against God?

ARTICLE 16: A PASTORAL RESPONSE TO THE FEAR OF REPROBATION

> Those who do not yet experience a lively faith in Christ, an assured confidence of soul, peace of conscience, an earnest endeavor after filial obedience, and glorying in God through Christ, efficaciously wrought in them, and do nevertheless persist in the use of the means which God hath appointed for working these graces in us, ought not to be alarmed at the mention of reprobation, nor to rank themselves among the reprobate, but diligently to persevere in the use of means, and with ardent desires devoutly and humbly to wait for a season of richer grace. Much less cause have they to be terrified by the doctrine of reprobation who, though they seriously desire to be turned to God, to please Him only, and to be delivered from the body of death, cannot yet reach that measure of holiness and faith to which they aspire; since a merciful God has promised that He will

> not quench the smoking flax nor break the bruised reed. But this doctrine is justly terrible to those who, regardless of God and of the Savior Jesus Christ, have wholly given themselves up to the cares of the world and the pleasures of the flesh, so long as they are not seriously converted to God.

Article 16 is closely related to article 12, which dealt with the assurance of election. Article 16 addresses the very important, pastoral topic: the fear of reprobation.

Three kinds of people are addressed in this article.

First, there are those who do not yet experience the assurance of their salvation. Second, there are those who are dissatisfied with their spiritual progress. Third, there are those who are careless and openly ungodly.

Article 16 presupposes that reprobation is being preached, for it speaks of "the mention of reprobation." This is a condemnation of many preachers and churches where the doctrine of reprobation is buried in guilty, cowardly silence. The Arminians used the doctrine of reprobation to discredit the Reformed faith. Because the Arminians hated the sovereignty of God, they painted it in the worst possible light, which is still their tactic today. They hoped to make godly members of the churches afraid of the doctrine of reprobation so that they would reject it and embrace the Arminian error. In the conclusion to the Canons, some of these slanderous accusations against reprobation are set forth and answered. The effect of the slander of the Arminians, combined with the legitimate preaching about reprobation in the Reformed churches, could be a cause for concern in the hearts and minds of sincere church members.

Some hearers might be afraid that they belong to the number of the reprobate. The Canons answer these fears in a warm, pastoral, comforting manner.

The first category of troubled souls do not yet experience lively faith in Christ; assured confidence of soul; peace of conscience; an earnest endeavor after filial obedience; and glorying in God through

Christ. These things are "efficaciously wrought" in God's children. We should take note of the fact that the article does not say that these things are absent, but that they are not *experienced*. We should also notice that the people described here *know* that they do not yet experience these things and are *troubled* at that lack. They long for and desire to experience these things. There are church members like this: they are afraid that they might be hypocrites and even reprobates. There are preachers who foster such fears in their hearers. A faithful pastor must deal gently and compassionately with such troubled sheep. The Reformed fathers did not say to such a soul, "There is nothing that you can do. You cannot know one way or the other. If you are reprobate, you will be damned, whatever you do. You must wait for God to give you a new heart."

The Reformed fathers instead gave encouragement to such a soul.

First, these desires are the fruit of God's grace. A hypocrite or a reprobate is not troubled, for he does not care about sin. That a person is concerned shows that this person is already a believer: "Lord, I believe; help thou mine unbelief" (Mark 9:24). We see this in the article itself: the counsel of the Reformed fathers was to wait for *further* grace. This means that God's grace is already working in such a person. You have grace. Wait for a season of richer grace.

Second, this person must not be alarmed at the mention of reprobation, that is, the preaching of reprobation must not terrify or frighten him. The doctrine of reprobation is awe-inspiring, but it is never used to frighten God's people (1 Thess. 5:9; 2 Thess. 2:12–14).

Third, such a person must not rank himself among the reprobate. He must never include himself among the reprobate either as a reason for despair and terror or as a reason for sin. There are two attitudes of people who label themselves as reprobates. Some say, "I am reprobate, so there is no point in believing, repenting, or living in a godly way. I will eat, drink, and be merry, for tomorrow I die." Such a person uses or misuses reprobation as an excuse to continue in sin, which he loves. Others say, "I am terrified that I will go to hell, but there is nothing I can do. God has rejected me, and there is no hope for me." Such a person finds in reprobation an occasion to despair. Both reactions, although very different, amount to the same thing: unbelief.

Those whom God has eternally rejected in his decree of reprobation not only never believe, repent, or live in godliness, they also do not *desire* to believe, to repent or to live in godliness, and they are not troubled at the fact that they have no desire to believe, to repent, or to live in godliness.

Fourth, this person should "diligently...persevere in the use of means." The pastoral response of the Canons is *not* fatalism, the idea that God has either chosen or reprobated you, so that there is nothing that you can do. Rather, the Canons direct the troubled soul to God's means of grace, for God uses those means for the working of faith, for assurance, and for the strengthening of faith. The person in view here already uses the means of grace. The advice of the Reformed fathers was "diligently to persevere in the use of means, and with ardent desires devoutly and humbly to wait for a season of richer grace." Keep attending the preaching and do not stop. Keep using the sacraments and do not stop. Keep using the means of prayer and do not stop. Seek out the fellowship of the saints, attend public worship, and do not stop. The very worst thing that a weak saint can do is to neglect public worship and stop his personal and family devotions, for "faith cometh by hearing, and hearing by the word of God" (Rom. 10:17; see also 1 Thess. 2:13).

The second kind of person is a sincere believer, whose growth in grace is, in his own estimation, slow and unsatisfactory. But what Christian is ever satisfied with his spiritual progress? This is the normal Christian who experiences sorrow over sin, who struggles with the corruption of his flesh, and who has a small beginning of the new obedience. Do not permit pietistic, charismatic perfectionists to give you unrealistic expectations of the Christian life.

This second category is described thus: first, they seriously desire to be turned to God; second, they seriously desire to please God only; and third, they seriously desire to be delivered from the body of death. Notwithstanding these serious desires, they experience distressing spiritual symptoms: "[they] cannot yet reach that measure of holiness and faith to which they aspire." Again, this is a description of all believers in Jesus Christ; it is the *normal* Christian life (Rom. 7:14–25; Gal. 5:16–17).

The pastoral answer of the Canons is beautiful: "much less cause have they to be terrified by the doctrine of reprobation." Much less! They have less reason to be afraid than the first category—and they had none. Such sensitive Christian souls are bruised reeds and smoking flaxes, which a merciful God promises not to break nor to quench (Isa. 42:3; Matt. 12:20). The "bruised reed" is a weak believer, crushed and almost broken under sin; while the "smoking flax" is a believer with much corruption, barely flickering in the darkness. God will not destroy the one in whom he has begun the work of his grace. Therefore, such a struggling saint must not become discouraged or fearful (Phil. 1:6). Since God will not crush the bruised reed or quench the smoking flax, it is the duty of Christian pastors to deal gently with such troubled souls. This was exactly the approach of the theologians at Dordt. How inaccurate is the caricature of the hard-nosed Reformed preacher who supposedly delights in terrifying people with nightmares about reprobation.

The third category is the wicked or ungodly man. The Canons describe such men thus: first, they disregard God and the savior Jesus Christ; second, they give themselves wholly up to the cares of the world and the pleasures of the flesh; and third, they are not seriously converted to God. Such people scoff at the gospel, live for this world, and do not have any sorrow over sin. These people live "regardless of God," for they are unconcerned about spiritual things. Only this category of the three has good reason to fear reprobation: "this doctrine is justly terrible" to them. As long as they remain unbelieving, they have no right to presume upon God's favor. They must be warned that God's wrath abides on them, as the Heidelberg Catechism teaches:

> The kingdom of heaven is shut...against unbelievers...when it is declared and testified to all unbelievers, and such as do not sincerely repent, that they stand exposed to the wrath of God and eternal condemnation, so long as they are unconverted; according to which testimony of the gospel God will judge them, both in this and in the life to come.[17]

Even then, the Reformed fathers did not dare to label such people as reprobate, for while they are unconverted, unbelieving, and impenitent, we cannot tell if they are in the number of the elect. If they are, God will certainly bring them to saving faith, for which we hope and pray.

Jerome Zanchius (1516–90) wrote,

> That there are reprobate persons is very evident from Scripture...but who they are is known alone to Him, who alone can tell who and what men are not written in the Lamb's book of life. I grant that there are some particular persons mentioned in the Divine Word of whose reprobation no doubt can be made, such as Esau and Judas; but now the canon of Scripture is completed, we dare not, we must not pronounce any man living to be non-elect, be he at present ever so wicked. The vilest sinner may, for aught we can tell, appertain to the election of grace, and be one day wrought upon by the Spirit of God. This we know, that those who die in unbelief and are finally unsanctified cannot be saved, because God in His Word tells us so, and has represented these as marks of reprobation; but to say that such and such

17 Heidelberg Catechism A 84, in *Confessions and Church Order*, 118.

individuals, whom, perhaps, we now see dead in sins, shall never be converted to Christ, would be a most presumptuous assertion, as well as an inexcusable breach of the charity which hopeth all things.[18]

ARTICLE 17: A PASTORAL RESPONSE TO GRIEVING PARENTS

> Since we are to judge of the will of God from His Word, which testifies that the children of believers are holy, not by nature, but in virtue of the covenant of grace in which they, together with the parents, are comprehended, godly parents have no reason to doubt of the election and salvation of their children whom it pleaseth God to call out of this life in their infancy.

Article 17 addresses a very emotive subject, namely, the election and salvation of children. More specifically, the article concerns the children *of believers*. More specifically still, the article addresses the children of believers who die in infancy. There were good reasons that the synod addressed this subject here.

First, this was an urgent pastoral concern, especially in that day. Miscarriages and infant deaths were a stark reality in Europe in the seventeenth century, much higher than in our day. Because infant mortality was so very high, pastors were called to bring a word of comfort on such occasions. What could be said to grieving parents whose dear child had died of an illness shortly after its birth?

This pastoral comfort was necessary, moreover, because the Arminians used the occasion of the death of children to slander the Reformed faith. They charged the Reformed fathers of teaching that "many children of the faithful are torn, guiltless, from their mother's

---

18 Jerome Zanchius, *Absolute Predestination* (London: Silver Trumpet Publications, 1989), 69.

breasts and tyrannically plunged into hell, so that neither baptism, nor the prayers of the church at their baptism, can at all profit them."[19] The Arminians delighted, and still delight, in painting the Reformed faith in the worst possible light.

The issue for the Arminians was the election and reprobation of children. The Arminians taught, and most Arminians still teach, that all children, whether those born to believers or those born to unbelievers, are numbered among the elect. Arminians, therefore, denied the reprobation of children because in their view salvation is conditional. Since children cannot be guilty of unbelief or fulfill the condition of faith, all of them must be automatically included in God's salvation. Arminianism denied, and still denies, contrary to Psalm 51:5, Romans 5:12, and other passages of the word of God, that children are guilty in Adam. If children are not guilty in Adam, there is no reason for them to perish. Indeed, if children are not guilty in Adam, and if they are not corrupted through original sin, which was the view of Pelagius, they do not even *need* salvation, for from what would they be saved? Many modern Arminians teach that all children before the age of accountability are saved. There is no consensus among Arminians on the exact point at which a child passes from unaccountable to accountable. Some Arminians believe that the age of accountability is seven years; others suggest twelve years; others even suggest eighteen years or older. Nevertheless, the age of accountability theory, so attractive to Arminians, has no basis whatsoever in the word of God.

On the face of it, the Arminian theory, although attractive to our emotions, is absurd. Should we believe that all the children who drowned in Noah's flood, who perished in Sodom and Gomorrah, who were slain in the tenth plague in Egypt, and who suffered God's vengeance in the conquest of Canaan, were taken by God into heaven? Besides that, the very fact that those children *died* demonstrates that

---

19 Canons of Dordt conclusion, in *Confessions and Church Order*, 179.

they were sinners, for "the wages of sin is death" (Rom. 6:23). In the case of those children, the wages of *Adam's sin* imputed to them was death. "Death reigned from Adam to Moses, even over them that had not sinned after the similitude of Adam's transgression, who is the figure of him that was to come" (Rom. 5:14). Death reigned over all the children who died from Adam to Moses, and death still reigns over children today, whether newborns, toddlers, teenagers, or the youth, if we stretch the age of accountability to its limits.

The only hope for children—for any children—is the grace of God. If children are saved, it is not because they are innocent, or not yet accountable to God. It is because God is gracious; it is because Christ redeemed children; and it is because the Holy Spirit regenerates and sanctifies children. But we have *no reason* to believe that Christ redeemed or the Holy Spirit regenerated and sanctified the children who perished under the judgments of God mentioned in the previous paragraph. We do, however, have *every reason* to believe that God is gracious to, has redeemed, regenerates, and sanctifies the elect children of believers born in the church.

The Canons do not address the issue of the children of unbelievers who die in infancy. Instead, the synod sought to comfort "godly parents." First, our Reformed fathers reminded us "to judge of the will of God from His Word." In such a sensitive subject believers must not speculate. When faced with such grief godly parents need solid promises from God's word. Second, the Canons appeal to the truth of our children's *holiness*. Since without holiness no man shall see the Lord (Heb. 12:14) and since nothing unclean shall enter the heavenly city (Rev. 21:27), this is a vitally important truth. The holiness here is opposed to "uncleanness" in 1 Corinthians 7:14. Therefore, it is not mere external holiness, a kind of setting apart, but real, internal, spiritual holiness, the holiness that makes a child a saint with his parents in the church of God. Third, the Canons are quick to point out the source of our children's holiness: "not by nature, but in virtue of the covenant of grace in which they, together with the parents, are comprehended." Believers' children are *not* exempt from original sin. They are not naturally better than unbelievers' children. Every godly parent can testify to the truth of Proverbs 22:15: "Foolishness is bound in the heart of a child." Every godly parent mourns to see his own sins reflected in his children. The Reformed parent clings to the truth of Heidelberg Catechism answer 74: "Redemption from sin by the blood of Christ, and the Holy Ghost, the author of faith, is promised to them [the children] no less than to the adult."[20] Fourth, the Canons urge parents, especially grieving parents, to view their children from the perspective of the covenant. They are, the Canons remind us, "comprehended" with their parents in the covenant of grace.

Reformed theology, including the Reformed theology of Dordt, where the five points of Calvinism were formulated, is covenantal theology. Although the Canons do not present a detailed, systematized doctrine of the covenant, they do mention it in key places (Canons 1.17; 2.8; 2, errors 2, 4–5; and 5, error 1). Head one, article 17 is the first time the word "covenant" is explicitly mentioned.

The covenant of grace is the bond or relationship of friendship and communion that God establishes with his people in Jesus Christ. In the covenant, God declares that he is our God and the God of our seed after us in our generations for an everlasting covenant. This means that God promises to be the God of our children *as children*, not merely when they grow up to be adults who believe the truth of the gospel and confess Christ. This is abundantly taught throughout scripture (Gen. 17:7; Deut. 30:6; Ps. 8:2; 22:9–10; 71:5–6; Isa. 54:13; 59:21; Jer. 32:39–40; Mark 10:13–14; Luke 18:15–16; Acts 2:39; 1 Cor. 7:14; Eph. 6:1–3; Col. 3:20, and other passages). The other confessions also teach this, for the Heidelberg Catechism declares, "[Children], as well as the adult, are included in the

20 Heidelberg Catechism A 74, in ibid., 111.

covenant and church of God."[21] The Belgic Confession insists upon the same truth:

> We believe [that the children of believers] ought to be baptized and sealed with the sign of the covenant, as the children in Israel formerly were circumcised upon the same promises which are made unto our children. And indeed Christ shed His blood no less for the washing of the children of the faithful than for adult persons.[22]

The baptism form used in Reformed churches teaches the same truth on the basis of the same promises of God's covenant:

> God the Father witnesseth and sealeth unto us that He doth make an eternal covenant of grace with us...the Son sealeth unto us that He doth wash us in His blood from all our sins...the Holy Ghost assures us, by this holy sacrament, that He will dwell in us and sanctify us...And although our young children do not understand these things, we may not therefore exclude them from baptism, for as they are without their knowledge partakers of the condemnation in Adam, so are they again received unto grace in Christ.[23]

Notice, however, that the Bible uses the term *seed* deliberately, for God's promise is to save the *elect* children. This is clear from Romans 9:6–8; Galatians 3:16, 29; and Acts 2:39. Election must be presupposed when we read the Canons, for the creeds promise that the children of believers are washed in the blood of Christ. We know from head two that Christ shed his blood only for the elect: "It was the will of God that Christ by the blood of the cross, whereby He confirmed the new covenant, should effectually redeem...all those,

21 Heidelberg Catechism A 74, in ibid.
22 Belgic Confession 34, in ibid., 69–70.
23 Form for the Administration of Baptism, in ibid., 258–59.

and those only, who were from eternity chosen to salvation."[24] Moreover, the Holy Ghost, the author of faith, is given *only to the elect*. (Canons 1.6). Therefore, God does not promise to save all the children of believers on condition that they believe, but he promises to save the elect children of believers *so that they believe*. God makes no promise to reprobates, whether to reprobate adults or to reprobate children.

What, then, do the Canons say to grieving parents as they stand by the grave of their little ones? First, the Canons appeal to God's sovereignty: "whom it pleaseth God to call out of this life in their infancy." The Reformed fathers were careful in their wording: the devil did not take the child; the child did not simply die, tragic as the death was; but God called the child out of this life because it pleased him. Every believer, whether parent or not, must rest in God's good pleasure. Our lives and the lives of our children are in his hands. He determines our days and the days of our children for our good and for his glory. Second, the Canons give solid comfort to grieving parents. Godly parents "have no reason to doubt of the election and salvation of their children." Godly parents *ought not* to doubt. Godly parents *must not* doubt. Instead of doubting, godly parents *must believe* and *be assured*. They must believe and be assured of the election and salvation of their children who die in infancy. They must believe and be assured of the election and salvation of the particular child whose death they are grieving.

They must be assured, not because the child was cute or sweet (most likely it was), not because the child was innocent (it most certainly was *not*), not because the child was by nature holy (it was not), but because of God's covenantal promise, which can be paraphrased in these words: "I will be your God and the God of your seed after you, including your seed which I am pleased to call out of this life in their infancy. When I call your seed out of this life in their

24 Canons of Dordt 2.8, in ibid., 163 (emphasis added).

infancy, although it breaks your heart, you must trust me. You must not doubt my promise, for I am your God."

The objection to this, of course, is the truth of reprobation. Is it not true that the line of election and reprobation cuts through families, so that there are reprobates born to believing parents? Was there not an Esau born to godly Isaac and Rebekah? Was there not an Absalom born to godly David? Was not godly Eli's heart broken by the wickedness of his two sons, Hophni and Phinehas, sons of Belial? And are there not reprobates among the children of believers today? No one who reads the word of God or scans church history can deny it. Nevertheless, article 17 stands firm, for God does not call the reprobate children of believers out of this life in their infancy. God causes the reprobate seed to grow to maturity, so that they can fill up the cup of their iniquity, and so that God can be justified in their destruction. Such was the case with Esau, with Absalom, with Eli's wicked sons, and with all the reprobate in Israel. Such is the case also today. When a child of believers is called out of this life in its infancy, we have no reason to doubt—we ought not doubt, we must not doubt—of its election and salvation. That is the hope, solid, well-grounded hope, that the Canons of Dordt give to grieving parents.

In fact, we have no reason to doubt, and must not doubt, the election and salvation of *any* member of the church, whether an adult or a child, unless unbelief and impenitence are manifested in a wicked or ungodly life. What solid comfort we have in life and in death because we, with our children, belong to our faithful and merciful God.

ARTICLE 18: THE TWOFOLD RESPONSE TO ELECTION AND REPROBATION

> To those who murmur at the free grace of election and just severity of reprobation, we answer with the apostle: *Nay, but, O man, who art thou that repliest against God?* (Rom. 9:20), and quote the language of our Savior: *Is it not lawful*

> *for me to do what I will with mine own?* (Matt. 20:15). And therefore, with holy adoration of these mysteries, we exclaim in the words of the apostle: *O the depth of the riches both of the wisdom and knowledge of God! how unsearchable are his judgments, and his ways past finding out! For who hath known the mind of the Lord? or who hath been his counsellor? or who hath first given to him, and it shall be recompensed unto him again? For of him, and through him, and to him, are all things: to whom be glory for ever. Amen* (Rom. 11:33–36).

In article 4 the Canons identified two distinct responses to the gospel: faith and unbelief. Similarly, men react in two different ways to the truth of predestination, or as the Canons put it, to the "free grace of election and just severity of reprobation." Election is by "free grace," which excludes all merit, whether real or potential, in man. Reprobation is severe, but just.

The first response is negative—some people murmur at it. In every age, wicked men have complained about predestination. The proud heart of man cannot stand the truth that salvation is entirely in the hands of God. The Canons remind such murmurers of the rebuke of the apostle Paul in Romans 9:20, "Nay but, O man, who art thou that repliest against God?" That is the only answer scripture gives: since you are a creature, you have no right to complain about God. Get off your high horse and humble yourself in the dust before your Creator.

The second response is positive—believers adore it. They exclaim, said the fathers at Dordt, "with holy adoration of these mysteries." They echo the words of the apostle,

> 33. O the depth of the riches both of the wisdom and knowledge of God! how unsearchable are his judgments, and his ways past finding out!
> 34. For who hath known the mind of the Lord? or who hath been his counsellor?

35. Or who hath first given to him, and it shall be recompensed unto him again?
36. For of him, and through him, and to him, are all things: to whom be glory for ever. Amen. (Rom. 11:33–36)

Is that the response of your adoring heart? May it be so by God's grace.

Discussion questions on the first head of doctrine

1. Why do Arminians often concentrate their attack on reprobation when they discuss the scriptures with the Reformed? Why do the Canons not begin there? Should they begin there?
2. Would you begin your witness with these words, "Did you know that God does not love everyone?" Why/why not?
3. Which truths are foundational to a biblical treatment of predestination?
4. Do the Arminians *really* believe that God is not obligated to save anyone?
5. Why is the word *world* such a battleground between Arminians and the Reformed? See the scriptural texts on the meaning of *all men* and *world* listed at the end of chapter two. Can you think of any other texts seized upon by Arminians in an effort to teach universal salvation or at least a chance of universal salvation? Reserve judgment on these texts until the end of the Canons.
6. What is the meaning of the word "whosoever" in John 3:16?
7. Why is the gospel "[the] most joyful tidings"? Is it joyful tidings for *you*?
8. What hope is there for the heathen who never hears the gospel? How do passages such as Romans 1:18–25, Acts 14:11–18, and 17:22–34 address this question?
9. How do the Canons consistently demonstrate that unbelief is the sinner's—and not God's—fault? Why is it important to demonstrate this?
10. What does it mean that faith is the "gift" of God? Does God promise to give a person salvation *if he believes*? Does God

promise to give a person faith *if he believes*? Explain your answer.

11. Which steps does God take in order to save his elect for whom he has decreed salvation?
12. Does God take any of these steps for the reprobate? What is the implication?
13. Identify and define the main words used in the Bible to describe God's eternal decrees.
14. A common objection to predestination is that God is not a "respecter of persons." What does this mean? Prove that it is an invalid objection.
15. Why do the Canons call God's decree of election "discrimination"? What does this mean and why is such a word so offensive today?
16. How is the truth of election abused? What comfort does it afford God's people? What comfort does it afford *you*?
17. What is the main difference between the Arminian concept of election and the biblical truth of election explained in the Canons?
18. What is the significance of the phrase in Canons 1.7 that Christ is the "Head of the elect"?
19. Why is the statement of the Arminians that God has decreed "to save those who would believe and would persevere in the obedience of faith," while true, inadequate to explain what God's decree of election actually *is*?
20. How is the oneness of God's will, as set forth in Canons 1.8, contradicted by both the teaching of the well-meant offer and the teaching of dispensationalism?
21. The Arminians of the seventeenth century were convoluted in their theology, as is evident from the errors and rejections. Are

modern Arminians convoluted also? Evaluate the statement: "The truth is simple; heretics make it complicated."

22. What is the difference between conditional and unconditional election?
23. Is it true that God foresees who will believe? Why does God foresee it?
24. What does the Bible mean by the term *foreknowledge*? How do Arminians abuse this term?
25. What is the difference between God's foresight of a person's faith and God's foreknowledge of his people? What is the significance of the verb *know* in this connection?
26. Some Reformed theologians of the past used *condition* in an orthodox sense. In what unorthodox sense do Arminians and other theologians use the word? Should we simply avoid the word altogether?
27. What is your impression after reading Canons 1, errors and rejections 4–5?
28. What is the "good pleasure" of God? Why is there no deeper cause than God's good pleasure?
29. Faith is "from its very nature undeserving." While this is true, explain why it is *not* true when combined with the other teachings of Arminianism. Arminians will commonly argue, "God offers you salvation as a free gift, which is yours if you accept it." Explain how Arminianism makes salvation a work of man.
30. To which attributes of God did Dordt appeal in Canons 1.11 to prove the certainty of election? How does this show that Arminianism is an attack on the attributes of God?
31. Calvin warned that any doctrine of predestination that goes beyond the scriptures is a "fatal abyss." Discuss.

32. What was the Arminians' doctrine of assurance? Why is it inadequate to have an assurance of one's salvation without an assurance of one's eternal, unchangeable election?
33. How do some preachers undermine their listeners' assurance? How can—and should—preachers encourage their hearers to be assured?
34. Demonstrate from Canons 1.12 that assurance is the norm for all believers.
35. What is the meaning of the qualifying phrase "in various degrees and in different measures"?
36. How do believers attain assurance? Why do the Canons refer to "the infallible fruits of election"?
37. What are the serious spiritual effects of a lack of assurance in a person's life and in the life of the congregation?
38. How, according to Arminianism, can a person be assured of eternal salvation?
39. Examine the fruits described in Canons 1.13. How can you grow in these graces?
40. What disastrous effects did the Arminians predict in those assured of their eternal election (Canons 1.13). Did they have a point?
41. Discuss the danger of an "idle and wanton trifling with the grace of election" (Canons 1.13). Is that a threat to your spiritual life? What steps can you take to avoid this sin?
42. Calvin called the enemies of election "dogs" and "hogs." What did he mean, and was he right?
43. Why is predestination so infrequently preached from pulpits today? How does this compare with the practice of the past? What encouragement could you give to your pastor to preach more often on this doctrine?

44. What is the *purpose* of the preaching of predestination, and what is the effect on the congregation that hears such preaching? What effect does it have on *you*?

45. Why did the fathers at Dordt wait until Canons 1.15 to treat reprobation?

46. Is it possible to hold to *single* predestination, that is, to believe election *without reprobation*? How do the Canons make election and reprobation inseparable?

47. Explain the difference between reprobation and damnation. Do the ungodly perish simply because it pleases God to destroy them?

48. What do infra- and supralapsarianism have in common? Can you name any famous infralapsarians or supralapsarians, whether contemporary or of the past?

49. Explain the meaning of the statement, "Reprobation serves election." If you can, give examples from the Bible to illustrate this truth.

50. What would it mean for God to be "the author of sin"? Why do the Canons abhor such an idea with such vehemence?

51. How would you use Canons 1.16 to comfort a doubting believer?

52. Should we ever be terrified at a sermon about reprobation? Explain your answer.

53. What comfort must a godly grieving parent take from Canons 1.17? Is such a statement *necessary* in a Reformed creed? Why did the fathers at Dordt deem it necessary to include it in the first head on predestination?

54. Having studied the first head on predestination, what is your response? Do you murmur or do you adore?

Proof texts for the first head of doctrine

Deuteronomy 4:37
Deuteronomy 7:7–8
Deuteronomy 10:14-15
Deuteronomy 14:2
Psalm 65:4
Psalm 89:3
Psalm 105:6
Psalm 147:19-20
Isaiah 41:8
Isaiah 42:1
Isaiah 43:1
Isaiah 44:1
Isaiah 45:4
Isaiah 48:9
Isaiah 49:16
Matthew 11:25
Mark 13:20, 27
John 6:37-45
John 10:25-30
John 15:16
John 17:2–6, 9–11, 24
Romans 8:28–34
Romans 9:11–24
1 Corinthians 1:28–29
Ephesians 1:3–5, 11
Colossians 3:12
1 Thessalonians 1:4
2 Thessalonians 2:13
2 Timothy 1:9
2 Timothy 2:10
Titus 1:1
1 Peter 2:8–9
2 Peter 1:10
Revelation 13:8
Revelation 17:14

The Second Head of Doctrine on the Death of Christ and the Redemption of Men Thereby

INTRODUCTION

We must take note of the fundamental difference between Arminianism and the Reformed faith with respect to the death of Christ.

The Reformed faith teaches *substitutionary atonement*, which means that Christ paid the penalty for sin in the place of a certain definite people (the elect) who are saved by that sacrifice. The Arminians taught that Christ died for all men, but that his death was *not* a payment for the sins of anyone in particular. Instead, Christ died in order *to make it possible* for God to offer salvation to all men on a certain condition, a condition that he (God) would determine. Modern Arminians are less subtle in their theological distinctions and inconsistently confess some form of substitutionary atonement. They teach that Christ died for all men in order to make salvation possible for all men, but not to secure salvation for anyone in particular. Therefore, a modern Arminian will make such statements in his evangelism: "Christ died for you, just as he died for all men. Christ died in your place. Christ paid the penalty for your sins. Now you must make him your own and personal savior by accepting what he has done for you." Nevertheless, the Arminian will concede that, if you do not believe in Christ, and if you do not accept Christ as savior, his death on the cross will not save you. Some modern Arminians are more consistent, even chiding their less consistent brethren for falling into the "error" of substitutionary atonement. For example, J. Kenneth Grider wrote:

> A spillover from Calvinism into Arminianism has occurred in recent decades. Thus many Arminians whose theology is not very precise say that Christ paid the penalty for our sins. Yet such a view is foreign to Arminianism, which teaches instead that *Christ suffered for us*. Arminians teach that what Christ did he did for every person; therefore, what he did could not have been to pay the penalty, since no one would then ever go into eternal perdition. Arminianism teaches that *Christ suffered for everyone* so that the Father could forgive the ones who repent and believe.[1]

Before I begin to examine the articles of head two, I need to prepare the ground by discussing the subject of the atonement in general, for the Bible has a lot to teach about the significance and importance of Christ's death. Arminians have historically held to different views of the atonement, especially the governmental view and the moral influence view. As noted above, for an Arminian to hold to substitutionary atonement, albeit inconsistently, is a modern phenomenon.

The governmental view is a development of the theology of Hugo Grotius (1583–1645). According to this theory of the atonement, Jesus died as an example in order to display the justice of God. In other words, God punished Jesus to show what he could do to sinners if they do not repent. The death of Christ, then, serves to display God's

---

1 J. Kenneth Grider, "Arminianism" in *Evangelical Dictionary of Theology,* ed. Walter Elwell (Grand Rapids, MI: Baker Academic, 1984), 80 (emphasis added).

displeasure at sin, to exert God's moral government over the universe, and to make it possible for God to forgive sinners on some condition or other, the condition chosen being repentance and faith. However, the governmental view denies that Christ bore the punishment that sinners deserved to endure. It denies that Christ made satisfaction to God to pay the penalty for sin as a substitute for sinners.

William Booth (1829–1912), the founder of the Salvation Army and a vehement anti-Calvinist, held to the governmental view of the atonement. He wrote:

> The Scriptures teach that Christ on the Cross, in virtue of the *dignity of His person*, the *voluntariness of His offering*, and the *greatness of His sufferings*, did make and present, on behalf of poor sinners, a sacrifice of *infinite* value. And that this sacrifice, by showing all worlds the terrible *evil* of the sin man had committed, and the *importance* of the *law man* had broken, did make it possible for the love and pity of God to flow out to humanity by forgiving all those who repent and return in confidence to Him, enabling Him to be just and yet the justifier of him that believeth in Jesus.[2]

Perhaps this sounds like substitutionary atonement to the reader, but do not be deceived. Booth did *not* believe that Christ paid the penalty for sinners, for he was astute enough to understand that such a view would lead inevitably to limited atonement or particular redemption, a position that Booth abhorred. He continued:

> You will sometimes hear people talk about the finished work of Christ. What is meant by it?
>
> That Christ, when He died on the Cross, put Himself in the place of the sinner and bore the *exact amount of punishment* which he deserved, thus actually *paying the debt* that

2 William Booth, "The Finished Work of Christ," section 6, in *The Doctrines of the Salvation Army: Prepared for the Training Homes* (London, 1891), 26.

> the sinner owed to Divine justice. And that if the sinner will only *believe* this, he is forever *free* from the claims of the law, and can never be brought into condemnation either here or hereafter.
>
> Is this so?
>
> We think not…If it were so, if Christ did literally pay the sinner's debt, in this sense, God cannot justly demand payment *twice* and consequently *no one will be sent to Hell*, and *all* will be saved…If a debt is paid, it is paid, and the sinner's *unbelief* does not in any way affect the *fact*. If I owe a man £25, and some one pays it for me, my creditors cannot *sue me* for the sum. I am all right, seeing the debt is paid, whether I believe it or no…Any one can see that if all the sinner's debt has been paid, all the sin of *unbelief* must have been paid also, otherwise how can his *past* unbelief be forgiven, and if *all his unbelief* has been atoned or paid for, how can he be sent to hell for that, any more than for any other sin?[3]

The second view, the moral influence view, is less popular. According to this view, popularized by the medieval theologian Peter Abelard (1079–1142), Christ died to inspire men to moral excellence. When men contemplate the cross, they see the wonderful love displayed therein. They will then be moved to obey God, to love him, and to love the neighbor. Nevertheless, this view also denies that Christ died to pay the penalty for the sins of anyone in particular. It also fails to reckon with man's depravity, for the cross does not move men emotionally to repentance. Instead, the cross

---

3 Ibid., 24–25. Elsewhere, Booth remarked, "To me there was one God, and John Wesley was his prophet. I had devoured the story of his life. No human compositions seemed to me to be comparable to his writings, and to the hymns of his brother Charles, and all that was wanted, in my estimation, for the salvation of the world was the faithful carrying into practice of the letter and the spirit of his instructions" (Quoted in F. De L. Booth-Tucker, *The Life of Catherine Booth the Mother of the Salvation Army* (New York: Fleming H. Revell Company, 1892), 1:74.

is an offense to fallen mankind, a stumbling block to the Jews and foolishness to the Gentiles (1 Cor. 1:23).

Another important consideration is the language used in the Bible to describe the purpose and fruit of Christ's death for sinners, words such as *atone* or *atonement*; *redeem*, *redemption*, or *ransom*; *reconcile* or *reconciliation*; *propitiate* or *propitiation*; *satisfy* or *satisfaction*; and *washing* or *purification* or *cleansing*.

The word *atonement*, which is used almost exclusively in the Old Testament (Romans 5:11 is the exception, but the better translation there is "reconciliation"), has the root meaning of covering. To atone is to cover over by means of a sacrifice, which happened in the Old Testament by blood (Lev. 1:4). The word *redeem* means to deliver or release from slavery, bondage, or imprisonment. Redemption takes place by means of a ransom or a price. The one thus redeemed is set free or liberated from that which enslaved him, namely sin and Satan (Matt. 20:28; Eph. 1:7). Reconciliation is the restoration of alienated parties to friendship through the removal of the cause of their estrangement. The result is the restoration of a previously fractured relationship. Since the offense was sin, elect sinners were reconciled to God when Christ gave his life for them on the cross (Rom. 5:10–11; 2 Cor. 5:18–19). The words *propitiate* and *expiate* are close in meaning. Someone is propitiated, appeased, or placated when his wrath is turned away by means of a sacrifice or a gift. Expiation adds to this the idea of the covering over of sin by means of a sacrifice and is, therefore, similar to the word *atonement*. Christ propitiated God, or turned away his wrath from his people, by his death on the cross (1 John 4:10). Satisfaction is the full payment of a debt owed to the offended justice of God, so that the one for whom satisfaction is made is not obligated to pay (Isa. 53:10–11). To wash, purge, or purify is to remove the pollution or filth of sin from sinners so that they are clean (1 Cor. 6:11; Eph. 5:25–26; 1 John 1:7).

The Bible teaches that Christ truly made atonement, thus covering over with the sacrifice of his blood the sins of all for whom he died. The Bible teaches that Christ truly redeemed his people, by paying the ransom price, thus truly liberating all those for whom he died from the bondage of sin and Satan. The Bible teaches that Christ truly reconciled his people to the Father, by shedding his precious blood, thus restoring the friendship between God and all those for whom Christ died. The Bible teaches that Christ truly propitiated God by his death on the cross, thus removing the wrath of God from all those for whom Christ died. The Bible teaches that Christ truly made satisfaction to God's justice, by bearing the punishment due to their sins, thus removing the guilt of sin from all those for whom Christ died. The Bible teaches that the blood of Christ really washed away sin, purified sinners, and cleansed souls, thus removing the filth of sin from all those for whom Christ died.

Arminianism, however, posits an atonement that does not atone; a redemption that does not redeem; a reconciliation that does not reconcile; a propitiation that does not propitiate; a satisfaction that does not satisfy; and a washing that does not wash. All of these benefits, which are supposedly available to all, are *only made possible* by the death of Christ, for everything depends on the free will of the individual sinner. Therefore, according to Arminianism, Christ died for many who will ultimately perish in the lake of fire. John Wesley (1703–91), the founder of Methodism wrote,

> What! Can the blood of Christ burn in hell?…I answer...one who was purchased by the blood of Christ may go thither. For he that was sanctified by the blood of Christ was purchased by the blood of Christ. But one who was sanctified by the blood of Christ may nevertheless go to hell; may fall under that fiery indignation which shall for ever devour the adversaries.[4]

---

4 *The Works of John Wesley* (Grand Rapids, MI: Baker Publishing Group, 1996), 10:297.

In the second point of the Remonstrance, the Arminians declared,

> That, agreeably thereto, Jesus Christ, the Saviour of the world, died for all men and for every man, so that he has obtained for them all, by his death on the cross, redemption, and the forgiveness of sins; yet that no one actually enjoys this forgiveness of sins except the believer, according to the word of the Gospel of John iii. 16: "God so loved the world that he gave his only-begotten Son, that whosoever believeth in him should not perish, but have everlasting life." And in the First Epistle of John ii. 2: "And he is the propitiation for our sins; and not for ours only, but also for the sins of the whole world."[5]

I must address one further argument before beginning the study of the second head—the Bible's use of the words *world* and *all men* with respect to the death of Christ. If Jesus died only for the elect, why does the Bible speak so often about the world and all men? The simple answer is that by these terms the Holy Spirit is not teaching that Christ died for everyone head for head, but for all kinds of people, both Jews and Gentiles, or for all people in a specific group, which is usually made clear in the context.[6]

As the Reformed fathers at Dordt began head one by building a foundation, not mentioning election until article 6 and reprobation until article 15, so they began head two by laying the groundwork for the doctrine of the atonement. The fundamental concepts underlying the doctrine of the atonement are the necessity of satisfaction, the impossibility of the creature's making satisfaction, the satisfaction made by the Son of God, the suitability of Christ

---

5 Five Arminian Articles 2, in Schaff, *Creeds of Christendom,* 3:546.

6 For examples of how the Bible uses such seemingly universalistic expressions (*world, all men, every, any,* and the like), see the scriptural texts on the meaning of *all men* and *world* listed at the end of chapter two.

to make satisfaction, and the value of Christ's satisfaction. Limited atonement itself, the famous *L* of TULIP, the fathers did not mention until head two, article 8.

ARTICLE 1: THE NECESSITY OF DIVINE SATISFACTION

> God is not only supremely merciful, but also supremely just. And His justice requires (as He hath revealed Himself in His Word) that our sins committed against His infinite majesty should be punished, not only with temporal, but with eternal punishment, both in body and soul; which we cannot escape unless satisfaction be made to the justice of God.

Article 1 begins with God, for in theology everything must begin with God. It begins with two of God's attributes, his mercy and his justice: "God is not only supremely merciful, but also supremely just."

God's mercy is an attribute, which means that God's mercy is who or what he *is*: "God is… supremely merciful." If God were not merciful he would not be God. Therefore, irrespective of the creature, God *is* merciful. God's mercy is his perfection according to which he is, knows himself to be, and wills himself to be, the most blessed forever.[7] As the merciful God, he delights in himself. Because God's mercy is an attribute, it is eternal and unchangeable: "O give thanks unto the LORD; for he is good: for his mercy endureth forever" (Ps. 136:1).

---

7 Herman Bavinck wrote about God's goodness, "[God] receives nothing, but only gives. All things need him; he needs nothing or nobody. He always aims at himself because he cannot rest in anything other than himself. Inasmuch as he himself is the absolutely good and perfect one, he may not love anything else except with a view to himself. He may not and cannot be content with less than absolute perfection. When he loves others, he loves himself in them: his own virtues, works, and gifts...The goodness of God, when shown to those in misery, is called *mercy*" (Herman Bavinck, *Reformed Dogmatics*, ed. John Bolt, trans. John Vriend, vol. 2, *God and Creation* [Grand Rapids, MI: Baker Academic, 2004], 211, 213).

God's mercy is also shown to the creature, for the merciful God desires to share his mercy and to show his mercy. God's mercy is his compassion or pity for the miserable or wretched creature. God's mercy is also his will or desire to deliver the miserable creature from misery and to make him blessed. And because we have in mind *God's* mercy, it is powerful mercy: it is God's power by which he actually does deliver his creatures from misery and makes them blessed.

An ineffectual pity that yearns to deliver a miserable person from wretchedness is the mercy of a creature (the mercy of a mother for her son in a hospital, for example, as she watches the body of her child wracked by fever, which pain she is powerless to stop or even alleviate), but it is not God's mercy, for God's mercy cannot be *ineffectual.* God's mercy powerfully delivers all those to whom it is directed.

The second attribute treated in article 1 is God's justice: "God is...also supremely just." When we think of God's justice, we view him as being fair or equitable in his dealings with men. As an attribute, however, God's justice is his absolute commitment to himself as the only and highest good. As the just and righteous God, Jehovah always acts in accordance with himself as the holy God. As the just God, Jehovah is the standard of righteousness, for there is no higher standard of justice to which he must conform.[8] That is why Paul reacted with such vehemence in Romans 9:14 to the idea that God could be unjust: "What shall we say then? Is there unrighteousness with God? God forbid." Moses sang of God's justice: "He is the

---

8 Louis Berkhof wrote about God's justice or righteousness, "But though there is no law above God, there is certainly a law in the very nature of God, and this is the highest possible standard, by which all other laws are judged. A distinction is generally made between the absolute and the relative justice of God. The former is that *rectitude of the divine nature, in virtue of which God is infintely righteous in Himself,* while the latter is *that perfection of God by which He maintains Himself over against every violation of His holiness, and shows in every respect that He is the Holy One*" (Louis Berkhof, *Systematic Theology* [Edinburgh, Scotland: Banner of Truth, repr., 2003], 74–75).

Rock, his work is perfect: for all his ways are judgment: a God of truth and without iniquity, just and right is he" (Deut. 32:4).

God's justice also means that he always punishes sin, never leaving sin unpunished, but punishing sin with exact punishment in accordance with the offense committed. God's justice cannot be changed and his just demands cannot be denied, even when the creature is unable to meet them. Therefore, for example, God *still* justly requires perfect obedience from fallen men and women who are incapable of obedience because of the depravity of their human natures.

Article 1 insists that God is *both* supremely merciful *and* supremely just. There is no conflict or disharmony between God's justice and mercy. God's justice is not opposed to his mercy, while God's mercy does not swallow up his justice. Both are true, for both are necessary to the being of God. A god who is mercy without justice or justice without mercy is not the God of the Bible, but a miserable idol invented by men.

God cannot show mercy at the expense of his justice. This truth regarding the unity and harmony of the attributes of God is called the *simplicity* of God. Arminianism denies the simplicity of God when it seeks to pit God's mercy against his justice, or when Arminians teach that God's mercy overcomes his justice. If that were true, there would be a conflict in the being of God between two of his attributes, which is impossible.

Since it is true that God is supremely merciful *and* just, the justice of God demands punishment where there is disobedience. Such punishment must be temporal and eternal in body and soul. Temporal punishment is punishment inflicted in time, while eternal punishment is punishment inflicted in eternity. The punishment must be exact, for it must fit the crime. God punishes neither excessively, beyond what sin deserves, nor insufficiently, letting the guilty sinner off lightly. And because God is perfectly omniscient and wise, he knows the appropriate punishment for every individual transgressor, for he understands not only which sins have been committed, but also the circumstances of every sin.

From a human perspective temporal and eternal punishment of body and soul might *seem* extreme, but humans have neither the right nor the competency to judge of such things: "O man, who art thou that repliest against God?" (Rom. 9:20). Such "extreme" (but not excessive) punishment is necessary because of the dignity of the God against whom we commit sin: "Our sins against his infinite majesty should be punished." This, too, is the teaching of the Heidelberg Catechism: "God is indeed merciful, but also just; therefore His justice requires that sin which is committed against the most high majesty of God be also punished with extreme, that is, with everlasting punishment of body and soul."[9]

This punishment is inescapable, "unless satisfaction be made to the justice of God." Satisfaction is the full payment of a debt so that a sufficient payment is made fully to meet the sinner's obligation. It is not to pay too little, nor is it to pay too much, but it is to pay exactly the amount required.

Therefore, man, when confronted with his obvious guilt, but not desiring to repent, appeals in vain to the mercy of God. Surely, says the sinner, if God is merciful, why not forgive *without satisfaction*? Nevertheless, God's mercy is not displayed in forgiveness without satisfaction, but in satisfying his justice by the substitutionary satisfaction of his Son. In other words, God is merciful in not requiring satisfaction *from his people*, but in providing satisfaction *in another*. By so doing God is both merciful *and* just—praise his name!

What would you think of a merciful but unjust judge? How would you react to a judge who, because he feels sorry for criminals, never punishes anyone for their crimes? Would you not despise such a person as a wicked, unjust, and foolish judge? God is the supremely just and merciful judge; therefore, to deny either of these

---

9 Heidelberg Catechism A 11, in *Confessions and Church Order*, 87.

attributes is to deny him. Do not be tempted to evade God's justice by denying it or criticizing it, for God will not deny himself. He remains just even when all men deny it (Heb. 9:22; 2 Tim. 2:12–13). Instead, let us seek out his mercy, which is a just mercy, for only in his mercy is there salvation for guilty sinners.

Article 1, however, leaves us in suspense. Satisfaction is necessary, but is it possible? That question the synod addressed in article 2.

ARTICLE 2: THE PROVISION OF CHRIST AS SURETY AND SUBSTITUTE

> Since, therefore, we are unable to make that satisfaction in our own persons, or to deliver ourselves from the wrath of God, He hath been pleased in His infinite mercy to give His only begotten Son for our surety, who was made sin, and became a curse for us and in our stead, that He might make satisfaction to divine justice on our behalf.

Having set forth the necessity of divine satisfaction, the Canons close the door against the notion that we could make satisfaction in our own persons. Article 2 assumes this, for the Reformed faith in Lord's Days 4–6 of the Heidelberg Catechism has already declared this to be the case. Before expounding the teaching of article 2, I will examine why this should be so. Why are we not able to make satisfaction for sin ourselves? Why do we need a substitute?

There are three main reasons.

First, the debt is too great, for the sinner's obligation toward God is to render to God perfect, lifelong obedience (Matt. 22:36–40; Gal. 3:10; James 2:10). Do not brush that aside too quickly—the demands of God's law are not that we do our best (and if we are truly honest, we must say that we actually *never* do our best; we could always make more effort), but that we obey all of God's commandments at all times and that we do so with the pure motive of love for God. Do you spend every waking moment serving God gladly from the heart, delighting in him as your creator, and dedicating your life to him as your lord? Do you deliberately abstain from all sin, so that your life is untainted by even the slightest transgression of God's holy law? If you do not—and Solomon wrote, "There is not a just man upon earth, that doeth good and sinneth not" (Eccl. 7:20)—you have not met your obligation toward God.

Second, the sinner's debt is steadily increasing, for every day the debt of obedience remains unpaid, while every day the sinner adds to his mounting burden of guilt. This morning you woke up a debtor. Take the example of a twenty-five-year-old man. Perhaps, we can venture to make a rough estimate of his debt. That young man owes God for all the *unpaid obedience* of the first twenty-five years of his life (in monetary terms he is in arrears). Let us imagine (by grossly underestimating the reality) that the young man commits three sins per day, one evil thought, one evil word, and one evil action. By the time he reaches age twenty-five, he has committed 27,375 transgressions. In addition to his actual sins, the young man is responsible for his guilt in Adam and for the depravity of his sinful nature. And the young man's conscience knows that he commits many more than three sins per day. If the young man reaches the age of fifty, he will, if he continues to sin at the rate of three sins per day, be responsible for 54,750 transgressions! If he dies at the age of eighty, he appears in the judgment with a "sin record" of 87,600 transgressions. In reality, of course, our debt is incalculable and ever increasing, for "who can understand his errors?" (Ps. 19:12). No wonder that the psalmist, crying from the depths, asked, "If thou, LORD, shouldest mark iniquities, O LORD, who shall stand?" (Ps. 130:3).

Third, the sinner has nothing with which to pay, for everything the sinner possesses he already owes to God (Ps. 49:6–9; 50:7–15; Luke 17:10). Perhaps the young man in the illustration realizes how much he owes to the justice of God. Instinctively, he looks for a way to escape the debt. What could he give God? He cannot give him money or any material possession, for the whole world and everything in it belongs to God. He cannot arrange to serve God in his spare time, for he does not have any spare time that does not already belong to God. Having squandered the first twenty-five years of his life in the service of sin, even if he served God perfectly for the next twenty-five years (which is impossible), he could not make up for the previous unpaid service or transgressions that he has accumulated. He cannot even offer God good works, prayers, and other religious activities, for even his best works are tainted with sin and he already owes God the obedience that he would offer: "When ye shall have done all those things which are commanded you, say, we are unprofitable servants. We have done that which was our duty to do" (Luke 17:10).

The result is that sinners cannot deliver themselves from the wrath of God. Death itself does not satisfy the justice of God. Even when the wicked suffer in hell, they do not satisfy God's justice there. Endless suffering in hell does not even begin to pay off the debt to God's justice, which is why the punishment of hell can never come to an end. Hell is not redemptive or remedial, but hell is punitive. The fires of hell do not cleanse the sinner or rehabilitate him so that he is ready to enter the society of heaven one day (such is the foolish teaching of the Roman Catholics with their dogma of purgatory); hell serves to punish the sinner.

Moreover, no mere creature can deliver the sinner or make satisfaction for him. Consider the alternatives. An animal cannot satisfy God's justice, for "it is not possible that the blood of bulls and of goats should take away sins" (Heb. 10:4). Imagine the millions and millions of animals slaughtered in the Old Testament. None of them could remove a single sin. God accepted animal sacrifices in the Old Testament merely as types and shadows of the sacrifice of Jesus Christ, but there is a great difference between an animal and a human being. God's justice cannot be satisfied through the death of a beast. God's believing children in the Old Testament understood that: they did not trust in the blood of bulls and goats, but in the

Messiah who was to come whose atoning death was prefigured in the sacrifices of the Old Testament law. In addition, an angel cannot satisfy God's justice, for God will not punish the innocent angels for the sins committed by men. A mere man cannot satisfy God's justice, for all men are already sinners with their own debts. Besides, no mere man is able to endure the wrath of God in order to deliver others from it. The terrible burden of God's wrath against sin is so great that a mere man would be crushed under it.

What a miserable creature is man. Hemmed in on every side by debt, he must die under the curse of God, unless God mercifully provides salvation for him.

Into that impossible situation God in his supreme mercy sent his only begotten Son Jesus Christ: "[God] hath been pleased in His infinite mercy to give His only begotten Son." Take note of the fact that the source of the gift of God's Son is the "infinite mercy" of God. It is not that God is reluctant to save sinners and that Jesus had to persuade God to show mercy to his people. Rather, God *in his infinite mercy* sent Jesus to satisfy his own justice. God's love and mercy are always *first* (Eph. 2:4–7; 1 John 4:10).

In expressing the truth this way, the Reformed fathers had their eyes on a caricature of the Arminians. Those wicked enemies of the truth sought to discredit the Reformed faith by portraying the God of the Reformed faith as stingy in his mercy. How false, for God sent his Son in his *infinite mercy.* If God saves only one person, he does so *in his infinite mercy*. God's mercy is not measured in the number of people he saves. Rather, God's mercy by definition is infinite, immeasurable, and unsearchable in its richness and depth because it is *God's* mercy. All the tongues of men and angels are insufficient to praise the greatness of God's mercy, which is why God has given us "the ages to come," in which he will "[show] the exceeding riches of his grace in his kindness toward us through Christ Jesus" (Eph. 2:7).

The source of the sending of the Son is the good pleasure of God, for "He hath been pleased…[to send]." God was under no obligation to send Christ, but he did so because he willed to send him. In turn, Christ did not come out of compulsion or unwillingly, but he came willingly, with a heart filled with love for his people and with a desire to fulfill the Father's will for their salvation: "Then said I, Lo, I come: in the volume of the book it is written of me, I delight to do thy will, O my God: yea, thy law is within my heart" (Ps. 40:7–8). "No man taketh [my life] from me, but I lay it down of myself" (John 10:18).

Article 2 introduces a very important biblical concept of "surety:" "[God] hath been pleased…to give his only begotten Son for our surety." A surety is one who represents another before the law and who undertakes to assume the legal obligations of that person (Gen. 43:9; 44:32; Prov. 6:1; Heb. 7:22). Sometimes a man might agree to be guarantor on a loan, but he must be very careful because if the person for whom he is a guarantor defaults on the loan, the guarantor is legally obliged to pay the loan. For that reason the book of Proverbs warns against becoming a surety (Prov. 11:15). Nevertheless, Jesus Christ became a surety out of love for his people and he knew exactly what it meant to become their guarantor. Christ's becoming a surety was not foolish, for it is part of the plan of salvation of the only wise God. Because God's people could not render to God the obedience that he required, Christ rendered that obedience for them in a life of righteousness under God's law. Because they could not bear the penalty that God's justice demanded, Christ bore that penalty for them in their stead in his lifelong sufferings and death on the cross. Christ (as their surety), therefore, represented them in his life, death, burial, resurrection, ascension, and session at God's right hand (Gal. 2:20; Eph. 2:5–6; Col. 2:12).

Arminianism denied that Christ is the surety because the Arminians understood that if Christ represented all men all men would be saved. To speak in monetary terms, if Christ as guarantor represented all defaulted debtors, all defaulted debtors would be set free from the obligation to pay their debts. Then God would not remand anyone to the debtors' prison of hell, which is clearly not the case, for the Bible teaches that many perish forever in hell.

In Arminianism Christ did something equally for all, but for none in particular. What he did falls far short of actually assuming responsibility for their debt, however. Therefore, the Arminian conception of Christ's death rules out the idea of a surety, for a surety is also a substitute and a surety is impossible without substitution.

As the surety, Christ establishes the covenant, for *surety* is a covenantal term, as the epistle to the Hebrews explains. Christ is qualified to be the surety of his people because he is both God and a real, sinless man. Therefore, he is both legally and organically related to them. Because they have transgressed the covenant so that they cannot inherit the blessings of the covenant, Christ died for them in order to purchase for them the blessings of God's covenant. The covenant is like a testament that can only be ratified through the death of the testator, and since Christ is divine, he is the testator (Heb. 9:15–17).

What does this mean for them? First, Christ represented some—and only some—in his death. Second, the sins of those people were imputed to, or reckoned to the account of, Christ, their surety and substitute. Third, the benefits that he purchased in his death are imputed to, or reckoned to the account of, all those whom Christ represented in his death. Fourth, Christ is the representative head of the members of the covenant, that is, only of the elect, which means that the covenant is established only with the elect.

The Canons state that in submitting to the death of the cross, Christ "became a curse for us and in our stead." The curse is God's word *against* sinners, for it is the word of God's wrath that effectually destroys sinners, making them eternally miserable. God's curse, which is the opposite of God's blessing, rests upon all sinners outside of Jesus Christ (Ps. 37:22; Matt. 25:41; Gal. 3:10). God's curse would rest upon us also, but for Jesus Christ. Article 2 teaches that Christ "became a curse" for us, echoing the words of Galatians 3:13.

When Christ became a curse, God addressed the word of his wrath *against his Son*. Christ tasted the misery of having God as his enemy. God's face was set against Christ to destroy him because he represented sinners. The result is that the curse is removed from us. This truth explains the cross, for Christ bore God's wrath and became a curse for all those whom he represented. Therefore, since he was cursed "for us and in our stead," we cannot be cursed.

The Arminians would not confess the language of Dordt that Christ died "for us and in our stead." Instead, the Arminians declared that Christ died *for our benefit*, that is, he died equally for the benefit of all men. However, that benefit was *not* that he paid the penalty of our sins. We shall see presently the supposed "benefit" purchased by the death of Christ in Arminianism. In Arminianism Christ died for all, but he did not bear the curse for all, for he did not remove the curse from all. In Arminianism there are some, indeed many, for whom Christ died who still endure the curse forever in hell.

The purpose of Christ's death for his people was "that He might make satisfaction to divine justice on our behalf." What we could not do, Jesus Christ did. That is the heart of the gospel. No wonder that Paul was determined to know nothing except Christ and him crucified! No wonder that Paul would not glory or boast in anything but the cross of Christ!

ERROR AND REJECTION 2: CHRIST'S ACQUIRING RIGHTS FOR THE FATHER

> Error 2: Who teach that it was not the purpose of the death of Christ that He should confirm the new covenant of grace through His blood, but only that He should acquire for the Father the mere right to establish with man such a covenant as He might please, whether of grace or of works.
>
> Rejection: For this is repugnant to Scripture, which teaches that Christ has become the Surety and Mediator of a better,

that is, the new covenant, and that a testament is of force where death has occurred (Heb. 7:22; 9:15, 17).

We have seen that the purpose of the death of Christ was to satisfy divine justice with respect to the sins of all those whom Christ represented as head, surety, and substitute. Now we must compare this with the heresy of Arminianism.

Arminianism denied that it was God's purpose with the death of Christ to "confirm the new covenant of grace through His blood" (a denial of Christ's words in Matthew 26:28). To understand this denial, we need to understand the covenant of grace. God has established one everlasting covenant of grace in Jesus Christ. This covenant is revealed progressively through history in the covenant with Adam, the covenant with Noah, the covenant with Abraham, the covenant with Israel, the covenant with David, and the new covenant prophesied in Jeremiah 31. God did not establish a brand new covenant on each of those occasions. Instead, there is one covenant, which has one head, one promise, and one surety, and is established with one people in the Old Testament and the New Testament. This covenant is established only with the elect, for the reprobate wicked are never in the covenant, although some of them (such as reprobate children born to godly parents) appear in the sphere of the covenant for a time (Rom. 9:6).

The Reformed faith teaches that Christ ratified or confirmed the new covenant with the shedding of his blood. In support of this truth, the Reformed fathers at Dordt appealed to Hebrews 7:22 and 9:15, 27. They could also have appealed to Galatians 3:15–23.

Against this the Arminians posited a different covenantal scheme. They argued that the old covenant, which they viewed as a covenant of works, required obedience to God's commandments. Nevertheless, because God saw that man could *not* fulfill the conditions of the old covenant, that old covenant was removed. Christ died in order to satisfy the demands of the old covenant so that it could be taken away. Because of what Christ has done by his death on the cross God now has the right to establish a new covenant, if he pleases. Since man's guilt and depravity made it impossible for God to offer a new covenant until the sins of mankind were removed, Christ has purchased for God the right to make a new covenant. Moreover, this new covenant could be on whatever condition God might choose, "whether of grace or of works." Thus the cross has redeemed the Father from having to uphold the demands of his own law. In other words, it could be said that the cross benefits God the Father, rather than sinners. It purchases nothing (at least nothing directly) for sinners, but it purchases something for the Father, the right to make a new covenant.

In response to that, the Reformed fathers exclaimed that this is "repugnant to Scripture," for it is a gross denial that Christ is the surety and mediator of the "better, that is, the new covenant," which is the covenant of grace.

ERROR AND REJECTION 3: CHRIST'S MERITING SALVATION FOR NO ONE

> Error 3: Who teach that Christ, by His satisfaction, merited neither salvation itself for anyone, nor faith, whereby this satisfaction of Christ unto salvation is effectually appropriated; but that He merited for the Father only the authority or the perfect will to deal again with man, and to prescribe new conditions as He might desire, obedience to which, however, depended on the free will of man, so that it therefore might have come to pass that either none or all should fulfill these conditions.
>
> Rejection: For these adjudge too contemptuously of the death of Christ, do in no wise acknowledge the most important fruit or benefit thereby gained, and bring again out of hell the Pelagian error.

Error 3 is a development of error 2. To understand what the wily Arminians were seeking to achieve by their novel theory of the atonement, we should first understand the biblical and Reformed faith.

The Reformed faith teaches that by virtue of the death of Christ certain blessings are merited or purchased for sinners: salvation itself, that is, salvation in the broadest sense (including justification, sanctification, eternal glory [Isa. 53:5; John 1:29; Rom. 5:9–10; Gal. 3:13; Eph. 1:7; Heb. 9:12], and faith [Phil. 1:29]). This is an important difference between the Reformed faith and Arminianism, for the Reformed faith teaches that *faith was purchased for the elect on the cross*. Remember, that head one taught that election is the fountain of every saving good, including faith. Head two teaches that the cross is the source of faith. Heads three and four will teach that the Spirit is the source of faith. Always, therefore, God, not man, is the source of faith.

In contrast, Arminianism teaches that faith is the *condition that man must fulfill* in order to receive salvation, for faith is supposedly man's part or contribution to salvation. I have already demonstrated that the Bible teaches that faith *itself* is part of salvation and something that God gives to sinners so that salvation is "effectually appropriated" ("unto you it is given *in the behalf of Christ*, not only to believe on him" [Phil. 1:29, emphasis added]). Thus there is no conflict between what Christ merited or purchased and what the Spirit applies. Arminianism teaches that Christ merited something for all—it was *not* salvation; we shall see what it is—but that it depends on the free will of the sinner for its appropriation or application.

According to the Arminians, then, *what* did Christ merit on the cross? First, Christ did not merit salvation for any sinner. Second, Christ did not merit faith for any sinner. In fact, Christ merited *nothing* for sinners. Instead, he merited something *for the Father*: first, "the authority or the perfect will to deal again with man"; second, the authority or the perfect will to "prescribe new conditions as He might desire." The obedience to these new conditions depends "on the free will of man." Therefore, it "might have come to pass that either none or all should fulfill these conditions."

This might all sound rather abstruse, so I quote Dave Hunt (1926–2013) to show that modern Arminianism is not a million miles away from this position. Dave Hunt came to fame in 2002 when he published *What Love Is This?*—a book that purports to be a refutation of Calvinism, when in reality it is a caricature of Calvinism. If Christ accomplished nothing for any sinner (neither salvation nor faith), how can Hunt pretend that Christ's death was actually worthwhile? I will allow him to explain:

> As a result of Christ's death *having paid the full penalty*, no one will spend eternity in the lake of fire because of his sins; they will be there for rejecting Christ and *the salvation He obtained* and freely offers to all…Even if no one believed in Him, Christ proved God's love, mercy and grace; He proved the sinfulness of sin, the justice of the penalty and glorified God *in paying in full for all*. Because of Christ's death on the cross, God has been fully vindicated in His creation of man and will be eternally glorified in those in hell…Christ did not die for individual sins only, but for sin itself, a penalty which had to be paid in order for anyone to be saved. But *His paying the penalty for sin itself* could not occur without *His paying for all sins* and providing for all mankind… There is no way that Christ's death could be limited to paying only for the elect's sins. To deliver even one person from eternal punishment, no matter how few or many the sins he may have committed, *Christ had to pay the penalty demanded by His infinite justice for sin*. By very definition, then, the death of Christ on the cross *paid the penalty for sin* itself which hangs over the heads of the entire human race. It could not be otherwise. Christ is the 'second man…the last Adam" (1 Cor. 15:45–47), the representative of the entire human race. Therefore, *what He did at Calvary had to be efficacious for*

> *all mankind. He paid for Adam's sin*, which brought death upon all, so *in paying that penalty* He has freed all who will receive the salvation He offers.[10]

Do not let the italicized phrases mislead you. Hunt's Arminianism leads him to make several errors. First, despite claiming that Christ's death was "efficacious for all mankind" and despite repeatedly referring to a penalty being paid, Hunt gives no solid purpose for the death of Christ and no infallible fruit of his death. Second, Hunt denies that God imputed specific transgressions to Christ, for Christ supposedly died for the nebulous concept of "sin" in general, but for nobody's sins in particular. Third, Hunt teaches that the only penalty that Christ paid was the original sin of Adam ("he paid for Adam's sin," which was that initial act of disobedience in the garden of Eden), and either denies or downplays the individual sins of men, but even here Hunt is inconsistent and confusing. Fourth, Hunt rightly views Adam as the representative of all men, but he fails to see that Christ is the representative only of his people, who are the elect. Lastly, Hunt denies that sinners are punished for their own sins—they are punished only for the sin of unbelief. Therefore, Adolf Hitler is not punished for the sin of mass murder, but only for the sin of unbelief; and there are no adulterers, idolaters, thieves, liars, and the like in hell—there are *only unbelievers*. The scriptures teach that God punishes every kind of sin, not only unbelief, with eternal damnation (1 Cor. 6:9; Eph. 5:5–7; Rev. 21:8, 27; 22:15). In fact, Hunt conceives it possible that *nobody* would be saved through the death of Christ and yet Christ's death would be fully efficacious, accomplishing everything that God intended in that death.

The response of the synod to this error was sharp. "These [the Arminians] adjudge too contemptuously of the death of Christ." To adjudge means to regard, to consider, or to deem. Contempt is the

---

10 Dave Hunt, *What Love Is This? Calvinism's Misrepresentation of God* (Sisters, OR: Loyal Publishing, 2002), 248, 250–51 (emphasis added).

disdaining or the despising of something. "These...do," charged the synod, "in no wise acknowledge the most important fruit or benefit" of Christ's death. The Arminians denied that there is any *immediate* benefit to any from the death of Christ, for remember that by his death he secured salvation for no one. Dordt's conclusion was devastating: "These...bring again out of hell the Pelagian error." Pelagius with his Pelagianism is in hell; the Arminians sought to resurrect him from the pit by repackaging his error in new clothes!

Strong words, indeed.

ERROR AND REJECTION 4: PERFECT OBEDIENCE NO LONGER REQUIRED

> Error 4: Who teach that the new covenant of grace, which God the Father, through the mediation of the death of Christ, made with man, does not herein consist that we by faith, inasmuch as it accepts the merits of Christ, are justified before God and saved, but in the fact that God, having revoked the demand of perfect obedience of the law, regards faith itself and the obedience of faith, although imperfect, as the perfect obedience of the law, and does esteem it worthy of the reward of eternal life through grace.
>
> Rejection: For these contradict the Scriptures: *Being justified freely by his grace through the redemption that is in Christ Jesus: whom God hath set forth to be a propitiation through faith in his blood* (Rom. 3:24–25). And these proclaim, as did the wicked Socinus, a new and strange justification of man before God, against the consensus of the whole church.

Error and rejection 4 further explain how the Arminians viewed the covenantal blessings made possible—not purchased—by the death of Christ. Again, notice a sharp contrast with the biblical and Reformed faith.

The teaching of the Reformed faith is that in the new covenant of grace the elect are "justified [by faith] before God and saved." They are justified by faith alone, "inasmuch as it [faith] accepts the merits of Christ." Therefore, the ground of justification and salvation is the merits of Christ (his lifelong obedience, atoning sufferings, and death), while faith is the instrument by which the sinner receives these merits of Christ. This instrument of faith is the gift of God purchased on the cross by Christ for his elect people. Christ is the mediator and surety of the new covenant: "The mediation of the death of Christ."

The Arminians denied all the aforementioned truths. According to them, the death of Christ accomplished the following: first, it made it possible for God to revoke the demand of perfect obedience to the law; second, it resulted in God's regarding a new condition of justification as satisfactory, for God regards "faith...and the obedience of faith, although imperfect, as the perfect obedience of the law." Therefore, the grace of God in the death of Christ is seen in God's revoking one difficult condition (perfect obedience) and replacing it with an easier condition (faith and the imperfect obedience of faith). God, then, esteems faith and the imperfect obedience of faith as "worthy of the reward of eternal life through grace." Therefore, this is "grace" for the Arminians—God makes it possible for sinners to save themselves or, at least, to contribute decisively to their own salvation.

The Reformed fathers vehemently rejected the Arminian error. This is a contradiction of the scriptures (Rom. 3:24–25) and this is the proclamation of "a new and strange justification of man." Dordt charged the Arminians with following wicked Faustus Socinus (1539–1604), a heretic who denied the deity of Christ, the Trinity, substitutionary atonement, and justification by faith alone. To be in the camp of two notorious heretics, Pelagius and Socinus, is not a good place to be. And remember that the Arminians appointed the

Socinian, Conrad Vorstius, to be the successor of Arminius in the University of Leiden. Additionally, the Arminians denied the justice of God, for God cannot revoke the just demands of his law and God cannot regard imperfect obedience as if it were perfect obedience and worthy of eternal life.

When God saves his people, he must do so in accordance with his mercy *and* justice. Therefore, perfect satisfaction must be made to the justice of God, which can only be accomplished by Jesus Christ. Any other justification is "strange," foreign to the scriptures, and must be rejected as dangerous heresy.

ERROR AND REJECTION 5: NO MAN CONDEMNED FOR ORIGINAL SIN

> Error 5: Who teach that all men have been accepted unto the state of reconciliation and unto the grace of the covenant, so that no one is worthy of condemnation on account of original sin, and that no one shall be condemned because of it, but that all are free from the guilt of original sin.
>
> Rejection: For this opinion is repugnant to Scripture which teaches that we are *by nature children of wrath* (Eph. 2:3).

The Arminians tried to make the death of Christ accomplish something. We have seen what, according to them, the death of Christ did *not* accomplish: it did *not* save anyone for whom he died; it did *not* purchase any of the blessings of salvation for anyone for whom he died; and it certainly did *not* purchase faith for anyone for whom he died. Instead, it purchased for God the possibility to offer a new covenant based upon easier conditions, which would still have to be fulfilled by man.

The Arminians taught, first, that by the death of Christ "all men have been accepted unto the state of reconciliation." Beware, as we proceed, of the extreme subtlety of the Arminian language. It is not for nothing that Paul wrote of heretics that they handle the word of God deceitfully (2 Cor. 4:2) and that "by the sleight of men, and cunning craftiness…they lie in wait to deceive" (Eph. 4:14). To teach that "all men have been accepted unto the state of reconciliation" is *not* the same as to teach that all men are truly reconciled, for not all men are reconciled to God. To be accepted unto the state of reconciliation is merely to be placed in a position in which reconciliation becomes possible, while to be reconciled is actually to be restored to fellowship with God. The latter the Bible teaches; the former, which *sounds* biblical, is an invention of Arminianism (Rom. 5:10; 2 Cor. 5:19; Col. 1:21). Second, the Arminians taught that all men are "accepted unto...the grace of the covenant." This does *not* mean that all men are in the covenant or that they actually enjoy fellowship with God. Instead, it means that all men are placed in a position where fellowship with God in the covenant becomes possible, if certain conditions are met.

Since the old, impossible demand of perfect obedience has been revoked and the new covenant conditioned on faith and imperfect obedience is offered to all men, all men are in a sense in favor with God. Therefore, contended the Arminians, "No one is worthy of condemnation on account of original sin." This is simply the denial of the doctrine of original guilt, which is reflected in the common evangelical view of children: all children are supposedly innocent and remain so until they reach the so-called age of accountability. Moreover, "no one shall be condemned because of it [original guilt]." For a conditional covenant to have any credibility, the doctrine of original sin must be removed, which is exactly what Arminianism does.

The Canons simply destroy this error with the scriptures to which it is "repugnant." Since we are by nature "children of wrath" (Eph. 2:3), we cannot be merely "accepted unto a state of reconciliation and unto the grace of the covenant." Many supposedly "accepted" are eternally damned. Therefore, Christ must have done more for his people, which is exactly what the gospel teaches, as we shall see as we study the gospel further.

Praise God that the elect are actually reconciled and that they actually enjoy covenantal fellowship with God in Jesus Christ on the basis of his shed blood.

ERROR AND REJECTION 7: CHRIST'S DEATH IS NOT NECESSARY

> Error 7: Who teach that Christ neither could die, needed to die, nor did die for those whom God loved in the highest degree and elected to eternal life, and did not die for these, since these do not need the death of Christ.
>
> Rejection: For they contradict the apostle, who declares: *Christ loved me, and gave himself for me* (Gal. 2:20). Likewise: *Who shall lay any thing to the charge of God's elect? It is God that justifieth; who is he that condemneth? It is Christ Jesus that died* (Rom. 8:33–34), namely, for them; and the Savior who says: *I lay down my life for the sheep* (John 10:15). And: *This is my commandment, that ye love one another, even as I have loved you. Greater love hath no man than this, that a man lay down his life for his friends* (John 15:12–13).

Here the Arminians simply denied the atonement: Christ *could not* die for those whom God loved in the highest degree; Christ *did not need to* die for God's elect; and Christ *did not* die for them. Since God loves them, the satisfaction of the cross is unnecessary and impossible, for the elect do not need the death of Christ for their salvation.

The Reformed fathers did not argue the point, for why argue about something so obvious? Instead, they simply proved from scripture that the death of Christ *is* necessary. God's love does not make the death of Christ unnecessary. On the contrary, because God loves his people who are sinners, his love *requires* the death of Christ. If God had not sent Christ in his great love, they would have perished in their sins. God never shows his love at the expense of his justice.

Christians are indebted to Christ of whom they confidently affirm, "[He] loved me, and gave himself for me" (Gal. 2:20).

ARTICLE 3: THE INFINITE VALUE OF THE DEATH OF CHRIST

> The death of the Son of God is the only and most perfect sacrifice and satisfaction for sin, and is of infinite worth and value, abundantly sufficient to expiate the sins of the whole world.

The background of this article is a slander of the Arminians against the Reformed faith. Because the Reformed fathers taught that Christ died for only a specific people, the Arminians accused them of undervaluing the cross of Christ. The same charge is made today—you are limiting the cross, you are limiting the power of Christ's blood, and you are limiting God's love when you teach limited atonement or particular redemption.

On the face of it, such a charge is absurd, for how is it possible to limit the infinite value of Christ's atonement? How is it possible to limit *infinite* love? But the Arminians by devious reasoning could make it sound plausible. How could the infinite God whose mercy is infinite have mercy on only some? How could the infinite God whose grace is infinite be gracious to only some? How could the infinite God whose love is infinite love only some? How could the death of Christ whose value is infinite save only some?

First, even if God *did* love all men without exception, the question would remain. How could the infinite God whose love is infinite love only a limited number (not an infinite number) of people? God cannot create an infinite number of people, for there is only one infinite, namely God. The Creator is infinite, while the creation, including mankind, is finite.

Second, the answer is found in God himself, for the infinite object of God's love is not humanity, not even the whole of humanity, but God. God is love, which means (among other things) that he loves himself within his perfect triune being of Father, Son, and Holy Spirit. Moreover, God's love does not flow automatically or spontaneously to everything and everyone that he has made. God's love is free and sovereign, for God *chooses* to love. If God loved nobody at all, he would still be infinite in his love, grace, and mercy. God revealed this humbling truth to Israel: "The LORD did not set his love upon you, nor choose you, because ye were more in number than any people; for ye were the fewest of all people: *But because the Lord loved you*" (Deut. 7:7–8, emphasis added). Why does the Lord love his people? Because he chose to do so. There is no other reason.

The atonement, called in article 3 "the only and most perfect sacrifice and satisfaction for sin," is limited by God himself. Christ's sacrifice is of infinite worth and value; therefore, it is abundantly sufficient to expiate the sins of the whole world. Nevertheless, God intends the sacrifice to expiate the sins of only the elect. It is not available, by God's own decree and design, for all men, although it would be sufficient for all men, if God had so pleased. We need not fear any defect, lack, or insufficiency in the cross, for it covers all the sins of all the elect.

The Canons extol the greatness of the value of the cross. First, it is the death of the Son of God, which is the emphasis of the next article. Second, the death of the Son of God is the only *sacrifice* and *satisfaction* for sin. Those two words are important, for the key to understanding the atonement is not to understand those for whom Christ died, but to understand what the sacrifice *was*—it was satisfaction, the payment of a price sufficient to answer, and which actually answered, all the demands of God's holy law, or the full payment of the debt. Arminianism, for all its pretended extolling of the atonement, denied that it was true satisfaction. Third, the death of the Son of God was the "most perfect" satisfaction for sin, or a satisfaction perfect to the highest degree. Fourth, the death of the Son of God was of infinite worth and value, for no limit can be placed upon the sacrifice. It is greater than the sacrifice of all men and all angels, indeed of the entire universe. And fifth, the death of the Son of God was "abundantly sufficient to expiate the sins of the whole world"—there is no insufficiency in the death of Christ. God could have, if he had been pleased to do so, saved ten thousand worlds by the sacrifice of Christ.

Who really limits the atonement of Christ, then? Surely, it is the Arminian who teaches that Christ died for all men without securing the salvation of any. He limits the atonement by robbing it of its power and efficacy, making it an atonement in name only. The Reformed man who teaches that Christ actually saves all those for whom he died does not limit the atonement, for he teaches that Christ made an atonement indeed.

ARTICLE 4: THE REASON FOR THE INFINITE VALUE OF CHRIST'S DEATH

> This death derives its infinite value and dignity from these considerations, because the person who submitted to it was not only really man and perfectly holy, but also the only begotten Son of God, of the same eternal and infinite essence with the Father and the Holy Spirit, which qualifications were necessary to constitute Him a Savior for us; and because it was attended with a sense of the wrath and curse of God due to us for sin.

This article explains why the death of Christ is of such infinite value that it is able to secure the salvation of all of God's people.

First, it is of infinite value and dignity because of the person who submitted to the death of the cross: he is the only begotten Son of God. Christ is the second person of the Trinity, which makes his death worth more than the death of all men and angels. Christ is "of the same eternal and infinite essence with the Father and the Holy Spirit." This orthodox doctrine of Christ, confessed by the church of all ages and enshrined in the ecumenical creeds of Nicea, Athanasius, and Chalcedon, is vital for an orthodox doctrine of the atonement. If Christ were merely a man, his death would not have any atoning value.

Second, the voluntariness of the submission of Christ gives his death value and dignity, for the Son *willingly* underwent suffering and death in loving obedience to the Father. "No man," Christ testified, "taketh it [my life] from me, but I lay it down of myself. I have power to lay it down, and I have power to take it again. This commandment have I received of my Father" (John 10:18).

Third, the spotlessness of the Son of God in the human nature makes the atonement offered by him of great price, for he is "really man and perfectly holy." The eternal, only begotten Son became incarnate in order to suffer and die in the human nature. His human nature consists of a real body and soul, so that the substitute for sinners is perfectly holy, free from original and actual sin. These qualifications were necessary and unique, for only one who is God and man in one divine person in two distinct natures can be the savior, something explained in detail in Lord's Days 5–6 of the Heidelberg Catechism.

Additionally, Christ's death has infinite value because of the nature of his suffering: "It was attended with a sense of the wrath and curse of God due to us for sin." Christ's sufferings, therefore, were not merely or even mainly physical. They were spiritual sufferings, for in his body and soul he felt the pain and anguish of being under the wrath and curse of God. The Belgic Confession expresses it thus: "*He...suffered, the just for the unjust*, as well in His body as in His soul, feeling the terrible punishment which our sins had merited."[11] Or consider these words of the Heidelberg Catechism: "That in my greatest temptations, I may be assured, and wholly comfort myself in this, that my Lord Jesus Christ, by His inexpressible

11 Belgic Confession 21, in *Confessions and Church Order*, 48.

anguish, pains, terrors, and hellish agonies, in which He was plunged during all His sufferings, but especially on the cross, hath delivered me from the anguish and torments of hell."[12]

Yet again, the Canons emphasize, against the Arminians, the substitutionary nature of the atonement: "The wrath and curse of God *due to us* for sin" (emphasis added).

Take a moment, believing reader, to praise God for the immeasurably great gift of his own, only begotten, eternal Son, the only one able and willing to make full satisfaction for all of your sins.

ARTICLE 5: THE PROMISE OF THE GOSPEL TO BELIEVERS

> Moreover, the promise of the gospel is that whosoever believeth in Christ crucified shall not perish, but have everlasting life. This promise, together with the command to repent and believe, ought to be declared and published to all nations, and to all persons promiscuously and without distinction, to whom God out of His good pleasure sends the gospel.

Articles 5–7 are closely related to one another and deal with the preaching of the cross. The Arminians argued that if there was no general atonement (if Christ did not die for everyone), there could also be no general preaching of Christ crucified and, therefore, no call to saving faith to all men.

In treating this important subject, Dordt began with the promise of God. God's promise is his sure or certain word in which he undertakes to do something or to give something. God's promise is not to be confused with a command, a call, or even an offer. In a call or a command, God calls the sinner to do something. An offer is conditional, that is, God will give something *if the sinner does something*. God does not make offers, but he makes promises and he issues commands or calls.

---

12 Heidelberg Catechism A 44, in ibid., 100.

The promise of God in the gospel must be clearly understood.

First, the promise is particular, for God does not promise salvation to all men but only to some men. To whom then does God promise salvation? The answer is to "whosoever believeth." The Canons do not teach a general offer of the gospel to all hearers. Notice the careful wording of article 5: "Moreover, the promise of the gospel is that whosoever believeth in Christ crucified shall not perish, but have everlasting life." God does not promise, "I will save everyone." Nor does God declare, "I promise to everyone of you that, if you believe, you shall be saved." God simply promises salvation *to all believers*, which is what "whosoever believeth" actually means. And since God's promises are sure and certain, all believers do actually receive the promised salvation.

Second, the promise is unconditional. God does not say, "If you believe, I promise to give you eternal life." Nor does God say, "Your act of faith and repentance is the condition or prerequisite to my giving you salvation." Instead, God says, "I promise to give eternal life *to whomsoever believeth*" or "I promise to give eternal life *to all believers*" (Acts 16:31). This identifies the recipients of the promise. The first head of doctrine demonstrated that only the elect believe, for God gives faith to only the elect in accordance with his eternal decree. The second head of doctrine also demonstrates that only the elect believe, for Christ has purchased the gift of saving faith only for the elect. Salvation therefore, which is decreed in election and purchased on Calvary, is promised only to the elect and never to the reprobate, not even conditionally to the reprobate. How could salvation be promised to the reprobate when it was neither decreed nor purchased for the reprobate? How could salvation be promised to the reprobate when they are eternally excluded from election and from the benefits of the cross?

This particular, unconditional promise must be preached. The heirs of God's promise, the elect, must come to hear of it. Notice how the Canons explain this: "This promise...ought to be declared and published to all nations, and to all persons promiscuously and without distinction." The promise is particular, but the preaching is promiscuous, general or unrestricted. With the promise a second truth must be preached, which is the command or the call: "This promise, *together with the command* to repent and believe, ought to be declared and published" (emphasis added). The promise is particular, but the preaching with the command or call to repent and believe is promiscuous, general or unrestricted. This is the response of Dordt to hyper-Calvinism, which is the belief and practice that the gospel should *not* be preached promiscuously, but only to the elect or to supposedly sensible sinners. Those who show signs of regeneration or receptivity to the truth are, in the minds of hyper-Calvinists, sensible sinners. To none other will a hyper-Calvinist issue the command or call to repent and believe.

The call or command published in the gospel is quite simple: repent of your sins and believe in Christ crucified and you shall be saved. The preacher does not command all hearers to believe that Christ died for them, for only a believer can know that Christ died for him personally. Instead, the unbeliever is commanded to believe that Christ is the perfect, sufficient, effectual savior from sin and death, and he is commanded to trust in that savior alone for the forgiveness of sins and life eternal. No reprobate person will ever believe that. No reprobate person can ever believe that. When reprobate people hear the gospel, they despise it, which increases their condemnation. When the elect hear the gospel, they will believe it, receive it, and trust in Christ revealed in it, for God works faith in their hearts. Only through faith can a person know that Christ died for him personally, which is why the Canons are so careful in their wording: "Whosoever believeth in Christ crucified" and not "whosoever believeth that Christ died for him personally." Nowhere in scripture are unbelievers addressed thus, "Believe that Jesus died for you." That is an Arminian, not a biblical and Reformed, presentation of the gospel, which is no gospel at all.

This promise (with the command) must be preached "promiscuously." What must be preached promiscuously? Not the general Arminian presentation—"God loves you! Jesus died for you! God wants to save you! God has a wonderful plan for your life! Open your life to Jesus! God promises to save you if only you will believe and accept Jesus!" But this—"God has sent his only begotten Son into the world to save sinners. Jesus died on the cross and has made a perfect atonement for sin. God raised Jesus from the dead. Believe in this Jesus and God promises that you who believe shall be saved!" I hope that the reader can discern the difference. The Reformed believe, in light of article 5, in the *promiscuous proclamation of a particular promise.*[13]

The only restriction on the preaching, therefore, is God's good pleasure. Since God determines where the preaching goes (Canons 1.3), not all men shall hear it. Nevertheless, the church must not restrict the preaching, but must seek to publish it by all lawful means for the salvation of souls and the glory of God. This compels the church to diligent, enthusiastic evangelism and missions. For, as Paul wrote in Romans 10:14, "How shall they hear without a preacher?" "The Lord gave the word: great was the company of those that published it" (Ps. 68:11).

ARTICLE 6: THE FAULT OF UNBELIEVERS FOR UNBELIEF IN THE GOSPEL

> And whereas many who are called by the gospel do not repent, nor believe in Christ, but perish in unbelief, this is not owing to any defect or insufficiency in the sacrifice offered by Christ upon the cross, but is wholly to be imputed to themselves.

---

13 The Declaration of Principles of the Protestant Reformed Churches states, "The Canons in [head] II, 5 speak of the preaching of the promise. It presents the promise, not as general, but as particular, i.e., as for believers, and, therefore, for the elect. This *preaching* of the particular promise is promiscuous to all that hear the gospel, with the *command*, not a condition, to repent and believe" (Ibid., 414).

Article 6 is similar to head one, article 5. In both places, the Reformed fathers were answering the Arminians: the unbelief of the hearers of the gospel is not God's fault. It is not the fault of the particular election in God's decree, and it is not the fault of the particular atonement of the cross, but it is the fault of man. Unbelief is *always* the fault of man.

The Canons make three important points here.

First, "many who are called by the gospel do not repent, nor believe in Christ, but perish in unbelief." There are more called through the gospel than only the elect. The reference is to the external call, the command to repent and believe. It is God's purpose in the promiscuous proclamation of the particular promise of the gospel that some of the reprobate wicked are also called, for Jesus says, "Many are called, but few are chosen" (Matt. 22:14). God does not graciously invite the reprobate to believe, but he does call, summon, or command them to believe. And many of the hearers reject the gospel to the eternal damnation of their souls.

Second, there is no defect or insufficiency in the sacrifice of Christ. Christ's death, we have seen in article 3, is "of infinite worth and value, abundantly sufficient to expiate the sins of the whole world." Besides that, there are no reprobate persons who sincerely desire to be saved and to believe in Jesus, but who are not saved because Christ did not die for them. Nobody ever comes to Christ and discovers that the death of Christ is insufficient to save him or her (Heb. 7:25). Paul wrote, "Whosoever believeth in him shall not be ashamed" and "Whosoever shall call upon the name of the Lord shall be saved" (Rom. 10:11, 13). Therefore, the call comes to you, dear reader, if you have not already believed in Jesus: believe in Jesus, call upon his name, and you shall not be ashamed, but you shall be saved.

Third, unbelievers are entirely to blame for their unbelief: "[It] is wholly to be imputed to themselves." Unbelief is wicked, sinful rebellion against God for which reprobate people stand guilty before God. Christ died for the unbelief of all his own people, as well as for their other sins, and he died to purchase for them the gift of faith by which they receive the benefits of salvation.

Reader, if you die without believing in Jesus, you have no one to blame but yourself.

ARTICLE 7: THE SAVING GRACE OF GOD IN THE GOSPEL

> But as many as truly believe, and are delivered and saved from sin and destruction through the death of Christ, are indebted for this benefit solely to the grace of God, given them in Christ from everlasting, and not to any merit of their own.

The great benefit of the death of Christ is salvation, nothing less than eternal salvation from sin, death, and hell. Believers are "delivered and saved from sin and destruction through the death of Christ." The source of this benefit is not their works, merits, or even their free will, but "solely the grace of God, given them in Christ from everlasting." This benefit includes that they "truly believe." True faith, I never tire of underlining it, is not the condition that sinners fulfill to be saved, nor is it the contribution that they make to their salvation, but it is the fruit both of election and of the atonement of Christ. Faith has its source not in the free will of man, but in the everlasting grace of God in Christ. Therefore, no person can boast that he has believed in Christ in distinction from his neighbor. Unbelief is the fault of the sinner, while faith is the gift of God.

Believing reader, you have come to Christ to be cleansed from your sins. You are a great debtor to the grace of God. Do not rob God of his glory by attributing your salvation to anyone else but him.

ERROR AND REJECTION 6: THE EFFICACY OF THE CROSS CONDITIONED ON FAITH

> Error 6: Who use the difference between meriting and appropriating, to the end that they may instill into the minds

> of the imprudent and inexperienced this teaching, that God, as far as He is concerned, has been minded of applying to all equally the benefits gained by the death of Christ; but that, while some obtain the pardon of sin and eternal life and others do not, this difference depends on their own free will, which joins itself to the grace that is offered without exception, and that it is not dependent on the special gift of mercy, which powerfully works in them, that they rather than others should appropriate unto themselves this grace.
>
> Rejection: For these, while they feign that they present this distinction in a sound sense, seek to instill into the people the destructive poison of the Pelagian errors.

The Arminians made a sharp distinction between "meriting" and "appropriating" or between what Christ purchased for sinners on the cross and what God applies to, or confers upon, sinners. This is the distinction between objective salvation and subjective salvation.

Christ died some two thousand years ago at which point he purchased salvation for his people. However, they do not receive that salvation immediately or at once. They come into possession of the purchased salvation when the Holy Spirit applies the benefits of salvation to them. This work of the Spirit occurs according to a certain, definite, logical order (Rom. 8:30).

The Arminians made several claims about the distinction between Christ's "meriting" and the sinner's "appropriating" salvation. First, they argued that Christ purchased the same benefits of salvation for all men. (Remember that according to Arminianism he did not actually purchase salvation for anyone, but only a mere possibility for God to offer salvation to everyone. Therefore, in Arminianism Christ purchased *nothing*—never forget that.) Second, God desires to apply the benefits equally to all men: "God, as far as He is concerned, has been minded of applying to all equally the benefits gained by the death of Christ." The benefits are there for everyone, but not everyone will receive (or accept) them. Third, it depends on the free will of man whether the benefits of Christ's cross are received or not, for remember that in Arminianism salvation is always dependent on man, not on God. God has done his best, but man must finish what God has started. Fourth, God offers these benefits equally to all men, and he even offers grace to all men to enable them to receive salvation. Some men cooperate with God's grace—their free will joins itself to this grace—while others resist this grace of God and perish. The subject of resistible grace will be discussed in heads three and four of the Canons. Fifth, God's grace or mercy is, therefore, not decisive to the question of whether one receives the benefits of the cross or not.

In making that confession, the Arminians rejected the Reformed faith that teaches the following. First, the Holy Spirit applies the benefits of salvation to the same people (and to them only) for whom Christ died. Second, God works powerfully in some men (the elect) rather than in others, which is the reason some (only) are saved and obtain the pardon of sin and eternal life. The Canons speak of "the special gift of mercy, which powerfully works in them, that they rather than others should appropriate unto themselves this grace." God leaves nothing to the fickle and uncertain free will of man, for God is determined that his people, whom he loves, whom he elected, and whom he redeemed, should be actually, truly, and eternally saved. In other words, there are no benefits gained by the death of Christ that are not applied to the elect for whom Christ died. And there are no benefits gained by the death of Christ for the reprobate.

In answering the Arminians the synod exposed the evil motives of the heretics. They used a legitimate theological distinction, but they twisted it. They pretended to use it in a sound sense, but they instilled a false teaching into the minds of the imprudent and inexperienced. They sought to instill into the minds of the people "the destructive poison of the Pelagian errors" (2 Cor. 11:3–4; Gal. 2:4; Eph. 4:14; Jude 4).

Error is destructive poison. Avoid theological error and those who teach it, as you would avoid a cyanide pill.

ARTICLE 8: THE PURPOSE OF THE DEATH OF CHRIST

> For this was the sovereign counsel and most gracious will and purpose of God the Father, that the quickening and saving efficacy of the most precious death of His Son should extend to all the elect, for bestowing upon them alone the gift of justifying faith, thereby to bring them infallibly to salvation; that is, it was the will of God that Christ by the blood of the cross, whereby He confirmed the new covenant, should effectually redeem out of every people, tribe, nation, and language all those, and those only, who were from eternity chosen to salvation and given to Him by the Father; that He should confer upon them faith, which, together with all the other saving gifts of the Holy Spirit, He purchased for them by His death; should purge them from all sin, both original and actual, whether committed before or after believing; and, having faithfully preserved them even to the end, should at last bring them free from every spot and blemish to the enjoyment of glory in His own presence forever.

Article 8 is pivotal and central to head two. All of the previous articles of this second head have been leading up to it, which is evident from the use of the conjunction "for." Article 8 gives the reasons for the previous articles, especially for articles 5–7. Why preach promiscuously a particular promise? Why are the elect indebted alone to the grace of God for salvation through the death of Christ? "For this was the sovereign counsel and most gracious will and purpose of God the Father." We should, therefore, carefully examine the meaning of this article.

First, article 8 teaches us about the *purpose* of Christ's death, for the death of Christ occurred according to "the sovereign counsel and most gracious will and purpose of God the Father." God intended that Christ should die, and he had a certain, definite, and specific purpose for that death. The Reformed fathers understood the cross as something decreed (1 Pet. 1:20; Rev. 13:8). God determined the cross, its attendant circumstances, and its fruit (Acts 2:23; 4:27–28). The cross of Christ has its source in "the most gracious will and purpose of God the Father." God sent Christ to the cross because of his grace toward his people, which grace is his beautiful attitude of favor toward them. This attitude of grace was not a fruit of the cross, but it preceded the cross (1 John 4:10). The purpose of the cross is with respect to salvation, for God does not have a secondary, non-saving purpose in the cross of his Son. God does not have a gracious purpose with the cross for the reprobate, for God is not gracious toward the reprobate. He does not have a purpose that contradicts his purpose of election.

Second, article 8 teaches us the *particularity* of the cross. God did not intend, will, desire, or purpose to save any but the elect by the death of Christ. It is God's purpose that the benefits purchased on the cross should "extend to all the elect" (Matt. 1:21). Article 8, therefore, contains a very important phrase, "and those only." For the elect alone Christ died. Christ did not die for the reprobate. On the elect alone God bestows all the blessings of salvation. God bestows no saving benefits on the reprobate. This is the clearest and most explicit creedal reference to limited atonement or particular redemption in the three forms of unity.

Third, article 8 speaks about the *efficacy* of the cross. Arminianism teaches a potential and ineffectual atonement, where Christ died for all men without making actual atonement for any. The Reformed faith, following the Bible, teaches an efficacious, effectual atonement. Notice the language of the Canons: "The quickening and saving efficacy of the most precious death of His Son." If something is "efficacious" or "effectual," it accomplishes what was intended.

God intended to save a certain people through the death of Christ, and because it was effectual or efficacious, that is exactly what Christ did. The efficacy of the death of Christ is "quickening," where to quicken means to make alive. The death of Christ with his subsequent resurrection is the source of life for all of the elect. Because Christ died for the elect, he is able to make them alive, and he does make them alive. This quickening efficacy extends to all of the elect. The article then speaks of an infallible bringing, for by virtue of the death of Christ God bestows "upon them [the elect] alone the gift of justifying faith, thereby to bring them infallibly to salvation" (Heb. 2:10; 1 Pet. 3:18). Notice the word "alone" again—God bestows justifying faith on the elect alone. Moreover, the article describes an effectual redemption, for by his death Christ should (and does) "effectually redeem" all of the elect. Again this is contrasted with Arminianism, which denies an effectual redemption, substituting for it a potential redemption, or a redemption that does not redeem. Furthermore, the article extols a faithful preservation, for Christ's death is not the source merely of the beginning of salvation, but it also guarantees the completion of salvation: "Having faithfully preserved them even to the end."

Fourth, article 8 underlines the *all-comprehensive* nature of the salvation purchased by the death of Christ. The efficacy of Christ's death extends to all the elect, on whom God bestows the following benefits: justifying faith; all other saving gifts (Eph. 1:3); forgiveness of sins, for he "purge[s] them from all sin, both original and actual, whether committed before or after believing" (1 John 1:7); and eternal glory, for "having faithfully preserved them even to the end, [He]...at last bring[s] them free from every spot and blemish to the enjoyment of glory in His own presence forever" (Eph. 5:25–27; Jude 24). Moreover, these benefits pertain to all the elect, who are redeemed "out of every people, tribe, nation, and language" (Rev. 5:9), and who are "from eternity chosen to salvation and given to [Christ] by the Father" (John 6:37). In summary, Christ shall bring to glory *all* of the elect to whom he has given *all* the blessings of salvation and *all* the saving gifts of the Holy Spirit and whom he purges from *all* sin free from *every* spot and blemish *forever.*

Fifth, article 8 makes clear that *faith was purchased on the cross* as part of the gift of salvation (Eph. 2:8; Phil. 1:29). Therefore, faith is not a condition that man must fulfill to obtain salvation. This gift of faith is bestowed upon the elect alone: "Bestowing upon them *alone* the gift of justifying faith" (emphasis added). All of the gifts of salvation were purchased for the elect on the cross. Christ, therefore, does not say to sinners, "I will give you salvation if you believe," but Christ gives faith, which he has purchased on the cross, so that the elect believe. The Heidelberg Catechism makes a similar point: "Redemption from sin by the blood of Christ, and the Holy Ghost, the author of faith, is promised."[14]

Sixth, article 8 teaches us about the covenant, its benefits, and its beneficiaries. "It was the will of God that Christ by the blood of the cross, *whereby He confirmed the new covenant*, should effectually redeem" (emphasis added). The New Testament makes clear that Christ confirmed the new covenant, or testament, the one promised in Jeremiah 31, by his blood (Matt. 26:28; Heb. 8:6–13; 9:14–17). Since the blood of Christ was shed to confirm the covenant, and since Christ died only for the elect, we conclude that the covenant is made only with the elect (Gal. 3:16, 29). Since faith is purchased for the elect alone through the blood of the cross, whereby Christ confirmed the new covenant, faith cannot be the condition that the covenantal member must fulfill in order to enter the covenant or in order to remain in the covenant. Remember that this article was framed with the conditional covenant of Arminianism in mind, which was a covenant with all men on condition of faith. Since the Canons reject that conditional covenant, they also reject a conditional covenant made with all the children of believers in the church

14 Heidelberg Catechism A 74, in ibid., 111.

on the condition of faith. Conditional covenant theology is Arminian, not Reformed, theology.

Having read this magnificent statement concerning the death of our Savior, what can we do but sing the praises of the Lamb? "Thou art worthy to take the book, and to open the seals thereof: for thou wast slain, and hast redeemed us to God by thy blood out of every kindred, and tongue, and people, and nation; and hast made us unto our God kings and priests: and we shall reign on the earth" (Rev. 5:9–10).

ARTICLE 9: THE EFFICACY OF THE DEATH OF CHRIST

> This purpose, proceeding from everlasting love towards the elect, has from the beginning of the world to this day been powerfully accomplished, and will henceforward still continue to be accomplished, notwithstanding all the ineffectual opposition of the gates of hell, so that the elect in due time may be gathered together into one, and that there never may be wanting a church composed of believers, the foundation of which is laid in the blood of Christ, which may steadfastly love and faithfully serve Him as their Savior, who as a bridegroom for his bride, laid down His life for them upon the cross, and which may celebrate His praises here and through all eternity.

The previous article expounded at length the sovereign, eternal, gracious purpose of God with respect to Christ's atoning work with particular emphasis on its particularity and efficacy. As a final nail in the coffin of Arminianism, in article 9 the fathers at Dordt insisted that the purpose of God in the cross has been perfectly *accomplished*. The Reformed faith rejects the possible subterfuge that, while article 8 describes God's purpose, perhaps God does not achieve his purpose. Such a notion is absurd on the face of it, for all of God's purposes are accomplished (Ps. 115:3; Eph. 1:11).

Notice the wording of the Canons.

First, "this purpose...has...been... accomplished," for the Bible knows nothing of any *unfulfilled* purposes of almighty God. This purpose is that the "quickening and saving efficacy of the most precious death of [God's] Son should extend to all the elect" (Canons 2.8). This is exactly what has happened, for all the elect from the beginning to the end of the world have been saved, are being saved, and shall be saved through the blood of Jesus Christ. Men like Abel, Noah, Abraham, David, and Daniel, who lived before the death of Christ, have been saved. Men like Peter, Paul, and John, who witnessed the cross and the resurrection of Christ, have been saved. Believers in every age, and in our age too, have been saved and are being saved. And that purpose of God "will, henceforward, still continue to be accomplished." God has an elect people who must be saved and Christ has a commission to save them. Therefore, they *shall* be saved.

Second, this purpose has been "*powerfully* accomplished" (emphasis added). God's almighty power in sovereign providence lies behind the efficacy of the cross. This powerful purpose is accomplished "notwithstanding all the ineffectual opposition of the gates of hell." All the hellish powers of darkness oppose the salvation of the elect, but they are ineffectual. They fail. Notice the contrast: with God there is efficacy, infallible bringing, effectual redemption, and powerful accomplishment; but with Satan there is ineffectual opposition. How that must thrill our souls and give us confidence, peace, and assurance.

Third, this purpose "proceed[s] from everlasting love towards the elect." This point has been emphasized repeatedly, but the Canons state it again: God did not need the cross to persuade him to love his people, for the love of God was first, indeed, eternal and everlasting, and stood behind the cross. Therefore, because God loved them, he gave them Christ. In addition, the Canons know nothing of a love of God toward the reprobate, but confess only the everlasting love of

God toward the elect, a love that is irresistible, powerful, and cannot be thwarted, so that none of the beloved can be lost.

Fourth, the fruit of this powerful, loving, effectual purpose of God is that there is and there always shall be a church to confess the truth of God's word. The Reformed fathers expected there to be a true church faithful to Christ on the earth until the end of history. However, the Arminians taught that it was by no means certain that there would be a church, for it was conceivable that no one would believe. Since individual salvation depends on faith, said the Arminians, it follows that the existence of the church also depends on faith. To this the Reformed fathers responded with the Reformed conception of the church. "The elect in due time [shall] be gathered together into one." The church is the body of called out ones, not a collection of volunteers for Jesus. Because of the powerful work of Christ there "[shall] never…be wanting [or lacking] a church composed of believers." The "foundation" of the church is "laid in the blood of Christ," for without the cross there can be no church. This church, which is grounded in the blood of Christ and gathered by the Spirit through the preaching of the gospel, "steadfastly love[s] and faithfully serve[s] Him as their Savior." The relationship of Christ to his church is bridegroom to bride (Eph. 5:25–27). This church thus preserved shall "celebrate his praises here and through all eternity."

Are you part of that blood-bought church? Add your voice to that happy throng!

ERROR AND REJECTION 1: NO DECREE FOR SALVATION IN CHRIST'S DEATH

> Error 1: Who teach that God the Father has ordained His Son to the death of the cross without a certain and definite decree to save any, so that the necessity, profitableness, and worth of what Christ merited by His death might have existed, and might remain in all its parts complete, perfect,

> and intact, even if the merited redemption had never in fact been applied to any person.
>
> Rejection: For this doctrine tends to the despising of the wisdom of the Father and of the merits of Jesus Christ, and is contrary to Scripture. For thus saith our Savior: *I lay down my life for the sheep, and I know them* (John 10:15, 27). And the prophet Isaiah saith concerning the Savior: *When thou shalt make his soul an offering for sin, he shall see his seed, he shall prolong his days, and the pleasure of Jehovah shall prosper in his hand* (Isa. 53:10). Finally, this contradicts the article of faith according to which we believe the catholic Christian church.

We have come to the end of the second head of doctrine, which sets forth the Reformed view of the atonement of Christ. Perhaps nowhere more than here do we see the lines so sharply drawn between Arminianism and the biblical, Reformed faith. In articles 8–9 the Canons have extolled the wonders of God's eternal, efficacious, gracious purpose in the cross of Christ, but here we see how the Arminians viewed God as having no distinct purpose in the cross at all: he sent his Son to die "without a certain and definite decree to save any."

Arminianism, therefore, severs the cross from God's eternal decree. The Arminians did not believe in a certain and definite decree, but in an indefinite and a conditional decree. Christ would die, according to this indefinite and conditional decree, for all without exception, so that all *might* be saved *if they believed*. However, God did not determine who those believers might be, for potentially, all might have believed, or alternatively, none might have believed. The fruit of Christ's death, therefore, depends on the free will of sinners. The result is that, even if nobody believed (something entirely possible if the efficacy of the cross depends on man), the cross would still have accomplished everything that God planned or purposed.

That can be true in the Arminian scheme only because Arminianism teaches no definite purpose of God, for if God did not purpose the salvation of any (except conditionally), the cross is still "effectual" if nobody is saved. Seemingly with a straight face, the Arminians could claim that "the necessity, profitableness, and worth of what Christ merited by His death might have existed, and might remain in all its parts complete, perfect, and intact, even if the merited redemption had never in fact been applied to any person."

Recall what the Arminians confessed in point two of their Remonstrance. Their doctrine of the atonement (conditioned on faith) is agreeable to their prior doctrine of predestination (also conditioned on faith):

> That, agreeably thereto, Jesus Christ, the Savior of the world, died for all men and for every man, so that he has obtained for them all, by his death on the cross, redemption and the forgiveness of sins; yet that no one actually enjoys this forgiveness of sins except the believer, according to the word of the Gospel of John iii. 16: "God so loved the world that he gave his only-begotten Son, that whosoever believeth in him should not perish, but have everlasting life." And in the First Epistle of John ii. 2: "And he is the propitiation for our sins; and not for ours only, but also for the sins of the whole world."[15]

Here we see the audacity of heretics. The Arminians accused the Reformed of debasing the value of the cross of Christ, but what did the Arminians do? First, while speaking in grandiose terms of the "necessity, profitableness, and worth" of the cross, they denied the cross altogether, for the cross has accomplished *nothing*. The whole world might perish (because no one believes), but the cross would still be necessary, profitable, and valuable. The crux of Arminianism is this—any profitableness depends on man. Christ merited redemption for all, but the application of redemption depends on

---

15 Five Arminian Articles 2, in Schaff, *Creeds of Christendom*, 3:546.

faith, man's faith, which is the condition that he fulfills. This scheme robs the cross of its saving power and attributes all saving power to the supposedly sovereign will of man.

In response, the Reformed fathers pointed out that Arminianism is an insult to the Almighty. "This doctrine tends to the despising of the wisdom of the Father and of the merits of Jesus Christ."

First, it leads men to despise God's wisdom. If God's wisdom is his perfect ability to adapt his infinite knowledge to attain the highest purpose by the use of the best possible means, what wisdom is there in sending Jesus Christ *without a certain and definite decree to save any*? Either God did not know the outcome, which is impossible; or God did know the outcome but sent his Son to suffer the hellish agonies of the cross knowing that multitudes would still perish despite his best efforts. That is the foolish action of a foolish deity, not the perfect wisdom of our God and Father.

Second, this Arminian doctrine leads men to despise the merits of Christ, for Christ merited nothing by his death. He merited the mere possibility that God might do something, but he merited nothing for you, or for me, or for any sinner. The death of Christ, then, is a redemption that does not redeem, a propitiation that does not propitiate, a reconciliation that does not reconcile, and an atonement that does not atone. In short, the merits of Christ are worthless, for they depend upon man's free will. Who can stand such a blasphemy?

Third, this doctrine is opposed to the simple creed of all Christians who confess, "I believe an holy catholic church," for there might be no church if nobody believes in Jesus.

Finally, this doctrine is opposed to the word of God (Isa. 53:10–11; John 10:15, 27).

Two doctrines of the cross of Christ, irreconcilably opposed to one another, have been contrasted in head two. The conclusion is clear—Arminianism is a denial of the cross of the Savior, for the one who dies on the cross is not a Savior, unless words have lost all meaning.

Discussion questions on the second head of doctrine

1. Many people believe that the difference between Arminianism and the Reformed faith is that the former teaches that Christ died for everybody, while the latter teaches that Christ died for the elect only. Explain why that explanation is inadequate.

2. In the phrase, "Christ died for sinners," explain the preposition "for"? How does the Arminian explain the preposition "for"?

3. Arminianism teaches that Christ *paid for* the sins of everybody. True or false?

4. What is the governmental view of the atonement? Name some famous advocates of this view.

5. In the verse, "He is the propitiation for our sins: and not for ours only, but also for the sins of the whole world" (1 John 2:2), the Arminian places the emphasis on the words "the whole world," while the Reformed stress the word "propitiation." Explain the significance of this difference in emphasis.

6. The Arminian believes in a redemption that does not redeem. Explain.

7. Dordt did not address the extent of the atonement until Canons 2.8. Which important theological concepts did the fathers explain first and why?

8. Why is an understanding of both the mercy and the justice of God necessary for the doctrine of the atonement?

9. Why is it impossible for us to make satisfaction for our own sins? How is Christ uniquely qualified to be the mediator?

10. Is it true to say that Christ's death is "sufficient for all, but efficient for some"? Explain.

11. Explain the theological term *surety*. For whom is Jesus the surety?

12. According to classic Arminianism, what did Christ *accomplish* by his death?

13. Arminianism teaches that the outcome of Christ's death could be the salvation of absolutely no one. How is this consistent with the basic premise of Arminianism?

14. "Unbelief is the only sin that keeps a person out of heaven." True or false?

15. Christ died for the original sin of all men, but for the actual sins of only some men. True or false?

16. Christ died for the sins of all men, except for their unbelief. True or false?

17. The error of Arminianism places the Arminians into the heretical camps of Pelagianism and Socinianism. What did those two heresies teach and in what way are they similar to Arminianism? Is the Canons' designation of Arminianism as "Pelagian" fair?

18. What did the cross of Christ *not* accomplish according to Arminianism?

19. Some theologians such as John Piper teach that Christ died for all men in a certain sense in order for God to be able to make to all men "a bona fide offer of salvation." Do the Canons allow for this view? Is Piper's view correct? Discuss.

20. Both the Reformed faith and Arminianism "limit" the atonement. Explain.

21. Is limited atonement, the *L* of TULIP, an acceptable name for the doctrine? If not, what name is preferable?

22. What gives infinite value to the sufferings and death of Christ on the cross?
23. What is the relationship between the promise and the preaching of the gospel?
24. The Reformed believe in the "promiscuous proclamation of a particular promise." Explain.
25. Is an unbeliever commanded to believe that Jesus died for him personally? If he is not commanded to believe that, what is he commanded to believe? Explain.
26. If Christ did not die to purchase faith for the reprobate, how can the reprobate be condemned for not believing the gospel of Christ?
27. What phrase in Canons 2.8 is the clearest creedal statement in the three forms of unity on the particularity of the atonement?
28. What does Canons 2.8 teach about the covenant? What is the significance of this?
29. How is the Arminian view of the atonement inconsistent with the justice and wisdom of God?
30. How is Arminianism inconsistent with the Apostles' Creed, "I believe an holy catholic church"?

Proof texts for the second head of doctrine

Isaiah 53:4–6, 8, 10–12
Matthew 20:28
Matthew 26:28
John 1:29
John 3:14–18
John 6:51
John 10:11, 15, 17–18
John 11:49–52
John 12:23–24, 32
John 13:8–11
John 19:30
Acts 2:23–24
Acts 5:30–31
Acts 20:28
Romans 3:24–25
Romans 4:25
Romans 5:6–11
Romans 6:6–10
Romans 7:4
Romans 8:3, 32–34
Romans 15:3
1 Corinthians 1:17–18
1 Corinthians 5:7
1 Corinthians 6:11, 20
1 Corinthians 7:23
1 Corinthians 15:3
2 Corinthians 5:14–15, 18–21
2 Corinthians 8:9
Galatians 1:4
Galatians 2:20–21
Galatians 3:13
Galatians 4:4–5
Galatians 6:14
Ephesians 1:7
Ephesians 2:13–16
Ephesians 5:2, 25–27
Colossians 1:20–22
Colossians 2:14–15
1 Thessalonians 1:10
1 Thessalonians 5:10
1 Timothy 1:15
1 Timothy 2:6
2 Timothy 1:10
Titus 2:14
Hebrews 1:3
Hebrews 2:9, 17
Hebrews 7:27
Hebrews 9:12, 14, 26–28
Hebrews 10:10–20
Hebrews 12:2
Hebrews 13:12
1 Peter 1:2, 18–20
1 Peter 2:21–25
1 Peter 3:18
1 Peter 4:1–2
1 John 1:7
1 John 2:2
1 John 4:10
Revelation 1:5
Revelation 5:9–10
Revelation 7:14
Revelation 14:4

Scriptural texts on atonement, redemption, reconciliation, propitiation, satisfaction, *and* washing

Atone, atonement

Leviticus 1:4

Redeem, redemption, ransom, purchased/bought

Leviticus 25:52
Matthew 20:28
Acts 20:28
Romans 3:24–25
1 Corinthians 6:20
1 Corinthians 7:23
Galatians 3:13
Galatians 4:4–5
Ephesians 1:7
Colossians 1:14
1 Timothy 2:6
Titus 2:14
Hebrews 9:12
1 Peter 1:18–20
Revelation 5:9–10
Revelation 14:4

Reconcile, reconciliation

Leviticus 8:15
Daniel 9:24
Romans 5:10–11
2 Corinthians 5:18–19
Ephesians 2:15–16
Colossians 1:20–22

Propitiate, propitiation, expiate, expiation

Genesis 32:20
Romans 3:24–25
1 John 2:2
1 John 4:10

Satisfy, satisfaction

Isaiah 53:10–11

Wash, washing, purify, sanctify

1 Corinthians 6:11
Ephesians 5:25–26
Titus 2:14
1 John 1:7
Revelation 1:5

Scriptural texts on the meaning of **all men** *and* **world**

Does the word *world* in scripture (Greek: *kosmos* [κόσμος]) mean the entire human race?

"If thou do these things, shew thyself to the world" (John 7:4).

"I speak to the world those things which I have heard of him" (John 8:26).

"Perceive ye how ye prevail nothing? behold the world is gone after him" (John 12:19).

"If the world hate you, ye know that it hated me before it hated you" (John 15:18).

"I have chosen you out of the world, therefore the world hateth you" (John 15:19).

"Ye shall weep and lament, but the world shall rejoice: and ye shall be sorrowful, but your sorrow shall be turned into joy" (John 16:20).

"I spake openly to the world; I ever taught in the synagogue, and in the temple whither the Jews always resort" (John 18:20).

"I thank God [...] that your faith is spoken of throughout the whole world" (Rom. 1:8).

"We are made a spectacle unto the world, and to angels, and to men" (1 Cor. 4:9).

"Which [the gospel] is come unto you, as it is in all the world..." (Col. 1:6).

"They are of the world: therefore speak they of the world, and the world heareth them" (1 John 4:5).

"And we know that we are of God, and the whole world lieth in wickedness" (1 John 5:19).

Do the words *all* and *all men* in scripture refer to the entire human race without exception?

"When Herod the king had heard these things, he was troubled, and all Jerusalem with him" (Matt. 2:3).

"Then went out to him Jerusalem, and all Judaea, and all the region round about Jordan, and were baptized of him" (Matt. 3:5–6).

"And ye shall be hated of all men for my name's sake" (Matt. 10:22).

"If we shall say, Of men; we fear the people; for all hold John as a prophet" (Matt. 21:26).

"And all the city was gathered together at the door" (Mark 1:33).

"When they had found him they said unto him, All men seek for thee" (Mark 1:37).

"[And he] began to publish in Decapolis how great things Jesus had done for him: and all men did marvel" (Mark 5:20).

"All men mused in their hearts of John, whether he were the Christ, or not" (Luke 3:15).

"Behold, the same baptizeth, and all men come to Him" (John 3:26).

"If we let him thus alone, all men will believe on him: and the Romans shall come and take away both our place and our nation" (John 11:48).

"Many of them also which used curious arts brought their books together, and burned them before all men" (Acts 19:19).

"This is the man, that teacheth all men every where against the people" (Acts 21:28).

"Thou shalt be his witness unto all men of what thou hast seen and heard" (Acts 22:15).

"For your obedience is come abroad unto all men" (Rom. 16:19).

Do the words *every man* (in context) refer to the entire human race without exception?

"After that he put his hands again upon his eyes, and made him look up: and he was restored and saw every man clearly" (Mark 8:25).

"The law and the prophets were until John: since that time the kingdom of God is preached, and every man presseth into it" (Luke 16:16).

"Every man at the beginning doth set forth good wine [...] but thou hast kept the good wine until now" (John 2:10).

"And every man went unto his own house" (John 7:53).

"And [they] sold their possessions and goods, and parted them to all men, as every man had need" (Acts 2:45).

"For I say, through the grace of God given unto me, to every man that is among you [...] to think soberly, according as God has dealt to every man the measure of faith" (Rom. 12:3).

"But the manifestation of the Spirit is given to every man to profit withal" (1 Cor. 12:7).

"But all these worketh that one and selfsame Spirit, dividing to every man severally as he will" (1 Cor. 12:11).

"Whom [Christ] we preach, warning every man, and teaching every man in all wisdom; that we may present every man perfect in Christ Jesus" (Col. 1:28).

"They shall not teach every man his neighbour, and every man his brother, saying, Know the Lord: for all shall know me, from the least to the greatest" (Heb. 8:11).

Is this interpretation of *all, every, anyone,* and *world* really so radical, or is it simply the normal way in which we use language?

"The whole world looked in horror as the Twin Towers crumbled to the ground."

"The world mourned the death of Marilyn Monroe."

"The world stood still to remember the tragedy which occurred last week."

"Everyone is invited to the youth center for pizza after the meeting."

"All are reminded to clear away the chairs after supper."

"After the visit to the museum, everyone is asked to be on the bus no later than 1 PM."

"Does everyone have a pen and a notepad?"

"Everyone! Get in the car!"

"Can anyone recommend a good butcher?"

"Is anyone interested in going to the park?"

The Third and Fourth Heads of Doctrine of the Corruption of Man, His Conversion to God, and the Manner Thereof

INTRODUCTION

The Canons of Dordt consist of five heads of doctrine because the Arminians wrote five heads in their Remonstrance of 1610, one year after Arminius died. The synod treated heads three and four together because the heresy of Arminianism only becomes clear when these two heads are combined. If you read the third and fourth heads of the Arminian Remonstrance together, you will notice several important points. First, the Remonstrance *appears* to deny man's free will and to affirm man's total depravity. In fact, very few modern Arminians would write such a strong statement on human depravity:

> That man has not saving grace of himself, nor of the energy of his free will, inasmuch as he, in the state of apostasy and sin, can of and by himself neither think, will, nor do anything that is truly good (such as having Faith eminently is);

> but that it is needful that he be born again of God in Christ, through his Holy Spirit, and renewed in understanding, inclination, or will, and all his powers, in order that he may rightly understand, think, will, and effect what is truly good, according to the Word of Christ, John xv:5: "Without me ye can do nothing."[1]

Second, any Reformed person could agree with the third head of the Remonstrance (quoted above), as long as it is read independently of the other heads. The fourth head of the Remonstrance really contradicts what the third head teaches about man's depravity. It does this in its affirmation of *resistible* grace, which is the hallmark of all forms of Arminianism. You can extol grace to the skies, as the Arminians pretended to do, but if you make grace resistible, salvation is ultimately and finally in the hands of man, which is exactly where the Arminians wanted to locate it.

> That this grace of God is the beginning, continuance, and accomplishment of any good, even to this extent, that the regenerate man himself, without that prevenient or assisting, awakening, following, and co-operative grace, can neither think, will, nor do good, nor withstand any temptations to evil; so that all good deeds or movements, that can be conceived, must be ascribed to the grace of God in Christ. *But as respects the mode of the operation of this grace, it is not irresistible*, inasmuch as it is written concerning many that they have resisted the Holy Ghost. Acts vii., and elsewhere in many places.[2]

The Arminians pretended to extol the grace of God, calling it "prevenient or assisting" and "awakening, following, and co-operative," but their fatal error was to deny its irresistibility: "As respects

1 Five Arminian Articles 3, in Schaff, *Creeds of Christendom,* 3:546–47.
2 Five Arminian Articles 4, in ibid., 3:547 (emphasis added).

the mode of the operation of this grace [of God in Christ], *it is not irresistible*." Resistible grace is the teaching that God by the operation of the Holy Spirit is seeking to bring everyone to salvation, especially all who hear the preaching. Thus Arminianism teaches prevenient grace, which is a grace that comes before, which helps, assists, or prepares men for salvation. This grace, however, is a grace with which man must and can cooperate by his free will. This grace can be and often is resisted, so that God does not accomplish the salvation that he desires. Arminius and his followers were more refined in their subtlety than modern Arminians, but the idea is basically the same.

The teaching of the biblical, Reformed faith is *irresistible* grace. The term itself is problematic because it might seem to be teaching that God forces himself upon the sinner and overpowers him. The standard caricature of irresistible grace is of God's dragging the sinner kicking and screaming against his will into heaven. A better term than irresistible grace is effectual grace or efficacious grace, which accurately expresses the truth that God accomplishes his purpose when his grace works in sinners. God's grace cannot be *successfully* resisted, for whom God has a mind to save he saves, but he saves in such a manner that his elect people come willingly (Ps. 110:3).

To the idea of irresistible grace, the Arminians countered Acts 7:51: "Ye stiffnecked and uncircumcised in heart and ears, ye do always resist the Holy Ghost: as your fathers did, so do ye." However, this text does not deny irresistible grace. Stephen accused the unbelieving Jews of opposing the Holy Spirit *in the prophets*, so that they rejected the Christ of whom the prophets preached and wrote. When the men before the flood resisted the preaching of Noah, they resisted the Holy Spirit (Gen. 6:3; 1 Pet. 3:20); when the Jews resisted the preaching of the prophets, they resisted the Holy Spirit (Mic. 2:6; 3:8); when the Sanhedrin resisted the preaching of Stephen, they resisted the Holy Spirit (Acts 6:5, 10; 7:52–53). This does not mean that the Spirit was graciously seeking to save those unbelieving Jews, which gracious seeking they successfully resisted. No one can successfully resist the Holy Spirit when he comes in his grace to save.

Another couple of passages should be addressed here. The first is Matthew 23:37: "O Jerusalem, Jerusalem, thou that killest the prophets, and stonest them which are sent unto thee, how often would I have gathered thy children together, even as a hen gathereth together her chickens under her wings, and ye would not!" Often, this passage is misquoted—"how often would I have gathered *thee* together," instead of "how often would I have gathered *thy children* together!" Two wills are in conflict in the text—Christ's will ("how often would I"), which is the will of God, for Christ came to do the will of God who sent him (John 6:38–40); and Jerusalem's will ("ye would not"). The conflict is not between Christ's will and the will of Jerusalem's children, but between Christ's will and Jerusalem's will, which is the will of the scribes and Pharisees, who were addressed with fearful woes in the immediate context (Matt. 23:13–36). Many Arminians present the text this way: Christ laments that he earnestly desired to save Jerusalem, but Jerusalem was not willing to be saved, but that is not the meaning of the passage. Instead, Christ was denouncing the scribes and Pharisees (Jerusalem) because they opposed (they did not desire) Christ's gathering of Jerusalem's children. Nevertheless, despite Jerusalem's opposition, Christ *did* indeed gather Jerusalem's children: "This spake he [Caiaphas] not of himself: but being high priest that year, he prophesied that Jesus should die for that nation; and not for that nation only, but that also he should gather together in one the children of God that were scattered abroad" (John 11:51–52; see also John 6:39). Powerful men in church and state might oppose the salvation of the elect, but God saves his people despite the ineffectual opposition of men and the devil.

The second passage is 2 Peter 3:9, which is almost always partially quoted as "not willing that any should perish, but that all should come to repentance." The context, however, determines the meaning of Peter's words, which are designed to comfort the church as she waits for the coming of Christ. The saints were asking, as they were mocked by scoffers, "Where is the promise of his coming?" (v. 4). In response, Peter reminded his readers of several truths: first, "One day is with the Lord as a thousand years, and a thousand years as one day" (v. 8); second, "The Lord is not slack concerning his promise" (v. 9); and third, the Lord is longsuffering (vv. 9, 15).

But *to whom* is the Lord longsuffering? Is he longsuffering to everybody, to the entire human race? The answer is found in verse 9—"but is longsuffering *to us-ward*" (emphasis added). These words refer to the "beloved" of verse 8 and "to them that have obtained like precious faith with us" (2 Pet. 1:1). Here then is the reason for the perceived delay in the coming of Christ: God is patient with his elect whom he loves and whose salvation he desires. Therefore, he wills that the elect—and *only* the elect—should not perish, but that all of the elect should come to repentance. Jesus delays his coming, therefore, so that the full number of the elect are born, regenerated, converted, and saved. When the elect are safely gathered in, then and only then will Christ return. The passage has nothing whatever to do with the notion that God sincerely desires the salvation of all men without exception—something the Bible nowhere teaches.

ARTICLE 1: MAN WHO WAS CREATED RIGHTEOUS FELL INTO SIN

> Man was originally formed after the image of God. His understanding was adorned with a true and saving knowledge of his Creator and of spiritual things; his heart and will were upright; all his affections pure; and the whole man was holy. But, revolting from God by the instigation of the devil and abusing the freedom of his own will, he forfeited these excellent gifts, and on the contrary entailed on himself blindness of mind, horrible darkness, vanity, and perverseness of judgment, became wicked, rebellious, and obdurate in heart and will, and impure in his affections.

To understand the whole subject of free will and salvation, we must first have a biblical view of man, or anthropology. The Canons do not begin in heads three and four with the bald assertion that man has no free will. Instead, as they did in the previous heads of doctrine, the fathers at Dordt carefully built a foundation by setting forth some fundamental truths of God's word. Again I say, we would do well in our discussions with Arminians today to emulate that wise approach.

Many Arminians today simply presuppose that man has a free will, but they do not show any understanding of the creation and fall of man, which is exactly where the Canons begin. Article 1 begins with the innocence of man before he fell into sin in the garden of Eden. We learn from this that man is a creature, not an evolved animal. (On this the Reformed and Arminians were largely in agreement. The Canons were written centuries before the modern heresies of evolutionism and theistic evolutionism.) Moreover, man, unlike the beasts, was created in the image of God (Gen. 1:26–27). Because the image of God is so fundamental, the Canons carefully explain what they mean by it.

The Canons' conception of the image of God is threefold. First, man's "understanding was adorned with a true and saving knowledge of his Creator and of spiritual things." Second, "his heart and will were upright." Third, "all his affections [were] pure." This is the standard biblical and Reformed view that the image of God is knowledge, righteousness, and holiness. In Ephesians 4:24 and Colossians 3:10, the apostle explains that the elect are renewed after the image of God with knowledge, righteousness, and holiness. If in regeneration they are renewed in that threefold way, the original image of God must have consisted of those three spiritual characteristics. This also fits with what the earlier Reformed creeds stated about the image of God in question and answer 6 of the Heidelberg Catechism and in article 14 of the Belgic Confession. Similarly, the Presbyterian Westminster Confession of Faith describes man's creation in the image of God thus: "After God had made all other creatures, he created man, male and female, with reasonable and immortal souls, endued with knowledge, righteousness, and true holiness, after his own image."[3]

Therefore, the image of God is not the following. First, the image of God is not something physical, material, or visible. Adam and Eve did not look like God, as if their erect posture on two legs was part of the image of God, for example. This should be obvious because God is spiritual (John 4:24). Second, the image of God does not consist in rationality, reason, logic, or in a sense of beauty or creativity. Third, the image of God is not man's free will. If the capacity to choose (free will) is the image of God, then the demons have the image of God, for they, too, possess the faculty of choice. The image of God according to the Bible and the Reformed confessions is *only* knowledge, righteousness, and holiness. To add other characteristics of humanity to the image of God only confuses matters.

Additionally, there is no essential difference between *image* and *likeness* in scripture, for the two terms are interchangeable (Gen. 1:26; 5:1; James 3:9). Nevertheless, a proper distinction between *image bearer* and the *image of God* proper can be made. A tree is not an image bearer and neither is a dog or a monkey. Not only do plants and animals not possess the image of God, but they also do not have the capacity to possess the image of God, for they are not image bearers at all. Man is different, for he was made in the image of God. But he remains even after the fall an image bearer, for he can bear an image, the image of God or the image of the devil.

The point of the Canons is that man was created not with a tendency to evil, and not even morally neutral, but positively good with true knowledge, righteousness, and holiness (Eccl. 7:29).

Let us examine further these three aspects of the image of God in which man was created.

3 Westminster Confession of Faith 4.2, in ibid., 3:611.

First, man's "understanding was adorned with a true and saving [beneficial; Latin: *salutari*] knowledge of his Creator and of spiritual things." Adam knew God because God revealed himself to him. (The following remarks are true of Eve also, but for the sake of simplicity I will mention only Adam.) This was the knowledge of love and fellowship, for we see how the Lord God walked in the garden with Adam in the cool of the day, communing with him in love (Gen. 3:8). In that knowledge Adam delighted. That knowledge included the creation, for Adam saw God's glory reflected in everything that God had made. This explains why Adam was able to name the animals, for he possessed the spiritual insight to identify the true nature of the creatures (2:19). Therefore, Adam was a prophet who declared the glory of God in all God's works. When God saves his people, he renews them in knowledge: "The new man, which is renewed in knowledge after the image of him that created him" (Col. 3:10).

Second, man's "heart and will were upright." The heart is the spiritual center of man (Prov. 4:23). Uprightness is righteousness (or conformity) and harmony with God's revealed standard. Because Adam was furnished with an upright heart and will, he sought God and his glory in all things and all of his thoughts, words, and deeds were always in harmony with God's commandments. Thus Adam was perfectly and positively righteous with an inherent righteousness. Therefore, Adam was a king who ruled himself and the creation for God's honor. When God saves his people, he recreates them "in righteousness" (Eph. 4:24).

Third, all the affections of man were "pure; and the whole man was holy." Holiness is devotion, consecration, and dedication to God. Adam loved God, delighted in him, and had no inclinations or desires within him for anything else. He did not lust after evil, but all his affections (desires and emotions) were pure, holy, undefiled, and untainted by any evil. Therefore, Adam was a priest who consecrated himself and the creation to God's glory. When God saves his people, he renews them according to the image of "true holiness" (Eph. 4:24). Moreover, the purpose of God in the salvation of his people is to make them conformable to the image of his Son, who is the image of God (Rom. 8:29; 2 Cor. 4:4; Col. 1:15).

Therefore, if evil would come upon man, or if man were to commit evil, that evil must come from the outside. There was no internal bias toward evil in Adam, for there was no moral flaw in man in his creation. God created him with true knowledge, perfect righteousness, and pure or unsullied holiness. Scripture calls this the image of God because knowledge, righteousness, and holiness were reflected in Adam in such a way that he was *like* God.

Nevertheless, Adam did not remain in that state of innocence. All Christians of whatever stripe believe in some sense in the fall as recorded in Genesis 3, although many today (wrongly) view it as a non-historical account or as an allegory. The Reformed fathers viewed it as true, biblical history, the history of our first father and our first mother, Adam and Eve. Nevertheless, few Christians have given the fall much thought—what actually happened and what effect did the fall have on Adam? It appears that many Christians believe that the fall did not really bring about any significant change. Many believe that after the fall man is *still* good, *still* holy, *still* righteous, and *still* possesses the gifts with which Adam was created. The Arminians believed that, despite the fall, man *still* possessed the power of free will, which for Arminians is absolutely crucial for their doctrine of salvation.

The Canons remind us about what truly happened in the fall, how it affected Adam, and crucially, how it affects us, who are Adam's descendants: "Revolting from God by the instigation of the devil." This wording is similar to the earlier creeds in questions and answers 7 and 9 of the Heidelberg Catechism and in article 14 of the Belgic Confession.

The reasons for the fall are threefold. First, "the instigation of the devil": Satan introduced the idea of evil to holy Eve, who then convinced her holy husband Adam to eat of the forbidden fruit (Gen. 3:6; 1 Tim. 2:14). Second, Adam was guilty of "abusing the freedom of his own will." Adam was able to eat or not to eat, but he chose to disobey God despite the clear warning of God and despite God's goodness to him (Gen. 2:17). Third, Adam was guilty of willful rebellion ("revolting from God"), for Adam's act of taking and eating the forbidden fruit was treachery, a violation of his covenantal relationship with God, and wicked insubordination by an officebearer of God. Therefore, it was not an accident or a mistake. The Belgic Confession expresses it thus: "[He] willfully subjected himself to sin, and consequently to death and the curse, giving ear to the words of the devil."[4]

The consequences for Adam were severe. First, "he forfeited these excellent gifts." To forfeit something is to lose a privilege as a penalty for doing wrong. A teenager might forfeit his driving privileges for breaking his curfew. A thief forfeits his freedom for stealing. Adam forfeited something much more precious: he forfeited the knowledge of God; he forfeited the uprightness of his heart and will; he forfeited the purity of his affections; he forfeited the holiness of the whole man—in short, he forfeited and lost the image of God, and he had no way of restoring it.

Notice what this does *not* mean: Adam did not lose his mind (he still had a mind, the faculty of reasoning and thought); he did not lose his will (he still had a will, the faculty of making choices); he did not lose his affections (he still had affections, feelings, and emotions). In short, Adam was still a rational, moral, emotional, willing creature, even after he fell into sin and misery. The fall did not make Adam a beast or a devil, for he remained a human being. Nevertheless, he lost the *spiritual gifts* of knowledge, righteousness, and holiness (the image of God) in which he was created.

Moreover, the image of God in which he was created and which

---

4 Belgic Confession 14, in *Confessions and Church Order*, 38.

he forfeited was changed into its opposite—he did not become morally neutral, but positively and actively evil. He did not become a blank slate, but he adopted the image of the devil (John 8:44). The image of God, which he forfeited and lost, can only be restored through regeneration (Eph. 4:24; Col. 3:10). Adam became the opposite of what he had been and the opposite of what God had created him to be. The result was immediate estrangement, for Adam could no longer fellowship with the holy God as he once did, and he knew this too, for knowing that was naked, he sought to hide from God out of fear (Gen. 3:8; see also Belgic Confession 17).

The Canons spell out the horrible reality. First, he entailed upon himself blindness of mind, horrible darkness, vanity, and perverseness of judgment. Second, he became wicked (or evil), rebellious, obdurate in heart and will, and impure in his affections (Gen. 6:5; Isa. 1:6; Jer. 17:9; John 3:19–20; Rom. 3:11–12; 8:7–8; 1 Cor. 2:14; Eph. 2:1–3; 4:17–20; Col. 1:21; 2:13; Titus 3:3).

Given that dreadful reality, the doctrine of free will is a nonstarter. After the fall man retained a will, which is his faculty of choice—man can choose a host of things, subject to the sovereign decree of God, of course. Nevertheless, because of the fall man is spiritually unable to do anything good or even to will to do anything good. Man's will is a slave to his wicked nature. Therefore, man's will is *not* free, but corrupt, depraved, and even obdurate.

From what a height man has fallen—one who was positively righteous and holy is now actively evil, depraved, and wicked. One who possessed the true knowledge of God has been plunged into wretched darkness and blindness. Only a sovereign and gracious God could deliver man from such misery.

ERROR AND REJECTION 2: MAN'S WILL EXEMPT FROM THE EFFECTS OF THE FALL

> Error 2: Who teach that the spiritual gifts, or the good qualities and virtues, such as goodness, holiness, righteousness,

> could not belong to the will of man when he was first created, and that these, therefore, could not have been separated therefrom in the fall.
>
> Rejection: For such is contrary to the description of the image of God which the apostle gives in Eph. 4:24, where he declares that it consists in righteousness and holiness, which undoubtedly belong to the will.

Before we proceed, we need to look at what the Arminians taught concerning the will of man before the fall. As we shall see, Arminianism must protect its cherished doctrine of free will at all costs. Quite simply, the Arminians believed that the will of man was morally neutral both *before and after the fall.* For the Arminians the will of man is a faculty of choice by which he is able to choose whatever good or evil might be offered to it. Therefore, argued the Arminians, this morally neutral will could not have possessed the gifts of goodness, holiness, and righteousness, and (here is the crucial point) his will, therefore, could not have *lost* these gifts.

The Arminians went further. First, they taught that man was created with a natural inclination toward evil, but with the power of will to resist evil. Second, they argued that there was a disorder in the affections, but that the will was perfectly free. Third, this was necessary if the test to which Adam was subjected in the garden of Eden should be genuine. John Owen, in his masterful work, *A Display of Arminianism*, cited several of the Remonstrants, including Arminius himself, on this point: "There was an inclination in man to sin before the fall, though not altogether so vehement and inordinate as it is now…It was not fit that man should have a law given him, unless he had a natural inclination to what was forbidden by the law."[5]

---

5 John Owen, "A Display of Arminianism," in *The Works of John Owen*, ed., William H. Goold (Edinburgh, Scotland: Banner of Truth, repr. 1993), 10:87.

The Arminians' contention was that one cannot speak of a good will or of an evil will, but simply of a will or even a free will, because the will of man is *always neutral and always free*. This is the Arminian attempt to exempt the will from the corruption of man's nature. Nevertheless, the Bible does not teach that we can divide man in this way, for *the entire man* with *the entire human nature* (including his will) fell and was corrupted in man's fall into sin.

The answer of the Canons is that the Arminian conception of the neutrality of the will is contrary to the description of God's image in the Bible (Eph. 4:24). The Arminians in their anthropology (their doctrine of man) are philosophers, not exegetes. The Reformed fathers appealed to sacred scripture, for only God can tell us what we truly are. We cannot separate these qualities from the will. When we fell, therefore, our whole nature fell. That is our misery—not a morally neutral will, not a free will, but a will bound to sin, something Martin Luther termed "the bondage of the will."

ERROR AND REJECTION 3: MAN'S WILL HINDERED BUT NOT CORRUPTED

> Error 3: Who teach that in spiritual death the spiritual gifts are not separate from the will of man, since the will in itself has never been corrupted, but only hindered through the darkness of the understanding and the irregularity of the affections; and that, these hindrances having been removed, the will can then bring into operation its native powers, that is, that the will of itself is able to will and to choose, or not to will and not to choose, all manner of good which may be presented to it.
>
> Rejection: This is an innovation and an error, and tends to elevate the powers of the free will, contrary to the declaration of the prophet: *The heart is deceitful above all things, and it is exceedingly corrupt* (Jer. 17:9); and of the apostle:

> *Among whom* (sons of disobedience) *we also all once lived in the lusts of the flesh, doing the desires of the flesh and of the mind* (Eph. 2:3).

The Arminians were wrong about man's nature before the fall. Unsurprisingly, the Arminians were also wrong about man's nature after the fall. According to Arminianism the fall had the following effects upon man. First, the understanding is (somewhat) darkened and needs to be instructed. Second, the affections are (somewhat) irregular and need to be reordered or redirected. These irregularities hinder the will of man, but the will has not been corrupted and has not lost its native powers. Compare this with article 1: "Blindness of mind, horrible darkness, vanity, and perverseness of judgment...and impure in his affections."

If man's will is only hindered, he does not need regeneration. Instead, he only requires that the "hindrances" should be removed. These irregularities or hindrances can be removed by education, by persuasion, by an appeal to reason, or by an appeal to the emotions, all with the "help of grace." The will of man, insists Arminianism, has retained its native powers: "The will of itself is able to will and to choose, or not to will and not to choose, all manner of good which may be presented to it."

This view of man's will explains the practices of Arminianism. Man must be persuaded because man is not really depraved. Therefore, in Arminian preaching and evangelism the appeal to man's will and, preferably, the manipulation of man's emotions are critical. However, the scriptures teach that nothing short of sovereign regeneration is required to bring the sinner to believe in Christ. He does not need to be persuaded, convinced, or even manipulated. He needs to be born again. Peculiarly, Arminians teach that the new birth occurs *after faith* or even *in response to faith*, which would mean that the sinner is alive before he is made alive. Billy Graham (1918-2018), the famous Arminian evangelist, is representative:

> The context of John 3 teaches that the new birth is something that God does for man *when man is willing to yield to God*...Any person *who is willing to trust* Jesus Christ as his personal Savior and Lord *can receive the new birth now... All you have to do* to be born again is to repent of your sins and believe in the Lord Jesus as your personal Lord and Savior...*Repentance is* first, and absolutely necessary, if we are to be born again...The Holy Spirit will do everything possible to disturb you, draw you, love you—*but finally it is your personal decision.*[6]

Another passage that is greatly misunderstood in Arminian circles is John 1:12. Many Arminians interpret the text this way as a proof that the new birth is a consequence (even a reward) of faith: "But as many as received him [accepted Christ by free will], to them gave he power [ability] to become the sons of God [to be born again as a result of their freewill decision], even to them that believe on his name [who accepted Christ by free will].

The proper interpretation of John 1:12–13 is as follows:

> 12. But as many as received him [exercised saving faith, which is a gift of God], to them gave he power [the authority or legal right] to become the sons of God [to be legally adopted as an aspect of justification by faith alone], even to them that believe on his name;
> 13. Which were born, not of blood, nor of the will of the flesh, nor of the will of man, but of God [that is, sovereign regeneration without the free will of man].

---

6 Billy Graham, *How to be Born Again* (London: Hodder and Stoughton, 1977), 133, 136, 140, 144, 146 (emphasis added). The clue that this would be a bad book is in the title—How *to be Born Again*? If a gynecologist wrote a book for the unborn entitled *How to be Born*, it would be no less absurd than for a theologian to write a book giving instructions to the spiritually dead how to be born again.

Many Arminians misconstrue verse 12 and ignore verse 13, which teaches sovereign regeneration. The order is not saving faith, regeneration; but regeneration, saving faith, justification, and adoption.

The answer of the Canons to this teaching of Arminianism is threefold. First, this is an innovation and an error; second, this elevates the power of free will; and third, this is contrary to scripture (Jer. 17:9; Eph. 2:3). Beware of a teaching that elevates man's powers, for such a teaching does not glorify the grace of God. Indeed, such a teaching renders the grace of God ultimately unnecessary.

ARTICLE 2: THE TRUTH OF ORIGINAL SIN

> Man after the fall begat children in his own likeness. A corrupt stock produced a corrupt offspring. Hence all the posterity of Adam, Christ only excepted, have derived corruption from their original parent, not by imitation, as the Pelagians of old asserted, but by the propagation of a vicious nature.

Article 1 explains the creation and fall of Adam, but what does that have to do with us? The answer is original sin, perhaps one of the most offensive, and yet one of the most important, doctrines of scripture. Original sin is a two-part doctrine: original guilt and original pollution. The Reformed confessions generally stress original pollution over original guilt, for this is where the heart of the controversy lay at the time the confessions were written (Heidelberg Catechism Q&A 7; Belgic Confession 15).

In article 2 the Reformed fathers taught original guilt and original pollution. Sadly, the clause concerning original guilt is not included in many English translations of the Canons—"By the just judgment of God."[7] The sentence of article 2 should read, "Hence all

---

7 With reference to this article Philip Schaff wrote: "'*justo Dei judicio*' [in consequence of a just judgment of God]—omitted in the translation of the Reformed Dutch Church" (Schaff, *Creeds of Christendom*, 3:588).

the posterity of Adam, Christ only excepted, have derived corruption from their original parent…*by the righteous judgment of God*."

The doctrine of original guilt is simply this: the guilt of Adam's first transgression was imputed or reckoned to all of Adam's posterity, to us, so that we are guilty on account of Adam's first transgression. To understand how this could be so, we need to understand who Adam was. Adam was created not as a private individual, but as the head of the human race, or as some writers have explained it, a public person. Therefore, in the garden of Eden Adam was not acting merely on his own behalf, but on behalf of the whole of humanity. Adam was both the representative (federal) head and the organic head of the human race (Acts 17:26).

This is why his actions in the garden of Eden were so serious and so catastrophic for the human race, for because of Adam's transgression, all men are born into this world guilty, polluted, and totally depraved sinners. Because of his transgression, all men have lost all of the excellent gifts with which Adam was created. Because of his transgression, all men are devoid of the knowledge of God, they are unholy, and they are unrighteous—that is, they are deprived of the image of God, which Adam forfeited for them—from birth, even from conception. Because of his transgression, all men come into this world burdened with "blindness of mind, horrible darkness, vanity, and perverseness of judgment" and they are "wicked, rebellious, and obdurate in heart and will, and impure in [their] affections" (Canons 3–4.1).

Adam's headship is taught especially in two passages of the New Testament: Romans 5 and 1 Corinthians 15. The relevant verses of 1 Corinthians are the following: "Since by man came death, by man came also the resurrection of the dead. For as in Adam all die, even so in Christ shall all be made alive. And so it is written, The first man Adam was made a living soul; the last Adam was made a quickening spirit (vv. 21–22, 45).

From these verses, we learn that Adam affected all men, for in

Adam, *all men die*. We also learn that Christ is another head like Adam, indeed, the second Adam or the last Adam. What Christ did affected all men (or rather it affected all the men whom he represented, or all of the elect), for in Christ, *all shall be made alive*.

A more detailed explanation of the doctrine of original sin is found in Romans 5:12–21. This passage compares and contrasts two representative heads, Adam and Christ. Adam was the head of "his people," which is the whole of humanity. Christ is the head of "his people," which is the elect church. (Incidentally, because Christ is the head, he cannot be under the headship of Adam; in fact, he is the head *of Adam*). Paul drew a parallel between these two heads, for Adam was "a figure [or type] of him that was to come" (v. 14). "Wherefore, as by one man sin entered into the world, and death by sin; and so death passed upon all men, for that all have sinned. For if through the offence of one [the] many be dead [or the many *died*]... Judgment was by one to condemnation...By one man's offence death reigned by one...By the offence of one judgment came upon all men to condemnation...By one man's disobedience [the] many were made [or *constituted*] sinners" (vv. 12, 15–19). Notice how Paul repeatedly referred to "one offence" and "one man." The one man is Adam and the one offense is the act of disobedience and rebellion by which Adam fell in the garden.

The parallel between Adam and Christ is clear—as the one act of rebellion by Adam plunged the human race into guilt and misery, so the one act of obedience by Christ brought righteousness and salvation to the whole elect church: "Much more the grace of God, and the gift of grace, which is by one man, Jesus Christ, hath abounded unto [the] many. Even so by the righteousness of one the free gift came upon all men unto justification of life. So by the obedience of one shall [the] many be made [or *constituted*] righteous" (vv. 15, 18–19).

The fifth chapter of the epistle to the Romans is pivotal to Paul's explanation of justification. He demonstrated that God's people are justified in Christ *in the same way in which they became sinners in*

Adam: by the imputation of guilt on the one hand and the imputation of righteousness on the other. Thus the guilt of Adam was imputed to them *because he represented them*, and the righteousness of Christ is imputed to them *because he represented them*. You cannot confess one without the other, for they both stand or fall together.

As a consequence of this guilt, Adam's guilt righteously imputed to all men, God punishes the whole human race with original pollution. They forfeited these gifts: God stripped Adam of his image. God punished Adam with "blindness of mind, horrible darkness, vanity, and perverseness of spirit." The result was that he was "wicked, rebellious, and obdurate in heart and will, and impure in his affections" (Canons 3–4.1). And because Adam represented the whole human race and his guilt was imputed to all men, they are also punished with original pollution. This pollution is passed through the human race from parents to children, for "a corrupt stock produce[s] a corrupt offspring." Adam did not beget children in God's image, but in his own fallen image (Gen. 5:3). The Canons call this "the propagation of a vicious nature" (Ps. 51:5; 58:3; Rom. 5:14).

Therefore, all children born into this world are guilty and depraved—*totally* depraved—from the womb. Many Arminians teach that there is an age of accountability after which children become accountable to God and are subject to or liable to punishment, but before which age children are innocent before God. This is the invention of our modern sentimental age, for there is no such notion in the scriptures. All human beings, as creatures, are accountable to God from the very beginning of their existence, that is, from conception. The Canons explain it this way: first, "Man after the fall begat children in his own likeness" (Gen. 5:3); second, "All the posterity of Adam, Christ only excepted, have derived corruption from their original parent"; and third, this "propagation of a vicious nature" is *by the just judgment of God* (as noted above, these words are found in the original version of the Canons and should be included in the English version).

We can briefly contrast this with three errors.

First, Pelagianism views the universal prevalence of sin as the result of "imitation." Pelagius, a heretic whom we have met before in the Canons, taught that Adam fell alone and independently of all men, so that his fall had no real effect upon anyone else. The fall did not affect Adam's nature and it certainly did not affect the nature of his posterity. The reason that sin is common is that other people provide bad examples for their children. Sin, therefore, concluded Pelagius, is not in man's nature, but is the product of his environment. Liberal secularists and liberal theologians, believing Pelagius' lies, have attempted to improve man's environment for generations, but they have not succeeded in eradicating the evil from man's nature.

Second, semi-Pelagianism does not go as far as Pelagius, but views man as seriously weakened by the fall, although not dead in sin. The semi-Pelagians will confess that man is very far gone from original righteousness or that man is sick or almost dead, or dying, but they deny that man has lost all the powers of free will. The Roman Catholic Church is essentially semi-Pelagian, as are many modern Arminians:

> Although it is proper to each individual, original sin does not have the character of a personal fault in any of Adam's descendants. It is a deprivation of original holiness and justice, but human nature has not been totally corrupted: it is wounded in the natural powers proper to it, subject to ignorance, suffering and the dominion of death, and inclined to sin—an inclination to evil that is called "concupiscence." Baptism, by imparting the life of Christ's grace, erases original sin and turns a man back towards God, but the consequences for nature, weakened and inclined to evil, persist in man and summon him to spiritual battle.[8]

---

8 *Catechism of the Catholic Church*, paragraph 405 (Allen, TX: Thomas More Press, 1994), 102.

Many modern Arminians would agree with this paragraph of official Roman Catholic dogma, although they would differ with Rome on the subject of baptism. When you hear or read analogies in modern evangelicalism of drowning (but not drowned) men offered a lifeline or of sick (but not dead) men offered medicine, you should recognize the semi-Pelagian teaching.

Third, Arminianism teaches that man is corrupt and will even use the words *total depravity* or *radical depravity*, but the Arminian still believes that man has the power to cooperate with God's grace or that he has at least the power *not to resist it*. This teaching betrays Arminianism as a serious departure from the truth of the scriptures.

Given the truth outlined in article 2, Arminianism must fall at the first hurdle. No wonder that total depravity is such an important doctrine. All assaults on this truth are assaults on the grace of God, on grace's necessity, sufficiency, and efficacy.

ERROR AND REJECTION 1: ORIGINAL SIN NOT DAMNWORTHY

> Error 1: Who teach that it cannot properly be said that original sin in itself suffices to condemn the whole human race, or to deserve temporal and eternal punishment.
>
> Rejection: For these contradict the apostle, who declares: *Therefore as through one man sin entered into the world, and death through sin, and so death passed unto all men, for that all sinned* (Rom. 5:12). And: *The judgment came of one unto condemnation* (Rom. 5:16). And: *The wages of sin is death* (Rom. 6:23).

The Arminians denied the guilt of original sin, for they insisted that original sin is not something for which man can be condemned. Instead, original sin is merely an infirmity of the flesh. Arminians still deny original sin today because they are committed to the error of the innocence of children. Although we naturally pity children, we must confess what scripture confesses about them: children are guilty of Adam's transgression and they are born with a corrupt, totally depraved nature. If God willed, he would be perfectly just to condemn children and the whole human race to eternal destruction because of original sin: "Original sin…is so vile and abominable in the sight of God that it is sufficient to condemn all mankind."[9] The synod quickly dispatched the Arminian error with an appeal to the apostolic teaching of Romans 5:12 and 6:23.

ARTICLE 3: THE TRUTH OF TOTAL DEPRAVITY

> Therefore all men are conceived in sin, and by nature children of wrath, incapable of saving good, prone to evil, dead in sin, and in bondage thereto, and without the regenerating grace of the Holy Spirit they are neither able nor willing to return to God, to reform the depravity of their nature, nor to dispose themselves to reformation.

Article 3 outlines the severe consequences of the fall for the human race: all men are conceived in sin (Ps. 51:5); all men are by nature children of wrath (Eph. 2:3); all men are incapable of saving good (This must not be interpreted to mean that men are capable of non-saving good, a subject that will be discussed in article 4. Suffice to say that neither the Bible nor the Canons know of a non-saving good.); and all men are prone to evil (Gen. 6:5), dead in sin (Eph. 2:1), and in bondage to sin (John 8:34). Therefore, they are not able or willing to return to God; they are not able or willing to reform the depravity of their natures; and they are not able or willing to dispose themselves to reformation. The only power by which they could be changed is the "regenerating grace of the Holy Spirit." That is a very succinct and clear statement of the awful truth of total depravity, which fully agrees with the Heidelberg Catechism: "Are we then so corrupt that we are wholly incapable of doing any good, and inclined

9 Belgic Confession 15, in *Confessions and Church Order*, 40.

to all wickedness? Indeed we are, except we are regenerated by the Spirit of God."[10]

Dear reader, have you taken to heart the consequences of the fall? Do you understand what you have lost because of the transgression of our first father, Adam? Do you see what has become of your nature because of original sin? Does the knowledge of your depravity fill you with horror? It must if you are ever to find salvation in Jesus Christ. There is a reason believers in Christ still offer the fifth petition of the Lord's prayer, which the Heidelberg Catechism explains thus: "Be pleased for the sake of Christ's blood, not to impute to us poor sinners our transgressions, *nor that depravity which always cleaves to us*."[11]

ERROR AND REJECTION 4: MAN NOT UTTERLY DEAD IN SIN

> Error 4: Who teach that the unregenerate man is not really nor utterly dead in sin, nor destitute of all powers unto spiritual good, but that he can yet hunger and thirst after righteousness and life, and offer the sacrifice of a contrite and broken spirit, which is pleasing to God.
>
> Rejection: For these are contrary to the express testimony of Scripture. *Ye were dead through trespasses and sins* (Eph. 2:1, 5); and: *Every imagination of the thoughts of his heart was only evil continually* (Gen. 6:5; 8:21).

Moreover, to hunger and thirst after deliverance from misery and after life, and to offer unto God the sacrifice of a broken spirit, is peculiar to the regenerate and those that are called blessed (Ps. 51:10, 19; Matt. 5:6).

The Arminians detest the doctrine of total depravity, for it is a

10 Heidelberg Catechism Q&A 8, in ibid., 86.
11 Heidelberg Catechism A 126, in ibid., 139 (emphasis added).

deathblow to their cherished doctrine of free will. If total depravity is true, the whole system of free will salvation is destroyed. Therefore, total depravity must be denied at all costs. The Arminian teaching was as follows: "Unregenerate man is not really or utterly dead in sin"; unregenerate man is not "destitute of all powers unto spiritual good"; and unregenerate man can still please God. Moreover, the Arminians suggested that fallen man can do two things: he can "hunger and thirst after righteousness and life"; and he can "offer the sacrifice of a contrite and broken spirit."

The answer of the Reformed fathers was that the Arminians contradicted the scriptures. For example, Romans 8:8 and Ephesians 2:1 deny that fallen man can please God. In addition, the theologians at Dordt showed very deep insight into the scriptures, for "to hunger and thirst after deliverance from misery and after life and to offer unto God the sacrifice of a broken spirit" are "peculiar to the regenerate and those that are called blessed" (Ps. 51:10, 19; Matt. 5:6; Ps. 42:2; 63:1; 143:6; Isa. 55:1; John 7:37; Rev. 22:17).

This has important pastoral application, for if unregenerate people can hunger and thirst after righteousness and experience true sorrow over sin, how can the true child of God know that his sorrow over sin is genuine and not the sorrow produced by an unregenerate heart? If you, believing reader, have such a spiritual thirst and a heartfelt sorrow over your sins (and if you are a believer, you do), you must know that you have been born again of the Spirit of the living God.

ARTICLE 4: THE GLIMMERINGS OF NATURAL LIGHT

> There remain, however, in man since the fall the glimmerings of natural light, whereby he retains some knowledge of God, of natural things, and of the differences between good and evil, and discovers some regard for virtue, good order in society, and for maintaining an orderly external deportment. But so far is this light of nature from being

> sufficient to bring him to a saving knowledge of God and to true conversion, that he is incapable of using it aright even in things natural and civil. Nay further, this light, such as it is, man in various ways renders wholly polluted, and holds it in unrighteousness, by doing which he becomes inexcusable before God.

In articles 1–3 we have seen man's dreadful depravity. We have seen from what lofty heights man has fallen (we have fallen) and into what misery we have plunged ourselves in Adam. Articles 4–5 do not in any way give back to man what he has lost. They do not offer some concession to man as if he is not totally depraved after all or as if he retains some goodness after all.

This article has a significant history, for this article was misused in 1924 in the controversy over common grace. The Christian Reformed Church adopted the following three points of common grace: one, a general favor of God toward all men, including the reprobate, with a general offer of the gospel in which God expresses his desire to save everyone; two, a gracious restraint of sin that mitigates somewhat man's total depravity; and three, an ability through common grace in man by the Spirit without regeneration to perform civil righteousness, that is, good works genuinely pleasing to God. In defending common grace, the Christian Reformed Church appealed to only the first part of article 4, that is, to the part ending with the words "orderly external deportment."

According to this article, then, what does man retain after the fall? Has man perhaps become a devil or a demon? Has man perhaps become a beast? Does man now commit all possible sins so that life becomes impossible in the world? Conversely, is man *less than* totally depraved? Does man retain some remnants of the image of God? Is man still *partially* good? If that were the teaching of article 4, the Canons would be contradicting what they have just taught in articles 1–3.

The key phrase of article 4 is "the glimmerings of natural light." Before the fall Adam possessed and enjoyed a "true and saving knowledge of his Creator and of spiritual things" (Canons 3–4.1). That has been lost, for instead of knowledge there is blindness; instead of righteousness there is perverseness; instead of holiness there is depravity. The image of God is gone, for man has forfeited that image. Whatever these "glimmerings of natural light" are, they do not belong to the image of God.

The light in question is merely "natural." Everyone has natural light, which is the natural light of reason, but fallen man's natural light is but a "glimmering" or a dim flicker. In Adam it was pure light, but now because of sin only "glimmerings" remain. Is that not humbling to modern man? Man boasts of his enlightenment and of the progress he has made in knowledge and science. Supposedly, Adam was primitive, but we have evolved since then. The opposite is the truth: we have *devolved*, for Adam's mind was much brighter than man's darkened mind today. The Canons carefully delineate the power of this natural light of reason: "He retains some knowledge of God"; "he retains some knowledge...of natural things"; "he retains some knowledge...of the differences between good and evil"; and "he...discovers some regard for virtue, good order in society, and for maintaining an orderly external deportment."

Let us examine the "glimmerings" or the dim flickers of light in turn.

First, the natural man, while being totally depraved, retains *some knowledge of God*. This is not "a true and saving knowledge of his Creator," which knowledge he lost. This is not the knowledge of love and fellowship in the covenant, which covenant he violated in Adam. This is not the spiritual knowledge of appreciation and delight, for fallen man hates the God whom he knows. This is merely *natural* knowledge, the knowledge he derives from the creation around him, the knowledge he derives from within himself, and the knowledge that leaves even the most ardent atheist without excuse before his Creator (Acts 14:14–18; 17:24–30; Rom. 1:18–23; 1 Cor. 2:14; Eph. 2:12; 4:17–20).

Second, the natural man, although he is totally depraved, retains *some knowledge of natural things.* This is not "a true and saving knowledge…of spiritual things," which knowledge he lost. Sinful man can still engage in intellectual pursuits, for he can study the world that God has made. For example, he can become proficient in many fields of study, but all of his study is the pursuit of natural things without true spiritual understanding. Such pursuit is part of the so-called cultural mandate of Genesis 1:28: "Be fruitful, and multiply, and replenish the earth, and subdue it: and have dominion." Man pursues science, art, culture, and philosophy, but he does so *as totally depraved.* An unbelieving, cultured scientist with a PhD in physics is depraved, totally depraved, and he lacks the "beginning of [true] knowledge," which is the "fear of the LORD" (Prov. 1:7). There is no operation of grace in his pursuit of knowledge and the natural knowledge that he has (whether in science, philosophy, literature, history or even theology) does not in any way improve his nature so that he is anything less than totally depraved.

Third, the natural man, although he is totally depraved, retains *some knowledge of the difference between good and evil.* The totally depraved sinner knows the difference between sin and righteousness. For example, he knows that murder, theft, and adultery are wrong, and he knows that kindness, love, and generosity are good. (Even the atheist knows this, although he cannot account for why it should be so.) Moreover, the natural man has a conscience, his inner judge by which his deeds are either approved or condemned (Rom. 2:12–16). When Gentiles do the things contained in the law, they do not obey God's law, which is impossible (8:7), but they still display external virtue and avoid external vice. When they display "the work of the law written in their hearts" (2:15), this does not mean that God has written the *law* on their hearts—that would be regeneration (Jer. 31:33; Heb. 8:10)—but it means that God has written the knowledge of right and wrong in their hearts to which he testifies in their consciences. All men know the difference between right and wrong. This does not make them good, or even partially good, but inexcusable before their Creator and Judge.

Fourth, the totally depraved unbeliever *discovers some regard for virtue, good order in society, and for maintaining an orderly external deportment.* Even the basest of sinners prefer to live in a nation of laws. They see some need for a criminal justice system, even if they hope to escape human justice; and they see the benefit of complying with some moral code. Most people generally obey the law of the land of which they are the citizens. However, this is not civil righteousness, but it is self-preservation. Law is good for them and law is good for society. Most are astute enough to discern that lawlessness is counterproductive. Many are restrained by a natural sense of shame or a fear of punishment. But unless the Holy Spirit regenerates a sinner and writes God's law on his heart, that sinner will never serve God out of thankfulness from the heart in a way that pleases God.

However, the Synod of Dordt did not finish there. Here is how article 4 continues after the words "orderly external deportment":

> But so far is this light of nature from being sufficient to bring him to a saving knowledge of God and to true conversion, that he is incapable of using it aright even in things natural and civil. Nay further, this light, such as it is, man in various ways renders wholly polluted, and holds it in unrighteousness, by doing which he becomes inexcusable before God.

Notice those damning words. Not only do the "glimmerings of natural light" not improve totally depraved man, but they also actually make his judgment before God even worse because of his misuse of them. Man is "incapable of using it [the light of nature] aright even in things natural and civil." When man seems to fulfill the cultural mandate of Genesis 1:28, he sins. (In fact, none of his endeavors are a fulfilling of the cultural mandate, but the selfish pursuit of pleasure, wealth, power, and sin.) When man develops science, medicine, and technology, he sins. When man pursues any field of study, he sins. When man behaves in an outwardly moral fashion, even when he lets conscience be his guide, and when he follows God's law externally, he sins. When man lives as a law-abiding citizen, in faithfulness to one wife, and loves his children, he sins. Everything man does, he does in the service of sin. He cannot use natural light aright even in things natural and civil.

Of course, if instead of pursuing a cure for cancer, man makes and deploys an atom bomb, he sins even more. If instead of living in faithfulness to his wife, he commits adultery, or if instead of loving his children, he neglects or abuses them, he sins even more. If instead of living as a law-abiding citizen, he becomes a criminal, he sins even more. The issue is not between depravity and common grace, but between different expressions of depravity.

Moreover, "this light, such as it is [and it is not much], man in various ways renders wholly polluted, and holds it in unrighteousness." Man pollutes—he wholly pollutes—his intellectual gifts, his knowledge of God, his knowledge of good and evil, his conscience, and his natural sense of morality and external virtue. He wholly pollutes it.

The Synod of Dordt did not invent this distinction, but the fathers echoed the teaching of sacred scripture. Romans 1:18 states that unbelievers "hold the truth in unrighteousness," where the verb "hold" means to hold down or to suppress. 1 Timothy 4:2 describes those "having their conscience seared with a hot iron." Titus 1:15–16 warns, "Unto them that are defiled and unbelieving is nothing pure; but even their mind and conscience is defiled. They profess that they know God; but in works they deny him, being abominable, and disobedient, and unto every good work reprobate."

Romans 3:12 simply teaches, "There is none that doeth good, no, not one." No one does spiritual good, saving good, moral good, natural good, civil good, *or any other kind of good*. There is only one kind of good, the good that pleases God: "So then they that are in the flesh cannot please God" (8:8).

In summary, then, these "glimmerings of natural light" fall short of true righteousness. They do not constitute the image of God, or even a remnant of the image, which was wholly lost in the fall. They do not constitute true obedience; they do not enable the sinner to please God in any sense; and they are not good works, for they are not performed in obedience to God, from a heart purified by faith, or out of a pure motive to glorify God (Heidelberg Catechism Q&A 91). The world of unbelieving men might call the works of the wicked "good," and they might even praise their fellow unbelievers for their "good works," but they are not truly good works—not in the sight of God, whose is the only judgment that truly matters.

The conclusion is clear: man is inexcusable before God, so that even the most hardened atheist or the most darkened heathen has no excuse. God will justly condemn him, for he knows God while he suppresses the truth in unrighteousness. How necessary, then, is the grace—the saving grace—of God.

ARTICLE 5: THE WEAKNESS OF THE LAW

> In the same light are we to consider the law of the decalogue, delivered by God to His peculiar people, the Jews, by the hands of Moses. For though it discovers the greatness of sin, and more and more convinces man thereof, yet as it neither points out a remedy nor imparts strength to extricate him from misery, and thus, being weak through the flesh, leaves the transgressor under the curse, man cannot by this law obtain saving grace.

Natural light (the glimmerings thereof) is common to all men, but this is not common grace and (contrary to the theory of common grace) it does not enable man to do anything good. Although natural light (reason) is common to all men, the law of God is not common to all men. Article 5 moves from a consideration of natural light to "the law of the decalogue." What then does the decalogue do? The Canons indicate a similarity: "In the same light are we to consider the law of the decalogue."

The decalogue is the ten commandments. Is unregenerate man by means of the ten commandments, even if he succeeds in getting them displayed on public buildings, able to please God? By no means. Instead, the law of the decalogue accomplishes the following. First, it discovers (uncovers) the greatness of sin (Rom. 3:20; 7:7). Second, it more and more convinces man of sin. Indeed, the law incites man to commit sin, for the more the law declares, "Thou shalt do," the more defiantly man replies, "I shall not." The more the law forbids, "Thou shalt not do," the more defiantly man replies, "I shall" (Rom. 7:5, 8–13). Therefore, a billboard of the ten commandments only stirs up the enmity of man against God, which is why people oppose the posting of the ten commandments. It is also why the public display of the ten commandments will never change a man's heart. Moreover, it does not point out a remedy, and it does not impart strength to obey, for it is weak through the flesh (8:3); and it leaves the transgressor under the curse of God (Gal. 3:10). Therefore, we cannot attain saving grace by the law (Rom. 8:28; 4:15; Gal. 2:16, 21; 3:11–12).

Therefore, both the light of nature and the law of God leave the unbeliever without excuse and under God's wrath. No man is able to keep the law, for the law is not a means of salvation—not in the Old Testament, not in the New Testament, not now, not in the future, and not ever. That is why we need the saving, efficacious, sovereign grace of God.

ERROR AND REJECTION 5: MAN'S ATTAINMENT TO SAVING GRACE THROUGH NATURAL LIGHT

> Error 5: Who teach that the corrupt and natural man can so well use the common grace (by which they understand the light of nature), or the gifts still left him after the fall,

> that he can gradually gain by their good use a greater, namely, the evangelical or saving grace and salvation itself. And that in this way God on His part shows Himself ready to reveal Christ unto all men, since He applies to all sufficiently and efficiently the means necessary to conversion.
>
> Rejection: For the experience of all ages and the Scriptures do both testify that this is untrue. *He showeth his word unto Jacob, his statutes and his ordinances unto Israel. He hath not dealt so with any nation: and as for his ordinances, they have not known them* (Ps. 147:19–20). *Who in the generations gone by suffered all the nations to walk in their own ways* (Acts 14:16). And: *And they* (Paul and his companions) *having been forbidden of the Holy Spirit to speak the word in Asia, and when they were come over against Mysia, they assayed to go into Bithynia, and the Spirit suffered them not* (Acts 16:6–7).

The Arminians taught that God gave all men sufficient "common" grace through the light of nature to attain to saving grace. They taught that God was ready to give grace *if men would cooperate with him*. They taught that God was ready to reveal Christ to all men if they would only use his "common" grace (the light of nature) aright.

Notice the language. First, "corrupt and natural man can…use the common grace (by which they understand the light of nature), or the gifts still left to him after the fall." (We have seen already that man only retains faint "glimmerings" of natural light, which he is incapable of using aright, and which he wholly pollutes and suppresses.) Second, this light of nature the Arminians called "common grace," the only place where the term is used in the creeds, a term the Reformed fathers at Dordt rejected. Third, by a careful use of these gifts of "common grace" (the light of nature and the remnant of created gifts) man can gain "evangelical or saving grace and salvation itself."

The Arminian theory is that all men possess free will by which they can either use or improve or abuse "common grace" or the light of nature. This also applies to the law, for all men have the power of free will by which they can render obedience to the law. By doing this they can obtain a higher kind of grace—saving or evangelical grace, which is also resistible. Man must freely cooperate with and yield to this grace to be saved. If one is cooperative enough, he could even attain to salvation itself. This evangelical or saving grace, therefore, can be attained without the preaching of the gospel and without regeneration, but merely by the cooperation of free will with "common grace."

Fourth, God shows himself ready to reveal Christ to all men, for he desires to save all; he wants all to know him, and he is ready to reveal Christ to all who are worthy and show themselves to be worthy. (This view is not uncommon among Arminians today. It explains the so-called heathen problem. Do the heathen who have never heard the gospel perish? It seems unfair to many Arminians that God would condemn the heathen who never had a chance to be saved. Therefore, they are open to the possibility of other ways of salvation, and the cooperation of free will with common grace is attractive to some.) The Presbyterian creed the Westminster Confession of Faith warns against the error of teaching that those who are not called by the gospel can be saved:

> Much less can men, not professing the Christian religion, be saved in any other way whatsoever, be they never so diligent to frame their lives according to the light of nature and the law of that religion they do profess; and to assert and maintain that they may is very pernicious, and to be detested.[12]

---

12 Westminster Confession of Faith 10.4, in Schaff, *Creeds of Christendom*, 3:625–26.

Fifth, God applies to all "sufficiently and efficiently the means necessary to conversion." This sentence of the Arminians is surely nonsensical because it denies the very meaning of the word *efficient*. If something is efficient, it accomplishes the purpose for which it was sent. It cannot be applied sufficiently and efficiently if not all to whom it is applied are actually converted (Canons 1, error and rejection 9).

The Canons condemn the Arminian teaching, for scripture reveals that God is *not* ready to reveal Christ to all men. On the contrary, God reveals Christ to few and hides him from many according to his sovereign good pleasure (Ps. 147:19–20; Matt. 11:25–27; Acts 14:16; 16:6).

Has God revealed Christ to you? Fall on your knees in humble thanksgiving before him.

ARTICLE 6: THE POWER OF THE GOSPEL

> What therefore neither the light of nature nor the law could do, that God performs by the operation of the Holy Spirit through the Word or ministry of reconciliation, which is the glad tidings concerning the Messiah, by means whereof it hath pleased God to save such as believe, as well under the Old as under the New Testament.

By the natural light of reason the sinner cannot be saved. By the law the sinner cannot be saved. That was the teaching of articles 4–5, but now in article 6 we learn the real source of man's salvation—the Holy Spirit through the gospel. What we could not do by our own efforts, said the Reformed fathers, "God performs." That is the essence of the Reformed faith—salvation is of the Lord (Jonah 2:9).

Again the Reformed fathers at Dordt reminded us that God uses means: "God performs by the operation of the Holy Spirit through the Word or ministry of reconciliation, which is the glad tidings concerning the Messiah." The Bible emphasizes the importance of preaching, both the content (the message) and the method (the form).

Notice what the Canons teach about preaching. First, it is the "ministry of reconciliation," for through believing the gospel the rebellious sinner is reconciled to God who has reconciled sinners to himself through the death of his Son (Rom. 5:8–11; 2 Cor. 5:18–21). Second, preaching is "the glad tidings concerning the Messiah," for preaching is not advice for a happy life or political or social commentary, but the good news about Jesus Christ, who is the only savior of sinners. The preacher must emulate the apostle Paul, who affirmed, "We preach Christ crucified" (1 Cor. 1:23) and "I determined not to know any thing among you, save Jesus Christ, and him crucified" (2:2). Only such preaching is the ministry of reconciliation by which sinners are saved. The New Testament is full of texts that extol the preaching of the gospel: Romans 1:15–16, 10:11–17; 1 Corinthians 1:21–24, 2:2; Colossians 1:3–6; 1 Thessalonians 1:5, 2:13; and Titus 1:3 are only a sample.

If the means of conversion is the preaching of the gospel, the agent of conversion is the Holy Spirit, for he performs the saving work by which sinners are brought from darkness to light, from death to life, and from ignorance to saving faith. Even the preaching would be in vain if the Holy Spirit did not effectually call sinners through it. God saves "such as believe," that is, he does not save everyone who hears the gospel, but only those who believe. This is the identifying mark of those who are saved. God determines who the believers are, because faith is the fruit of election (Canons 1) and of the cross (Canons 2). Faith has always been the identifying mark of those who are saved, "as well under the Old as under the New Testament" (Gal. 3:8; Heb. 4:2, 6).

Therefore, we attribute our salvation solely to the effectual, saving, particular grace of the triune God: the Father ordained it, the Son purchased it, and the Spirit applies it.

ARTICLE 7: THE PARTICULARITY OF THE GRACE OF THE GOSPEL

> This mystery of His will God discovered to but a small number under the Old Testament; under the New (the distinction between various peoples having been removed) He reveals Himself to many, without any distinction of people. The cause of this dispensation is not to be ascribed to the superior worth of one nation above another, nor to their making a better use of the light of nature, but results wholly from the sovereign good pleasure and unmerited love of God. Hence they to whom so great and so gracious a blessing is communicated, above their desert, or rather notwithstanding their demerits, are bound to acknowledge it with humble and grateful hearts, and with the apostle to adore, not curiously to pry into the severity and justice of God's judgments displayed to others, to whom this grace is not given.

While the preaching of the gospel is the necessary means employed by the Holy Spirit to bring sinners to salvation, the preaching is restricted according to God's good pleasure. The gospel is here called the "mystery of [God's] will." A mystery in the Bible is not a riddle or an enigma, but something hidden in the secret counsel of God, which can only be made known by revelation, or something that was formerly hidden, but is now revealed. In the Old Testament God's mystery was revealed "to but a small number," for the word of God was restricted for the most part to one nation, the Jews, and to the relatively few Gentiles incorporated into that nation (Ps. 147:19–20; Acts 14:16; 17:30). In the New Testament "the distinction between various peoples" (such as Jews and Gentiles) has been "removed," for God now gathers a church from all nations.

Why, then, does God reveal the mystery of his will to only

some? It is not because of the superior worth of one nation over another (Canons 1, error and rejection 9). It is not because some make better use of the "light of nature" than others. Rather, the sovereign good pleasure and unmerited love of God determine the direction of the preaching of the gospel. Has God revealed the mystery of his will to you in distinction from others? Has God by the operation of his Holy Spirit opened your heart to believe the truth in distinction from others? Attribute that not to your merit, or to your worth, or even to your free will—attribute that only to the sovereign good pleasure and unmerited love of God.

Believers' response to this great truth is threefold. First, they acknowledge this great blessing "with humble and grateful hearts," for they know that this blessing is above what they deserve ("above their desert") and is despite their deserving the opposite, that is, condemnation ("notwithstanding their demerits"). Second, believers do not despise or neglect the preaching of the gospel, for it is an inestimable blessing given to them, and it is all the more precious since it is not common to all. Third, believers "adore...the severity and justice of God," for they see that God has deprived many of hearing the gospel, and he has not given all hearers of the gospel faith to believe it. When they do this, they do not "curiously...pry into" God's judgments, for they recognize that God is free to dispense his favors as it pleases him.

All around us men and women are perishing because there is a famine of the "hearing of the words of the Lord" (Amos 8:11), while we feed richly on the bread of life. Do we highly esteem such a great privilege? And if you lack such a privilege, are you seeking it in a true church?

ARTICLE 8: THE SERIOUS CALL OF THE GOSPEL

> As many as are called by the gospel are unfeignedly called. For God hath most earnestly and truly shown in His Word what is pleasing to Him, namely, that those who are called

> should come to Him. He, moreover, seriously promises eternal life and rest to as many as shall come to Him and believe on Him.

In article 7 we learned that God reveals the truth only to some by the Spirit through the gospel, which difference is not because of any merit in the nations and individuals who hear and believe the gospel, but is wholly due to the sovereign good pleasure and unmerited love of God.

Article 8 was written in response to the Remonstrants, who submitted their Opinions to the synod. The issue here is God's seriousness, for if the gospel only comes to some, and if God grants faith to only some who hear the gospel, is God *really serious* in the call of the gospel through the preaching? The Arminians contended that, if God did not intend to give salvation to all, if Christ did not purchase salvation for all, and if all sinners, either by nature or by means of so-called common grace, do not have the ability to choose salvation, then God must be hypocritical, insincere, and unserious in the preaching, promising something he does not have and which he does not intend to give.

The Opinions of the Remonstrants are very enlightening about what the Arminians understood by the call of the gospel:

> 8. Whomever God calls to salvation, *he calls seriously, that is, with a sincere and completely unhypocritical intention and will to save*; nor do we assent to the opinions of those who hold that God calls certain ones externally whom he does not will to call internally, that is, as truly converted, even before the grace of calling has been rejected.
> 9. There is not in God a secret will which so contradicts the will of the same revealed in the Word that according to it (that is, the secret will) He does not will the conversion and salvation of the greatest part of those whom He seriously calls and invites by the Word of the Gospel

> and by His revealed will; and we do not here, as some say, acknowledge in God a holy simulation, or a double person.[13]

Notice that it was the Arminians, and not the Reformed fathers at Dordt, who taught that God has a "sincere and completely unhypocritical intention and will to save" all those who hear the gospel. Arminians, not the Reformed, believe that God desires the salvation of all men without exception. More seriously, Arminians believe *contrary to the Bible* that God desires the salvation of all men without exception.

That background greatly clarifies the meaning of this article of the Canons. The key is the Latin word *serio*. Three times the word *serio* is used in heads three and four, article 8, translated by various adverbs in the official English version as "unfeignedly [*serio*] called"; "earnestly [*serio*]...shown"; and "seriously [*serio*] promises."

What *serio* does *not* mean is what the Arminians taught—"whomever God calls to salvation, He calls seriously, that is, with a sincere and completely unhypocritical intention and will to save." Some modern Calvinists, however, *do* define the gospel call (or offer, as they explain it) that way, as God's desire to save all, or as the sincere proposal of divine mercy to sinners in general, the so-called well-meant offer or free offer of the gospel.

Several observations can be made about *serio* (unfeignedly, earnestly, and seriously).

First, God is pleased with faith and repentance: "Those who are called should come to Him." The good pleasure here is not God's eternal decree, that which he is pleased to ordain. God is *not* pleased to ordain that all should repent and believe, for he has not decreed to give all men faith (Eph. 1:11; 2:8; Phil. 1:29). It is according to

---

13 Peter De Jong, ed., *Crisis in the Reformed Churches, Essays in commemoration of the great Synod of Dort, 1618–1619* (Grand Rapids, MI: Reformed Fellowship, Inc., 1968), 226–27 (emphasis added).

God's good pleasure that the elect receive the gift of faith and it is according to the same good pleasure of God that the reprobate do *not* receive it (Canons 1.6, 15). It is according to the good pleasure of God that Christ purchased faith for the elect and it is according to the same good pleasure of God that he did *not* purchase faith for the reprobate. In article 8 God's good pleasure is that which is pleasing in his sight or that in which he delights. It is that which he approves in his creatures, and therefore that which he commands his creatures to do (such as to obey the law and to exercise faith and repentance).

Second, God is serious or in earnest about this. God is not indifferent to sin and unbelief. We must not imagine that God does not care whether people believe or not. Will God send preachers, but remain indifferent as to whether sinners believe in Jesus? Will God remain unconcerned if sinners despise his Son in unbelief? Of course not. God is so serious about this that he threatens eternal damnation upon those who refuse to believe and to repent.

But the word *serio* certainly does *not* mean that God earnestly desires the salvation of all hearers. It cannot mean this because God did not elect all to salvation (in fact, he reprobated many of those who hear the gospel); Christ did not die for all men (in fact, God has nothing to offer the reprobate who hear the gospel, for Christ made no atonement for them); and the Holy Spirit does not work graciously in the hearts of all hearers to regenerate them and work faith in them (in fact, the Spirit hardens many who hear the gospel). Since the triune God does nothing for the salvation of the reprobate—he neither elects, nor redeems, nor regenerates them, but excludes, rejects, and hardens them—how could he, then, in the preaching of the gospel desire (even seriously, ardently, and passionately desire) the salvation of the same reprobate? Such is surely contradiction and confusion.

Moreover, the word "called" in article 8 does not mean invited or offered. There is a difference between an invitation or an offer and a call. If you invite someone, it is because you have a desire that he should come. If you offer something, it is because you have a desire that he receive the thing that you are offering. But a call is different because it does not express the desire of the caller, but it expresses *the obligation of the called*. When God calls, he says, "I *command* you to come. I *insist* that you come. You *must* come. Failure to comply with my command to come will have grave consequences." No one sends gracious invitations in that manner: "Mr. and Mrs. Smith cordially invite you to the marriage of their daughter, Veronica. Failure to come will result in your arrest and subsequent execution. Please RSVP by May 1." The difference in the illustration is between an invitation to a friend's wedding, which is a conditional, take-it-or-leave-it proposition with no serious consequences, and the command of a king, which you spurn at your peril.

Jesus illustrated this serious call of the gospel in the parable of the wedding feast in Matthew 22. In that parable "many are called, but few are chosen" (v. 14). Those who are called are *really* called (or to use the language of the Canons, "unfeignedly called"), for the king is *serious* in the call: "Behold, I have prepared my dinner: my oxen and my fatlings are killed, and all things are ready: come unto the marriage" (v. 4). Not to come to the wedding supper is to despise both the king and his son. Not to come is to anger the king: "When the king heard thereof, he was wroth: and he sent forth his armies, and destroyed those murderers, and burned up their city" (v. 7). Those who were unfeignedly, earnestly, truly, and seriously called were, to use the words of the parable, "not worthy" (v. 8). Therefore, God commanded his servants, "Go ye therefore into the highways, and as many as ye shall find, bid to the marriage" (v. 9). We must remember that there are serious, eternal consequences for those who do not believe the gospel or for those who despise the gospel call (Mark 16:15–16; Acts 13:38–41, 43–48).

Therefore, when God calls all to come to him through the preaching of the gospel, he is serious, truthful, and not hypocritical in his call. God is pleased that those who are called should repent and believe in Jesus Christ. God never rejects those who come to Jesus Christ (John 6:37). Because faith and repentance please God, he is displeased when those who hear the gospel continue in impenitence and unbelief.

However, the one who believes in the well-meant offer *does* make God out to be hypocritical, for God supposedly sincerely offers salvation to all hearers, while he does not have salvation to give. Christ did not die to purchase salvation for all sinners. How then can God offer salvation to all? How can God desire that sinners possess salvation that he did not ordain for them to have and that Jesus did not purchase for them on the cross? In fact, the Holy Spirit is determined *not* to give salvation to the reprobate. How then could God desire their salvation? This is why modern proponents of the well-meant offer are diluting the five points—they do not fit with the "well meant offer" and these proponents know it. Certainly, therefore, this article of the Canons does not fit with their modern well-meant offer theory, despite the fact that the Christian Reformed Church appealed to it in 1924 in support of its doctrine of the well-meant gospel offer.

With the call comes a promise, which we have encountered in head two, article 5. God promises eternal life and rest, and he is *serious* in that promise. But *to whom* does God make that promise in the gospel? God does not promise eternal life and rest to everyone, but "to as many as shall come to Him and believe on Him." In other words, God promises to save believers, or to express it differently, God promises to save the elect.

However, if the preacher declares, "I bring good news! God promises to save the elect," such a declaration, while true, does not identify the elect. Although we cannot name the elect, we can determine the elect from the spiritual characteristics set forth in holy scripture. The Bible does not name the heirs of the promise. Instead, the Bible describes the identifying features of the elect so that the reader or hearer can identify himself as one of the elect—he hungers and thirsts after righteousness; he has a broken and a contrite spirit; and above all he believes in Jesus Christ. We are believers because we are the elect; we are not the elect because we are believers.

Therefore, when the gospel goes forth, the preacher does not announce, "God promises salvation to every one of you" or "God promises to every one of you that, if you believe, you shall be saved." Instead, the preacher announces, "Here is what God has done for sinners in Jesus Christ. God commands you to repent and believe, and God promises—seriously promises—to give eternal life and rest to as many as shall come to Christ and believe on him. Therefore, believe in Jesus Christ, and you, too, shall enjoy rest and peace."

That promise God will surely keep. On that promise you can stake your eternal future.

ARTICLE 9: THE FAULT OF UNBELIEF IN THE GOSPEL

> It is not the fault of the gospel, nor of Christ offered therein, nor of God, who calls men by the gospel and confers upon them various gifts, that those who are called by the ministry of the Word refuse to come and be converted. The fault lies in themselves, some of whom when called, regardless of their danger, reject the Word of life; others, though they receive it, suffer it not to make a lasting impression on their heart; therefore their joy, arising only from a temporary faith, soon vanishes and they fall away; while others choke the seed of the Word by perplexing cares and the pleasures of this world, and produce no fruit. This our Savior teaches in the parable of the sower (Matt. 13).

This article reminds us whose fault it is that the gospel is *not* believed. The Arminians charged the Reformed with teaching that it is God's fault when certain sinners (the reprobate wicked) do not believe. The Arminians argued that (if the Reformed faith is true, which, of course, they denied), it is God's fault that the reprobate do not believe because he did not elect them to salvation; it is God's fault that the reprobate do not believe because Christ did not die to purchase salvation for them; and it is God's fault that the reprobate do not believe because God does not bestow saving faith upon them to enable them to believe. Along the same lines of argumentation as head one, article 5, and head two, article 6, the Canons emphatically deny that any fault can be imputed to God.

First, "it is not the fault of the gospel." It is not the case that the gospel is too deep or too difficult for certain sinners to grasp, so that God has made the gospel inaccessible to the common man. The gospel is good news, simple to grasp for even the simplest believer. A child can understand and believe the gospel, which is the testimony of many believing children and their parents.

Second, it is not the fault of "Christ offered therein." We should take note that the word *offer* has undergone a development in meaning over the centuries. In the days of the Synod of Dordt, the word *offer* commonly meant to present, to display, or to set forth. The modern use of the word *offer* includes the idea of a desire or intention in the one making the offer, as well as a presupposed ability in the one to whom the offer is made. These ideas are foreign to Dordt's meaning of the term. Unbelief is not the fault of Christ, for he is not to blame for the unbelief of the reprobate: he is the perfect savior, and there is no insufficiency in the atonement that he has made (Canons 2.3–4).

Third, it is not the fault "of God," for he calls the sinner, even the reprobate sinner, seriously in the gospel; and he confers upon the sinner "various gifts." These gifts are not saving gifts, nor are they gifts of common grace, but they are various gifts common to the reprobate such as reason, conscience, and discernment. God gives everything to the reprobate except grace. Some sinners come very close to salvation; they even "taste" it, but they do not receive it (Heb. 6:4–6).

Instead of attributing any fault, blame or guilt to God, the Canons place the blame where it belongs: "The fault lies in themselves." This is true for several reasons. First, the unbeliever refuses to come and be converted, for he has a wicked and stubborn heart. Second, the Canons refer to the various soils in the parable of the sower (Matt. 13:3–23). Some "regardless of their danger, reject the Word of life." These kinds of hearers are the "path" of the parable. Others "suffer it not to make a lasting impression on their heart[s]; therefore their joy, arising only from a temporary faith, soon vanishes and they fall away." These are the "stony ground" of the parable. Others "choke the seed of the Word by perplexing cares and the pleasures of this world." These are the "thorny ground" of the parable. These three kinds of hearers have this in common: they "produce no fruit," and they, not God, are responsible for their fruitlessness.

That unbelievers and hypocrites, despite being called by the ministry of the gospel, refuse to come, do not hear aright, and produce no fruit, is entirely their fault. "He that hath ears to hear, let him hear" (11:15).

ARTICLE 10: OBEDIENCE TO THE GOSPEL THROUGH GRACE ALONE

> But that others who are called by the gospel obey the call and are converted is not to be ascribed to the proper exercise of free will, whereby one distinguishes himself above others equally furnished with grace sufficient for faith and conversion, as the proud heresy of Pelagius maintains; but it must be wholly ascribed to God, who as He has chosen His own from eternity in Christ, so He confers upon them faith and repentance, rescues them from the power of darkness, and translates them into the kingdom of His own Son, that they may show forth the praises of Him who hath

> called them out of darkness into His marvelous light, and may glory, not in themselves, but in the Lord, according to the testimony of the apostles in various places.

If the fault of unbelief is the unbeliever's alone, it does not follow, as the Arminians alleged, that the credit for faith is the believer's. In article 9 there were some "called by the ministry of the Word [who] refuse to come and be converted." Now in article 10 the issue is "others who are called by the gospel [and who] obey the call and are converted." Take note that they *obey* the call; one does not obey a gracious invitation or a sincere offer. One obeys a call or a command. This fits with the explanation of the call in article 8.

The Arminians explained the difference between those who come and those who do not come along the following lines. God has furnished all equally with grace sufficient for faith and conversion. With the proper exercise of free will (joined to grace) one man can "[distinguish] himself above others." The Reformed fathers at Dordt dismissed such an error as "the proud heresy of Pelagius."

The Reformed explanation for this difference is to attribute it entirely to God: "It must be wholly ascribed to God." We do not give God partial praise, but we *wholly* ascribe our salvation to God. God has elected some from eternity in Christ. Christ redeemed them, and them only, by his blood on the cross. In time God "confers upon them faith and repentance." The result is that the glory of their salvation is God's alone. Notice the great works of God: "He…rescues them from the power of darkness," something free will is powerless to achieve; and he "translates them into the kingdom of His own Son" (Col. 1:13), something free will could never have accomplished. Therefore, following the apostles, we show forth God's praises and we do not boast in our own abilities. We glory, not in ourselves, but in God (Rom. 4:2; 1 Cor. 1:29–31). That is the very essence of the biblical and Reformed faith, contrary to the proud heresy of Pelagius *and Arminius*.

ARTICLE 11: THE INTERNAL WORKING OF THE SPIRIT IN REGENERATION

> But when God accomplishes His good pleasure in the elect, or works in them true conversion, He not only causes the gospel to be externally preached to them, and powerfully illuminates their minds by His Holy Spirit, that they may rightly understand and discern the things of the Spirit of God; but by the efficacy of the same regenerating Spirit pervades the inmost recesses of the man; He opens the closed and softens the hardened heart, and circumcises that which was uncircumcised, infuses new qualities into the will, which, though heretofore dead, He quickens; from being evil, disobedient, and refractory, He renders it good, obedient, and pliable; actuates and strengthens it, that like a good tree it may bring forth the fruits of good actions.

In articles 11–17 the Canons move from man's depravity to man's conversion or regeneration. At this point, therefore, the synod transitioned from head three to head four.

Man is totally depraved or dead in sin. Therefore, he must receive new life from God. Arminianism teaches either that such a new birth is not necessary, or that it is the work of man, or that it is the work of man cooperating with God's grace.

Article 11 begins with "[God's] good pleasure in the elect." This refers back to article 7, "the sovereign good pleasure and unmerited love of God." God's good pleasure is eternal, but he accomplishes his good pleasure in time in the elect. He does this by doing two things. First, he causes the gospel to be preached to them. The preaching of the gospel is the necessary means of conversion. God does not convert without the gospel, for he does not convert the non-evangelized heathen. Moreover, God is sovereign in the preaching of the gospel, so that the gospel is preached where God pleases.

Second, God powerfully illumines the minds of the elect by

the Holy Spirit. Remember that the mind of man is not merely hindered (as the Arminians alleged), but it is blind and horribly darkened. For example, in Romans 1:21 Paul taught that "their foolish heart was darkened," while in Romans 1:28 Paul referred to the "reprobate mind" of the ungodly (see also 1 Cor. 2:14; Rom. 8:7; Eph. 4:18; Titus 3:3). Powerful illumination is God's work of shining the light of the gospel into the darkened minds of his elect people (2 Cor. 4:3–4, 6), something that free will can neither accomplish nor resist.

The Arminian can agree so far: he agrees that God causes the gospel to be preached and that man's mind needs to be enlightened, but he insists that man's will *must also cooperate* with God's illumination. Man could, according to Arminianism, *resist* the illumination of God and render it ineffectual. This, of course, is absurd. Could the light resist God's creative command, "Let there be light"? (See the parallel between Genesis 1:3 and 2 Corinthians 4:6.) Therefore, to confound the Arminians and make the truth clearer and sharper, the Canons make it even more explicit: "Not only...but [also]."

In addition to the first two mentioned works, God "pervades the inmost recesses of the man." Clearly, the Reformed fathers were describing an internal work of the Holy Spirit. (Arminianism wants to keep God outside until man is willing to open the door, but God is not content to wait outside and to depend on the pleasure of man's will.) To pervade means to penetrate, to enter in, and to spread through. If a little leaven leavens the whole lump by spreading through the whole lump of dough (1 Cor. 5:6; Gal. 5:9), so in a positive way the influence of the Holy Spirit spreads through the whole inner being of man, so that nothing remains unaffected and so that the sinner is truly and radically transformed. The "recesses" of man are his secret and remote places, the places of the heart, mind, and will, which no man can reach. This pervasive action of the Holy Spirit is efficacious, for the Canons speak of "the efficacy of the same regenerating Spirit." The word "efficacy" means that the work achieves its appointed purpose. The Holy Spirit accomplishes in regeneration what God determined to accomplish.

In the inmost recesses of the man, the Holy Spirit performs several wonderworks. First, "he "opens the closed…heart" (Acts 16:14). Second, he "softens the hardened heart" (Ezek. 36:26–27). Third, he "circumcises that which was uncircumcised," which is a figurative expression meaning that he cuts away the sin from the heart (Deut. 30:6; Col. 2:11). Fourth, he "infuses new qualities into the will, which for the Arminian is the most controversial and contested point, for in Arminianism the will of man is *off limits*. To infuse is to put into or to introduce into something as if by pouring, or to cause to be filled with something. Since the Arminian denies that the will of man has any spiritual qualities, for it is strictly neutral (Canons 3–4, error and rejection 2), he denies that God could infuse spiritual qualities into it. Fifth, and finally, he "quickens" the will, which simply means that he makes the ("heretofore dead") will alive. Since the will, which is the faculty of choice, is an integral part of man, which cannot be separated from man, God converts *the whole person* (Acts 11:18; Phil. 2:13; Col. 2:13).

Notice the amazing transformation: a dead will becomes alive; an evil will becomes good; a disobedient will becomes obedient; and a refractory will becomes pliable. If something is refractory it is stubbornly resistant to authority like a horse that will not listen to its master (Ps. 32:9). A pliable will is easily shaped, molded, or influenced. The result of this is that God "actuates and strengthens" the will, or he moves it to action, with the result that a bad tree is made a good tree that bears good fruit (Matt. 12:33).

Believing reader, the fact that you believe in Jesus Christ is testimony to the fact that the Holy Spirit has performed these wonderworks in the deepest recesses of your heart. Without that work, your heart would still be closed, hard, and uncircumcised. Without that work, your will would still be evil, disobedient, refractory, and dead. If left to yourself, your evil will would ruin you. What debtors we are to God's sovereign, efficacious, irresistible grace.

ERROR AND REJECTION 6: NO NEW POWERS INFUSED INTO MAN'S FREE WILL

> Error 6: Who teach that in the true conversion of man no new qualities, powers, or gifts can be infused by God into the will, and that therefore faith, through which we are first converted and because of which we are called believers, is not a quality or gift infused by God, but only an act of man, and that it cannot be said to be a gift, except in respect of the power to attain to this faith.
>
> Rejection: For thereby they contradict the Holy Scriptures, which declare that God infuses new qualities of faith, of obedience, and of the consciousness of His love into our hearts: *I will put my law in their inward parts, and in their hearts will I write it* (Jer. 31:33). And: *I will pour water upon him that is thirsty, and streams upon the dry ground; I will pour my Spirit upon thy seed* (Isa. 44:3). And: *The love of God hath been shed abroad in our hearts through the Holy Spirit which hath been given us* (Rom. 5:5). This is also repugnant to the continuous practice of the church, which prays by the mouth of the prophet thus: *Turn thou me, and I shall be turned* (Jer. 31:18).

In rejection and error 2 the Reformed fathers answered the Arminian contention that good qualities do not belong to the will. Before the fall the will of man was not positively righteous, but morally neutral, claimed the Arminians. Therefore, argued the Arminians, it could not lose any moral qualities in the fall.

This supposed moral neutrality of the human will influenced the Arminian view of conversion as follows. First, no new qualities, powers, or gifts can be infused into the will in conversion. Second, faith is not and cannot be a quality or gift infused by God, but it is the work of man. Faith in Arminianism is *always and only* an act or activity of man. It is the act of man's free will; it is the contribution that man makes to his own salvation; it is the condition that man fulfills. Third, if faith can be called a gift, something that the Arminian does not like to admit, it is only a gift in this sense: God gives the power to attain to this faith, but if man resists God, he does not attain to the gift and believe. In short, according to Arminianism, God in the preaching of the gospel merely removes certain hindrances from the will of man so that he is able to believe of its own power.

The answer of the Canons is that Arminianism contradicts the scriptures, for God does indeed infuse "new qualities of faith, of obedience, and of the consciousness of His love into our hearts," as the passages quoted demonstrate (Isa. 44:3; Jer. 31:18, 33; Rom. 5:5).

ARTICLE 12: THAT REGENERATION SO HIGHLY CELEBRATED IN SCRIPTURE

> And this is the regeneration so highly celebrated in Scripture and denominated a new creation: a resurrection from the dead, a making alive, which God works in us without our aid. But this is in no wise effected merely by the external preaching of the gospel, by moral suasion, or such a mode of operation that after God has performed His part it still remains in the power of man to be regenerated or not, to be converted or to continue unconverted; but it is evidently a supernatural work, most powerful, and at the same time most delightful, astonishing, mysterious, and ineffable; not inferior in efficacy to creation or the resurrection from the dead, as the Scripture inspired by the Author of this work declares; so that all in whose heart God works in this marvelous manner are certainly, infallibly, and effectually regenerated and do actually believe. Whereupon the will thus renewed is not only actuated and influenced

> by God, but in consequence of this influence becomes itself active. Wherefore also, man is himself rightly said to believe and repent by virtue of that grace received.

Article 12 is really the centerpiece of heads three and four, for everything leads up to this magnificent statement on regeneration. Article 12 is not only a statement, a doctrinal explanation, but it is also a doxology, a word of praise to God for his wonderwork of grace. It begins with these words: "And this is the regeneration so highly celebrated in Scripture."

The article sets forth the following truths about regeneration. First, regeneration is the work of God alone: "Which God works in us *without our aid*" (emphasis added). We call that truth concerning our regeneration *monergism* or *monergistic regeneration*, which comes from two Greek words, *mono* (one) and *ergon* (work), the one work being the work of God. Second, scripture likens God's work of regeneration to other great works of God: a new birth (John 3:3–8); a new creation (2 Cor. 5:17); and a resurrection from the dead (Rom. 6:4, 13; 8:11; Eph. 2:1, 5). Since these three works are sovereign works of God in which man has no part, regeneration is also a sovereign work of God in which man plays no part. Man does not perform regeneration, he does not cooperate in regeneration, and he does not contribute to regeneration.

Third, the Canons describe this work both positively and negatively.

Negatively, God does not perform regeneration merely by the preaching: "This is in no wise effected merely by the external preaching of the gospel." God does not perform regeneration by "moral suasion," which is a kind of external persuasion or convincing (Ps. 58:4–5). God does not perform regeneration in such a way that the final decision is left to man: "Or such a mode of operation that after God has performed His part, it still remains in the power of man to be regenerated or not, to be converted or to continue unconverted." This statement is a direct assault on Arminianism, which maintains that God is trying to persuade everyone through the preaching, but that he is not able to convince everyone who hears to believe.

Positively, the work of regeneration is supernatural: "It is evidently a supernatural work." Supernatural means above or beyond nature: regeneration is the birth from heaven, it is birth to a life not of this earth, it is birth to the life of God, and therefore it remains outside the capacity of man to perform this work.

Fourth, because it is supernatural, the Canons pile up adjectives to describe it: "most powerful" (only divine omnipotence can raise the dead); "delightful" (it is sweet, pleasant, and wonderful—no one is forcibly regenerated against his will, but the elect sinner is made willing in the day of God's power); "astonishing"; "mysterious"; and "ineffable" (it cannot be expressed in words).

Of course it is! Can you explain God's work of creation; can you fathom the wonder of God's forming of a child in his mother's womb; can you comprehend the resurrection of the dead? Similarly, we cannot understand the wonder of regeneration—we marvel at it and we worship God because of it, but we cannot *understand* it.

Fifth, regeneration is "not inferior in efficacy to creation or resurrection from the dead." Notice the use of the word "efficacy," for God accomplishes regeneration everywhere he determines to regenerate sinners. He is *never* unsuccessful in regenerating his people. Notice, too, the strong statement on the inspiration of scripture: "As the Scripture inspired by the Author of this work declares."

The conclusion is obvious: "So that all in whose heart God works in this marvelous manner are certainly, infallibly, and effectually regenerated." The result is that they "do actually believe." Regeneration is the infallible cause of faith, and faith is the infallible fruit of regeneration. Without regeneration no man believes. With regeneration no man *fails to* believe (John 1:13; Eph. 1:19; 1 John 5:1). Moreover, by this power of the Holy Spirit the will of man becomes active: the will, declare the Canons, is "renewed," and it is not merely "actuated" and "influenced," but it becomes "active." This activity is faith, so that "man is himself rightly said to believe and repent by virtue of that grace received."

Therefore, we can answer the question, "Do *we* believe or does God believe *for* us?" The answer is that we do believe, but we only believe because God first worked in us to regenerate us, and by virtue of that work of regeneration, which is entirely the work of God, we believe.

Have you believed? Ascribe all the glory to God alone.

ERROR AND REJECTION 9: REGENERATION DEPENDENT ON MAN'S FREE WILL

> Error 9: Who teach that grace and free will are partial causes, which together work the beginning of conversion, and that grace, in order of working, does not precede the working of the will; that is, that God does not efficiently help the will of man unto conversion until the will of man moves and determines to do this.
>
> Rejection: For the ancient church has long ago condemned this doctrine of the Pelagians, according to the words of the apostle: *So then it is not of him that willeth, nor of him that runneth, but of God that hath mercy* (Rom. 9:16). Likewise: *For who maketh thee to differ? and what hast thou that thou didst not receive?* (1 Cor. 4:7). And: *For it is God who worketh in you both to will and to work for his good pleasure* (Phil. 2:13).

Sovereign regeneration is anathema to Arminianism because it is the deathblow to free will. Article 12 praises God for the work of regeneration. It excludes man entirely from regeneration, where he is entirely passive. The Arminians desired to share the glory of salvation—and they sought to claim the largest part of the glory for salvation for themselves.

Arminianism viewed the place of regeneration in salvation in the following way. First, "grace and free will are partial causes." Second, grace is not effectual grace, but advising or prevenient grace given to or offered to everyone. Third, of the two "partial causes" man's free will comes first, while God waits for man's free will to make the first move. If man shows a desire for salvation, God will give him helping grace to enable him to receive salvation, but only if man wills. Therefore, God will only assist the sinner *if he is asked*: "God does not efficiently help the will of man unto conversion until the will of man moves and determines to do this." Notice the weasel words "efficiently help." The Arminians did not believe in efficient help, but in conditional, ineffectual help.

This idea of Arminianism is expressed today in the gentleman analogy. God, we are told, is the perfect gentleman. Therefore, he will not enter our hearts without our permission. Instead, he is content to stand outside our hearts seeking admittance by knocking. A perversion of Revelation 3:20 has made this view popular today. God is the sovereign lord, the almighty creator, and the righteous judge—he is not a gentleman. Besides this, Revelation 3:20 has nothing to do with Christ's standing outside of unbelievers' hearts. In Revelation 3:20 Christ knocks on the door of the church of Laodicea to warn them that they are "wretched, and miserable, and poor, and blind, and naked" (v. 17). A passage which actually speaks about a sinner's heart is Acts 16:14 (notice the absence of the word "heart" in Revelation 3:20), where *God opens the heart* of Lydia.

The Canons respond to Arminianism with the charge of Pelagianism. They have done this before—the Arminian view of election is Pelagianism; the Arminian view of the cross is Pelagianism; and the Arminian view of regeneration is Pelagianism (Rom. 9:16; 1 Cor.

4:7; Phil. 1:6; 2:13; James 1:18). And remember the source of Pelagianism is hell.

ERROR AND REJECTION 7: GOD'S GENTLE ADVISING SUFFICIENT TO PRODUCE CONVERSION

> Error 7: Who teach that the grace whereby we are converted to God is only a gentle advising, or (as others explain it) that this is the noblest manner of working in the conversion of man, and that this manner of working, which consists in advising, is most in harmony with man's nature; and that there is no reason why this advising grace alone should not be sufficient to make the natural man spiritual, indeed, that God does not produce the consent of the will except through this manner of advising; and that the power of the divine working, whereby it surpasses the working of Satan, consists in this, that God promises eternal, while Satan promises only temporal goods.
>
> Rejection: But this is altogether Pelagian and contrary to the whole Scripture which, besides this, teaches yet another and far more powerful and divine manner of the Holy Spirit's working in the conversion of man, as in Ezekiel: *A new heart also will I give you, and a new spirit will I put within you; and I will take away the stony heart out of your flesh, and I will give you a heart of flesh* (Ezek. 36:26).

Biblical grace is effectual and irresistible. In contrast, Arminian "grace" is "a gentle advising." According to Arminianism, the grace of God cannot and may not be effectual, lest the abilities of man should be insulted. Far be it from man that he should be so depraved that only effectual grace can save him. This "gentle advising," as the Arminians understood it, "is most in harmony with man's nature," and therefore it surely should be enough to convert man. This is God's "noblest manner of working in the conversion of man." Notice how the Arminians pretended to praise God's grace while they actively sought to rob God of the power of his grace. This "gentle advising," which depends for its efficacy on the free will of man, is sufficient "to make the natural man spiritual." (Of course, by "natural man" Arminianism did not mean what the Bible teaches in John 3:19 and Romans 8:7.) By means of this "gentle advising" God is able to "produce the consent of the will." Nothing more is needed because man has a morally neutral free will and is not totally depraved.

The Arminians also compared and contrasted God's work with the work of Satan. We might ask the question, "Is God working harder to persuade sinners to believe in Jesus than Satan is working to tempt sinners *not* to believe in Jesus?" The answer of Arminianism is no. God and Satan are both battling for the souls of men, but the final vote or consent belongs to man. What, then, is the difference between God's operation and Satan's operation? Listen to the answer of the Arminians: "The power of the divine working, whereby it surpasses the working of Satan, consists in this, that God promises eternal life, while Satan promises only temporal goods." In other words, God has a better "sales pitch" than Satan—his "offer" is better than Satan's. But his power is not greater than Satan's, or God does not exercise his power more powerfully, effectually, and efficiently than Satan.

The fathers at Dordt responded with another indignant accusation of heresy: "This is altogether Pelagian." Moreover, Arminianism is contrary to scripture, which teaches "another and far more powerful and divine manner of the Holy Spirit's working in the conversion of man" (Ezek. 36:26).

ERROR AND REJECTION 8: REGENERATION REMAINING IN THE POWER OF MAN

> Error 8: Who teach that God in the regeneration of man does not use such powers of His omnipotence as potently and infallibly bend man's will to faith and conversion; but that all the works of grace having been accomplished, which

> God employs to convert man, man may yet so resist God and the Holy Spirit when God intends man's regeneration and wills to regenerate him, and indeed that man often does so resist, that he prevents entirely his regeneration, and that it therefore remains in man's power to be regenerated or not.
>
> Rejection: For this is nothing less than the denial of all the efficiency of God's grace in our conversion, and the subjecting of the working of Almighty God to the will of man, which is contrary to the apostles, who teach: *That we believe according to the working of the strength of his power* (Eph. 1:19). And: *That God fulfills every desire of goodness and every work of faith with power* (2 Thess. 1:11). And: *That his divine power hath given unto us all things that pertain unto life and godliness* (2 Pet. 1:3).

For the Arminian grace is resistible. How can the grace of God be resistible? First, Arminianism claims that God is omnipotent, but that in conversion he does not use the power of his omnipotence: "God in the regeneration of man does not use such powers of His omnipotence as potently and infallibly [to] bend man's will." In other words, God *could* act in his omnipotence, but he chooses not to act in an omnipotent manner. God chooses not to be omnipotent.

Nevertheless, this is impossible, for God's grace is by definition omnipotent, effectual, and irresistible. Whatever impotent, ineffectual, resistible grace is, it is not *divine* grace.

Second, God does not potently and infallibly *bend* man's will to faith and conversion. God, insist the Arminians, respects man's autonomy—and man's free will is off limits even to God.

Third, because God's grace is resistible, God might put forth great effort for the salvation of a sinner, but the outcome is left to man, for man might "resist God and the Holy Spirit." It might be the case that God "intends man's regeneration and wills to regenerate him," but because man does not consent to be regenerated, but instead resists God's attempt at regeneration, man "prevents entirely his regeneration." Since regeneration "remains in man's power," God is sometimes, indeed, often, frustrated in his attempts to regenerate sinners. This is simply the price that God is willing to pay in order to preserve man's autonomy and free will.

John Owen responded to this idea with masterful indignation:

> Take an instance in the great work of our conversion. "All unregenerate men," saith Arminius, "have, by virtue of their free-will, a power of resisting the Holy Spirit, of rejecting the offered grace of God, of contemning the counsel of God concerning themselves, of refusing the gospel of grace, of not opening the heart to him that knocketh." What a stout idol is this, whom neither the Holy Spirit, the grace and counsel of God, the calling of the gospel, the knocking at the door of the heart, can move at all, or in the least measure prevail against him! Woe be unto us, then, if when God calls us our free-will be not in good temper, and well disposed to hearken unto him! for it seems there is no dealing with it by any other ways, though powerful and almighty. "For grant," saith Corvinus, "all the operations of grace which God can use in our conversion, yet conversion remaineth so in our own free power that we can be not converted; that is, we can either turn or not turn ourselves;"—where the idol plainly challengeth the Lord to work his utmost, and tells him that after he hath so done he will do what he please. His infallible prescience, his powerful predetermination, the moral efficacy of the gospel, the infusion of grace, the effectual operation of the Holy Spirit, all are nothing, not at all available in helping or furthering our independent wills in their proceedings. Well, then, in what estate will you have the idol placed?[14]

14 Owen, "A Display of Arminianism" in *The Works of John Owen*, 10:117–18.

The fathers at Dordt objected that Arminianism denies "all the efficiency [efficacy] of God's grace in our conversion." In other words, Arminianism denies God's power, making the Almighty depend on finite creatures. Moreover, Arminianism is "the subjecting of the working of Almighty God to the will of man." This teaching is contrary to the word of God and an insult to the Almighty (Eph. 1:19; 2 Thess. 1:11; 2 Pet. 1:13).

Beware of any teaching that robs God of his power in order to ascribe more power to man's will.

ARTICLE 13: REGENERATION MYSTERIOUS BUT KNOWABLE

> The manner of this operation cannot be fully comprehended by believers in this life. Notwithstanding which, they rest satisfied with knowing and experiencing that by this grace of God they are enabled to believe with the heart, and love their Savior.

Article 13 urges the believer to be careful not to pry into the deep things of God's work of regeneration. We already learned in article 12 that regeneration is supernatural, powerful, delightful, astonishing, mysterious, and ineffable. Therefore, we know a lot about it, but we cannot fully comprehend it. A believer cannot fully comprehend his or her own regeneration—how it happened, when it happened, or why it happened.

The Canons urge Reformed believers to remember that they cannot "fully comprehend" the "manner of this operation," but they can be assured that God has regenerated them. The fathers at Dordt did not want them simply to know something about the doctrine of regeneration, but also to know that *they* are personally regenerated. Again, we see the emphasis of the Reformed faith on comfort and assurance: believers must be, and are, assured of their eternal election; they must be, and are, assured of their redemption in Christ; they must be, and are, assured of their regeneration: and as head five will teach, they must be, and are, assured of their perseverance in true faith.

Believers' limited understanding of their regeneration must not disturb them, however. Instead, it must humble them. And as they are humbled, they must rest assured in this: "By this grace of God they are enabled to believe with the heart and love their Savior." That is the infallible mark of regeneration—to believe from the heart and to love God, which is the infallible fruit of regeneration, which in turn is the infallible fruit of election (Rom. 5:5; 1 John 4:19). Do not look for any further evidence.

Do not allow anyone to lead you into the quagmire of doubt.

Do you believe? Be of good cheer: you are regenerate!

ARTICLE 14: FAITH AS THE GIFT OF GOD

> Faith is therefore to be considered as the gift of God, not on account of its being offered by God to man, to be accepted or rejected at his pleasure, but because it is in reality conferred, breathed, and infused into him; or even because God bestows the power or ability to believe, and then expects that man should by the exercise of his own free will consent to the terms of salvation and actually believe in Christ, but because He who works in man both to will and to do, and indeed all things in all, produces both the will to believe and the act of believing also.

Faith is the gift of God. Because this is a biblical expression (Eph. 2:8; Phil. 1:29), both the Arminians and the Reformed presented their explanation of it.

I begin with the negative. First, faith is not the gift of God in the sense that it is offered to man. By a gift Arminians often mean an offer. An offer can be accepted or rejected, but God does not offer faith to the sinner so that he can accept it or refuse it "at his pleasure." That would make faith, and therefore salvation, dependent on man. The idea is often expressed thus: "God wants you to believe; salvation is free for the taking; God is offering you help to believe, but you must be willing to accept it." However, nothing in scripture teaches that, for a *gift* in the Bible is not an offer, but something that God gives, which the one to whom he gives it therefore possesses.

In his 2012 Christmas message, the then Pope Benedict XVI expressed his views on man's free will, something with which many modern evangelicals would agree:

> "If we believe." Here we see the power of faith! God has done everything; he has done the impossible; he was made flesh. His all-powerful love has accomplished something which surpasses all human understanding: the Infinite has become a child, has entered the human family. *And yet this same God cannot enter my heart unless I open the door to him. Porta fidei!* The door of faith! We could be frightened by this, our inverse omnipotence.[15]

Freewill theology makes man omnipotent with a frightening "inverse omnipotence." God cannot enter a sinner's heart unless "inverse omnipotence," which is the power of the "door of faith," admits him entrance. What blasphemy against the omnipotent God. And yet many evangelicals could say a hearty amen to the former pope's sentiments, although they might be embarrassed if they knew that the words were the pope's. They ought not be surprised, however, for free will is a fundamentally Roman Catholic doctrine, one against which all the reformers resolutely stood.

Second, faith is not the gift of God in the sense that God "bestows the power or ability to believe, and then expects that man should by the exercise of his own free will consent to the terms of

---

15 *Urbi et Orbi* Message of His Holiness Pope Benedict XVI, Christmas 2012, accessed July 2, 2018, http://w2.vatican.va/content/benedict-xvi/en/messages/urbi/documents/hf_ben-xvi_mes_20121225_urbi.html (emphasis added).

salvation and actually believe in Christ." If God bestows the power or ability to believe, the person believes. If God bestows the power or ability to see, the person sees. If God bestows the power or ability to hear, the person hears. If God bestows the power or ability to live, the person lives. The Arminians in an attempt at subterfuge have invented a false dichotomy, as if one might have the power or ability to believe *without actually believing.*

Having cleared away the Arminian lies, the fathers at Dordt presented the truth positively. Faith is "in reality conferred, breathed, and infused into him [man]." If faith is conferred, the sinner believes; if faith is breathed into the sinner, he believes; if faith is infused into the sinner, he believes. And that is exactly the conclusion of the Canons, for God "produces both the will to believe and the act of believing also." Of course that is what God produces, for he is God. The Canons praise God's power, alluding to the scriptures in these words, "He who works in man both to will and to do, and indeed all things in all," performs this supernatural, powerful, delightful, astonishing, mysterious, ineffable, and marvelous work (1 Cor. 12:6; Phil. 2:13).

ARTICLE 15: GOD'S FREEDOM IN THE GIFT OF REGENERATION

> God is under no obligation to confer this grace upon any; for how can He be indebted to man, who had no previous gifts to bestow, as a foundation for such recompense? Nay, who has nothing of his own but sin and falsehood? He therefore who becomes the subject of this grace owes eternal gratitude to God, and gives Him thanks forever. Whoever is not made partaker thereof is either altogether regardless of these spiritual gifts and satisfied with his own condition, or is in no apprehension of danger and vainly boasts the possession of that which he has not. With respect to those who make an external profession of faith and live regular lives, we are bound, after the example of the

> apostle, to judge and speak of them in the most favorable manner. For the secret recesses of the heart are unknown to us. And as to others, who have not yet been called, it is our duty to pray for them to God, who calls the things that are not as if they were. But we are in no wise to conduct ourselves towards them with haughtiness, as if we had made ourselves to differ.

God's salvation is entirely gracious, for God is under no obligation to confer this grace upon anyone. God is, therefore, under no obligation to elect anyone, to redeem anyone, or to regenerate anyone. This is because God is sovereign and never indebted to the creature, as if God could ever *owe* the creature anything. By his sins, which are his demerits, man has forfeited everything. Even in his state of innocence before the fall, Adam was entitled to nothing. How much more is this not true for totally depraved man? Man has nothing of his own except "sin and falsehood." Man does not even have any desire or inclination toward God. Total depravity means that the sinner deserves only God's wrath, not his grace, for grace can never be deserved or merited. Since all men plunged into misery by their own fault in their first father Adam, God is not obligated to rescue them. If he chooses to rescue some, we praise his grace. If he chooses not to rescue others, we recognize his justice. Therefore, if you have received this grace, your attitude must be thanksgiving: "He therefore who becomes the subject of this grace owes eternal gratitude to God, and gives Him thanks forever."

The article then addresses those who are *not* partakers of this grace. There are two kinds of unbelievers mentioned in this article. First, there are the careless and profane, or the self-satisfied sinners. They do not care or they are "altogether regardless of these spiritual gifts." It is important to remember that there is no unregenerate sinner who desires to be regenerated. A broken and contrite spirit, and a hungering and thirsting after righteousness are marks of regeneration, not natural qualities in sinful man (Canons 3–4, error and rejection 4; Ps. 51:17; Matt. 5:6). Unregenerate sinners are satisfied to remain totally depraved and unregenerate, for sinners are willfully and wickedly sinful and rebellious (John 3:19). Second, there are the hypocrites. Such a hypocrite "is in no apprehension of danger and vainly boasts the possession of that which he has not." Such sinners claim to be believers and might even appear to others to be believers, but they do not truly believe.

The Canons give valuable pastoral instruction concerning how to view others in the church. We must adopt a certain charitable attitude toward professing Christians and church members. We do not know their hearts. Therefore, we judge them by their confession and walk. If they make an external profession of faith (they confess orthodox Christianity) and if they lead "regular lives" (lives free from obvious, gross, public sins, for example), we must "judge and speak of them in the most favorable manner" (Heb. 6:9).

The believer's attitude to unbelievers, however, must be as follows. First, he sees them as "not yet...called," that is, not yet effectually called. Second, his duty is to pray for them, for God can perform in any sinner the miracle of regeneration (Rom. 4:17). Third, he must not conduct himself with haughtiness, pride or arrogance, as if he had made himself to differ (1 Cor. 1:26–29; 4:7).

Believing reader, how would your unbelieving colleagues at work, your fellow students at school, your unbelieving family members, and the people of your neighborhood describe you—as *humble* or *haughty*? What attitude do your words and actions communicate—humility or haughtiness? Remember what Paul wrote about Christian love, "Charity vaunteth not itself, is not puffed up" (1 Cor. 13:4). To be "puffed up" is to have an over-inflated sense of one's own importance. To vaunt oneself is to *show* by one's speech and behavior that one has an over-inflated sense of one's own importance. The believer, understanding that even his faith is a gift of God and therefore that he did not make himself to differ from his unbelieving neighbor, is not haughty but humble.

ARTICLE 16: GOD'S OPERATION NOT UPON STOCKS OR BLOCKS

> But as man by the fall did not cease to be a creature endowed with understanding and will, nor did sin which pervaded the whole race of mankind deprive him of the human nature, but brought upon him depravity and spiritual death; so also this grace of regeneration does not treat men as senseless stocks and blocks, nor takes away their will and its properties, neither does violence thereto; but spiritually quickens, heals, corrects, and at the same time sweetly and powerfully bends it; that where carnal rebellion and resistance formerly prevailed, a ready and sincere spiritual obedience begins to reign, in which the true and spiritual restoration and freedom of our will consist. Wherefore, unless the admirable Author of every good work wrought in us, man could have no hope of recovering from his fall by his own free will, by the abuse of which, in a state of innocence, he plunged himself into ruin.

Article 16 is an answer to the Arminian objection to irresistible grace: "You make man a senseless stock or block." A stock is a stick, while a block is a lump of lifeless wood. The modern equivalent to this objection is to claim that the Reformed faith makes man a puppet or a robot. This article explains what man's will is and how God acts upon man's will without taking away its properties.

First, God created man as a rational, moral creature with understanding and will. As a human being he is rational and he has the faculty of choice, which never changes, even when he falls from the state of innocence in which he was originally created. Never is a human being a beast or a devil. Whether created in righteousness, fallen into sin, damned in hell, or glorified in heaven, he remains a human being with understanding, heart, will, and affections. He never becomes anything else. Second, man did not lose his humanity when he fell into sin and when he became totally depraved. Instead, the fall affected man morally or ethically, for now his heart, mind, understanding, affections, and will, although they are still fully human, are corrupted and the whole man is totally depraved. The Canons express it thus: "Man by the fall did not cease to be a creature endowed with understanding and will." Sin did not "deprive him of the human nature." The effects of sin are severe, but they did not rob him of his essential humanity—he was created as human; he fell as human; he is punished as human; and if God saves him, he is saved as human. Sin, however, "pervaded the whole race of mankind" and "brought upon him depravity and spiritual death," so that man is totally and actively, but humanly, evil, loving darkness rather than light, actively pursuing evil, and actively eschewing the good (Job 15:16; John 3:19; 8:44; Eph. 4:19).

This principle according to which sin does not change the essential humanity of man, although it renders him depraved, is applied to the truth of regeneration. When God regenerates a man, he does not rob him of his essential humanity either, for in regeneration man remains a rational, moral creature who retains his human understanding, heart, mind, affections, and will. Notice how the Reformed fathers at Dordt expressed this truth. First, "this grace of regeneration does not treat men as senseless stocks and blocks." Second, regeneration does not take "away [man's] will or its properties." Third, regeneration does not "[do] violence" to man's will.

The truth can be expressed this way: God regenerates *without* our will, but not *against* our will. Man does not ask God to regenerate him, because he is unaware of his need for regeneration and loves the darkness of his unregenerate state (John 3:19–20). But when God does regenerate him, by working graciously and miraculously in the deepest recesses of his heart, God causes the regenerated sinner to become conscious of the marvelous grace of regeneration. He knows that he has been born again, he knows that he has been resurrected from spiritual death, and he knows that he has become a new creature—and he is thankful for it. We do not ask for regeneration, nor are we active in it, but having been regenerated or born again we do become active, so that we "believe and repent by virtue of that grace received" (Canons 3–4.12).

What then does God do to the will in regeneration if he does not take away man's will, take away the will's properties, or do violence to the will? First, he "spiritually quickens" it, so that man's will that was dead becomes alive unto God. Second, he "heals" the will. Third, he "sweetly and powerfully bends" the will—who but God could be *sweet* in the exercise of his *power*. No wonder the psalmist could write, "Thy people shall be willing in the day of thy power" (Ps. 110:3), or that Paul could write, "It is God that worketh in you both to will and to do of his good pleasure" (Phil. 2:13).

The effect of this sweet, powerful, healing, and quickening operation of God in which he bends the will is the spiritual transformation of man's will. Before regeneration took place "carnal rebellion and resistance formerly prevailed." Without regeneration man rebels against God and resists his will, for he is "not subject to the law of God, neither indeed can be" (Rom. 8:7). After regeneration takes place "a ready and sincere spiritual obedience begins to reign." The regenerate man sincerely desires, by virtue of his healed, renewed, and quickened will, to obey God from the heart and to serve the Savior who has loved him.

The Canons call this not man's natural, fallen state, but regeneration, which brings about "the true and spiritual restoration and freedom of our will." Freedom is not the ability to do whatever you want, but it is freedom to do *what is good*. To be a slave to sinful lusts and pleasures is the very opposite of freedom, but it is the worst form of bondage. Therefore, the natural man is not free, but he is the worst kind of slave (John 8:34; Eph. 2:3; Titus 3:3). Only the regenerate Christian is free in mind, heart, and will to serve the God of heaven (John 8:34–36; Rom. 6:16–23).

The conclusion of the article is clear—regeneration is the only hope for man. Man was in a state of innocence, but "he plunged himself into ruin." Out of that ruin man has "no hope of recovering [himself]." Therefore, "unless the admirable Author of every good work wrought in us," man would have no hope of salvation.

Believers conclude by admiring the Author of their regeneration and by repudiating the proud error of Arminian freewill theology.

ARTICLE 17: SOVEREIGN CONVERSION NOT PRECLUDING MEANS

> As the almighty operation of God whereby He prolongs and supports this our natural life does not exclude, but requires, the use of means, by which God of His infinite mercy and goodness hath chosen to exert His influence, so also the before mentioned supernatural operation of God by which we are regenerated in no wise excludes or subverts the use of the gospel, which the most wise God has ordained to be the seed of regeneration and food of the soul. Wherefore, as the apostles and teachers who succeeded them piously instructed the people concerning this grace of God, to His glory, and the abasement of all pride, and in the meantime, however, neglected not to keep them by the sacred precepts of the gospel in the exercise of the Word, sacraments, and discipline; so, even to this day, be it far from either instructors or instructed to presume to tempt God in the church by separating what He of His good pleasure hath most intimately joined together. For grace is conferred by means of admonitions; and the more readily we perform our duty, the more eminent usually is this blessing of God working in us, and the more directly is His work advanced; to whom alone all the glory, both

of means and of their saving fruit and efficacy, is forever due. Amen.

This final article answers the very commonly repeated accusation that if God is sovereign in salvation and particularly in regeneration preaching is pointless and unnecessary. The simple response to this accusation is that God uses means both in the physical and the spiritual realm.

The article begins with an illustration from earthly life. God "prolongs and supports this our natural life" not without means, but with means. God's omnipotent providence upholds us (Heb. 1:3), so that he provides us with the air that we breathe, the water that we drink, the food that we eat, and with everything else necessary to life. Moreover, he powerfully works through such means to preserve our lives. The maintenance of our lives "does not exclude, but requires, the use of means." God "of His infinite mercy and goodness hath chosen to exert His influence" through these means. No one would be so foolish as to neglect or reject these means and then expect to live in this world. Although God can dispense with these means when it pleases him to do so, when he performs miracles, for example, his ordinary mode of operation is to keep us alive through air, water, food, and shelter. Therefore, we trust our heavenly Father to give us these things (Matt. 6:25–34).

This principle also applies to our spiritual life: the regenerating power of God, which has been described in the previous articles, "in no wise excludes or subverts the use of the gospel." Sovereign, efficacious, monergistic regeneration does not overthrow, destroy, or undermine the need for the preaching of the gospel. In the wisdom of God, he has determined that the preaching of the gospel should be the means by which he accomplishes salvation. The Canons call it "the seed of regeneration and food of the soul" (Isa. 55:10–11; Rom. 10:13–15; 1 Cor. 1:21; James 1:18; 1 Pet. 1:23–25; 2:2).

This is nothing new or novel invented by the Reformed fathers but has always been the practice of the true church: "The Apostles, and teachers who succeeded them, piously instructed the people concerning this grace of God." They did so and still do so to the glory of God and abasement of all pride. The goal and effect of faithful preaching are not to entertain, to tickle ears, to flatter, or to promote self-esteem, but to glorify God and to humble man in the dust before his Creator, and then to quicken and comfort God's children. Arminianism cuts the throat of humility, exalts the powers of man, and robs God of his glory in the work of salvation. Moreover, the same apostles and teachers "neglected not to keep them by the sacred precepts of the gospel, in the exercise of the Word, sacraments and discipline." The sovereignty of God in regeneration does not exclude the use of biblical instruction, the administration of the sacraments, or the exercise of Christian discipline, which are not only the means God uses to gather and build up the church, but also the marks of the true church (Belgic Confession 29).

Therefore, the fathers at Dordt warned against the grievous sin of tempting God. To tempt God, which was the heart of Satan's second temptation of Jesus in the wilderness (Matt. 4:5–7), is to ask God to do what he has revealed that he is *not* pleased to do. We tempt God when we expect him to work without means. Recklessly to endanger your life is to tempt God. Deliberately to trifle with sin is to tempt God. To neglect the instruction of your children is to tempt God. To forsake the true church and live separately from the means of grace is to tempt God. That is not faith—it is presumption. Article 17 warns that it would be tempting God to separate what God "of his good pleasure hath most intimately joined together." Can God save without means? Yes, theoretically and viewed abstractly, he can. Has God revealed that he is pleased to do so? No he has not, and it would be foolish presumption and a wicked tempting of God to expect him to do so.

The article ends with a beautiful explanation of the working of the grace of God. First, "grace is conferred by means of admonitions." God gives power to obey (his grace) by the command itself (admonition). God works faith through the call to faith. God works repentance through the call to repentance. God works sorrow for sin through warnings against sin. God preserves his people in holiness through commands to be holy. God preserves his people through warnings and threatenings (1 Tim. 4:13–16).

Second, "the more readily we perform our duty, the more eminent usually is this blessing of God working in us." This is not the condition that sinners must fulfill in order to have God's grace work in them, for there are no conditions to grace. Rather, God blesses *in the way of diligence*. God does not bless apathy, laziness, carelessness, or disobedience. God blesses obedience, diligence, prayerful study, and the use of means, both in preachers and in hearers. Remember the admonition of head one, article 16: "[They ought] diligently to persevere in the use of means, and with ardent desires devoutly and humbly to wait for a season of richer grace."

In this way the conclusion of article 17 is apt: "To whom alone all the glory, both of means and of their saving fruit and efficacy, is forever due. Amen."

Discussion questions on the third and fourth heads

1. Read independently of the rest of the Remonstrance, head three of the Arminian statement seems perfectly orthodox. Explain.
2. Resistible grace is the hallmark of Arminianism. What is it?
3. If grace is irresistible, how could Stephen accuse the Jews of resisting the Holy Spirit (Acts 7:51)?
4. Does God sincerely desire to save everyone, including the reprobate? Explain.
5. Why did Dordt in heads three and four not begin with a defense of the irresistibility of grace? Which doctrines should be explained first?
6. By means of irresistible grace, God drags unbelievers against their will to Christ. True or false? Explain your answer.
7. Why is a proper understanding of the biblical doctrine of man necessary before the subject of free will can be discussed?
8. How would you define the doctrine of free will? When Reformed believers reject the idea of free will, what exactly are they rejecting?
9. A horse is neither an image bearer, nor does it possess God's image. A man is an image bearer, and he can possess the image of God, although not all men do possess the image. Explain.
10. According to Abraham Kuyper, Adam would have become totally depraved, except for God's gift of common grace which provided an antidote to total depravity. True or false? Explain your answer.
11. Show from Genesis 3 how the fall into sin immediately affected Adam's relationship to his wife, to Satan, to God, and to the creation.

12. How does Adam's transgression affect us? Prove this using Romans 5.

13. What is the difference between Pelagianism and semi-Pelagianism?

14. Is it possible for an unregenerate sinner to hunger and thirst after righteousness? Explain.

15. What activities are possible for sinners who possess "the glimmerings of natural light" (Canons 3–4.4)?

16. What activities are impossible for sinners who possess "the glimmerings of natural light"?

17. If an unbeliever helps an old lady to cross the street, does he perform a good work? How does such a work fit with the truth of total depravity? Explain.

18. If the unbeliever robbed the old lady instead, how would God evaluate that work? Explain.

19. What does it mean for an unbeliever wholly to pollute natural light? How does Romans 1 explain this?

20. Do you believe that the "nice unbelievers" around you are totally depraved? How does the realization of this truth of total depravity affect your behavior with respect to your unbelieving neighbors?

21. Why is the preaching of the gospel *necessary* for the conversion and salvation of sinners?

22. How is the preaching of the gospel despised or neglected? Do you despise or neglect the preaching of the gospel? What are the implications of this for church membership?

23. What does it mean curiously to pry into God's judgments (Canons 3–4.7)? Why do the Canons warn against this?

24. What is hyper-Calvinism? Is hyper-Calvinism a threat to Reformed churches? Is it a threat to you? Discuss.

25. In what sense are all who hear the gospel preached "unfeignedly called" (Canons 3–4.8)? How do (a) the Arminian and (b) the hyper-Calvinist understand this?

26. What is the difference between the offer of the gospel and the call of the gospel?

27. Is God indifferent to the response of those who hear the gospel of his Son? Explain.

28. According to Canons 3–4.9, Christ is "offered" in the gospel. Explain.

29. The unbeliever is able to *refuse* to come to Christ, but he is unable to *choose* to come. Explain.

30. How would you answer the common Arminian presentation of Jesus' knocking on the unbeliever's heart, a presentation supposedly based upon Revelation 3:20?

31. How can regeneration be both powerful and delightful (Canons 3–4.12)?

32. The scriptures compare God's work of regeneration to which other powerful divine works?

33. All those whom God regenerates actually believe. True or false?

34. God desires to regenerate some who do *not* believe. True or false?

35. Do believers believe in Jesus or does God believe for them? Explain your answer.

36. Why would a "gentle advising" of God not accomplish the regeneration of a sinner?

37. Is it possible for God to act without using the powers of his omnipotence? Explain.

38. Is it possible for a believer to *know* that he is regenerate? How? Why is this important?

39. Is it possible for a reprobate ungodly person to *want* to repent and believe, but to be rejected because he is not elect? Explain Hebrews 12:17.

40. How in our communication and attitude do we appear haughty to others? What steps can we take to avoid appearing haughty to others? How does the truth of God destroy our pride and make our haughtiness inexcusable?

41. "The Reformed faith makes man a robot." What is your answer to this common Arminian objection?

42. God regenerates *without* our will, but not *against* our will. True or false? Discuss.

43. Why is it to tempt God to attempt to separate God's work of conversion from his use of means? How are you tempted to tempt God in this regard?

44. "Grace is conferred by means of admonitions" (Canons 3–4.17). Discuss.

Proof texts for the third and fourth heads

Genesis 6:5
Genesis 8:21
Job 15:16
Psalm 14:2–3
Psalm 51:5
Psalm 58:3–5
Psalm 110:3
Isaiah 1:6
Jeremiah 4:22
Jeremiah 13:23
Jeremiah 17:9
Jeremiah 31:33–34
Jeremiah 32:39–40
Ezekiel 36:25–27
Matthew 12:33
Matthew 15:18–20
John 1:12–13
John 3:3, 19–21
John 6:44, 65
John 8:34
Acts 11:18
Acts 16:14
Romans 1:28–32
Romans 3:9–20
Romans 5:12–19
Romans 6:16–20
Romans 8:5–8
Romans 9:16
1 Corinthians 2:14
1 Corinthians 4:7
2 Corinthians 4:3–4
2 Corinthians 5:17
Galatians 3:10
Galatians 5:19–23
Ephesians 1:19
Ephesians 2:1–10
Ephesians 4:17–20
Philippians 1:29
Philippians 2:12–13
Colossians 1:21–22
Colossians 2:13
Colossians 3:5–10
2 Timothy 2:24–26
Titus 1:15–16
Titus 3:3–7
James 1:18
1 John 3:7–9
1 John 5:1

The Fifth Head of Doctrine of the Perseverance of the Saints

INTRODUCTION

The Canons touched on the perseverance of the saints in heads one and two, but head five is the most detailed treatment of this important subject. "This elect number...God hath decreed to give to Christ, to be saved by Him...and having powerfully preserved them in the fellowship of His Son, finally to glorify them" (Canons 1.7). "It was the will of God that Christ...should effectually redeem... and, having faithfully preserved them even to the end, should at last bring them free from every spot and blemish to the enjoyment of glory in His own presence forever" (Canons 2.8).

This doctrine has different names: the perseverance of the saints, a name that emphasizes the truth that the saints come to heaven in the way of enduring to the end; the preservation of the saints, a name that emphasizes God's power in keeping the saints; eternal security, a name that emphasizes that the saints are perfectly and forever safe in God's hands; and once saved; always saved, a name that I do not prefer because it is favored by antinomians, for it omits the word "saints."

Arminianism teaches conditional salvation, conditional election, conditional redemption, conditional regeneration, and, you should not be surprised, conditional perseverance. The fifth point of the Remonstrance states:

> That those who are incorporated into Christ by a true faith, and have thereby become partakers of his life-giving Spirit, have thereby full power to strive against Satan, sin, the world, and their own flesh, and to win the victory, it being well understood that it is ever through the assisting grace of the Holy Ghost; and that Jesus Christ assists them through his Spirit in all temptations, extends to them his hand, and if only they are ready for the conflict, and desire his help, and are not inactive, keeps them from falling, so that they, by no craft or power of Satan, can be misled, nor plucked out of Christ's hands, according to the Word of Christ, John x.28: "Neither shall any man pluck them out of my hand." But whether they are capable, through negligence, of forsaking again the first beginnings of their life in Christ, of again returning to this present evil world, of turning away from the holy doctrine which was delivered them, of losing a good conscience, of becoming devoid of grace, that must be more particularly determined out of the Holy Scriptures, before we ourselves can teach it with the full persuasion of our minds.[1]

Notice several things about this statement. First, there is full power for every Christian to persevere in true faith to the end. Second, God is ready and willing to give his assisting grace to anyone who desires it. Third, whether God gives his grace and whether that grace is effectual in preserving anyone depends on the exercise of man's free will: "If only they are ready for the conflict, and desire his help, and are not inactive." Lastly, in 1610 the Arminians were not yet ready to commit to the possibility of the perishing of true believers. However, by the time of the Synod of Dordt, the Arminians *were*

---

1 Five Arminian Articles 5, in Schaff, *Creeds of Christendom,* 3:548–49.

committed to the teaching of the falling away of true saints into perdition.

Before studying the articles of the fifth head, I will make some general remarks about perseverance. First, the doctrine is called the perseverance or preservation *of the saints*, not of hypocrites, false professors, or ungodly sinners. Therefore, God preserves his people in holiness, not in sin; and they persevere in holiness and obedience, not in sin, disobedience, and depravity. Second, your definition of saint will determine your understanding of perseverance. A saint in the Bible is a holy one, a person set apart or separated to God, and in the Bible all of God's people, even the weakest of believers, are saints. A saint did not make himself holy, but God made of a sinner a saint, which is a work that he will bring to completion (Phil. 1:6). Holiness is decreed in election (Eph. 1:4), purchased at the cross (5:25–26), that to which believers are called (1 Thess. 4:7; 2 Tim. 1:9), and the fruit of Christ's intercession (John 17:17). Third, from the believer's point of view perseverance is not only unlikely, but it is also impossible, for the devil is too powerful, the world is too alluring, and the flesh is too deceitful, so that the believer must (if left to himself) perish:

> Which is the sixth petition?
>
> *And lead us not into temptation, but deliver us from evil*; that is, since we are so weak in ourselves that we cannot stand a moment; and besides this, since our mortal enemies, the devil, the world, and our own flesh cease not to assault us, do Thou therefore preserve and strengthen us by the power of Thy Holy Spirit, that we may not be overcome in this spiritual warfare, but constantly and strenuously may resist our foes, till at last we obtain a complete victory.[2]

2 Heidelberg Catechism Q&A 127, in *Confessions and Church Order*, 139.

However, the power of perseverance is in God, which makes perseverance not only likely, possible, or probable, but *certain* (John 10:28; 1 Pet. 1:5). Fourth, God uses means to preserve his people: he does not bring them to heaven except through struggles, trials, temptations, and a lot of stumbling. It is a miracle of grace that God's people persevere: "The steps of a good man are ordered by the Lord: and he delighteth in his way. Though he fall, he shall not be utterly cast down: for the Lord upholdeth him with his hand" (Ps. 37:23–24).

However, Arminianism sees it very differently. You make yourself a saint. You keep yourself in salvation. God is willing to help you. Nevertheless, salvation depends upon you. What a God-dishonoring and terrifying doctrine.

ARTICLE 1: SAINTS REGENERATED BUT NOT PERFECTLY SANCTIFIED

> Whom God calls, according to His purpose, to the communion of His Son, our Lord Jesus Christ, and regenerates by the Holy Spirit He delivers also from the dominion and slavery of sin in this life; though not altogether from the body of sin, and from the infirmities of the flesh, so long as they continue in this world.

Head five begins with a description of the believer as he lives in the midst of this world. It describes the believer as a saint who still struggles with the presence of sin. This is the saint who will persevere. This is the saint whom God will preserve.

Notice how the Canons describe the saints. First, they are called according to his purpose, which is God's sovereign purpose in election, redemption, and regeneration. The fifth head presupposes the previous heads of doctrine (Rom. 8:28–30; 9:11). Second, they are called "to the communion of His Son," which is fellowship and union with Christ, so that they share in all of the benefits that he purchased for them on the cross (1 Cor. 1:9; 1 Pet. 5:10; 1 John 1:3). Third, they are regenerated by the Holy Spirit (John 3:3). These privileges are only for the elect, redeemed children of God. Not all those who *claim* to be Christians possess these blessings. Hypocrites and false professors who are mixed in with believers in the church, but who are not in view here, are devoid of such graces: "We speak here not of hypocrites, who are mixed in the church with the good, yet are not of the church, though externally in it."[3]

By virtue of regeneration, we enjoy certain privileges. God delivers us from sin; from the guilt of sin, for Christ was punished in our place (1 Pet. 2:24); from the curse of the law, for Christ was made a curse for us (Gal. 3:13); from the pollution of sin, for Christ has washed us in his own blood (1 John 1:7; Rev. 1:5); and even from the dominion, power, bondage, or slavery of sin, for Christ's death has redeemed us from the devil who kept us in the chains of corruption (John 8:34–36; Titus 2:14).

Salvation is emphatically deliverance *from* sin, and not merely deliverance from the consequences of sin. Salvation is not deliverance *in* sin, but deliverance *from* sin, which is true blessedness. In the Christian's life sin no longer rules, for it no longer has dominion over him:

11. Likewise reckon ye also yourselves to be dead indeed unto sin, but alive unto God through Jesus Christ our Lord.
12. Let not sin therefore reign in your mortal body, that ye should obey it in the lusts thereof.
13. Neither yield ye your members as instruments of unrighteousness unto sin: but yield yourselves unto God, as those that are alive from the dead, and your members as instruments of righteousness unto God.

3 Belgic Confession 29, in ibid., 62.

14. For sin shall not have dominion over you: for ye are not under the law, but under grace.
15. What then? shall we sin, because we are not under the law, but under grace? God forbid.
16. Know ye not, that to whom ye yield yourselves servants to obey, his servants ye are to whom ye obey; whether of sin unto death, or of obedience unto righteousness?
17. But God be thanked, that ye were the servants of sin, but ye have obeyed from the heart that form of doctrine which was delivered you.
18. Being then made free from sin, ye became the servants of righteousness. (Rom. 6:11–18)

The Canons add a *but* or a "though": "Though not altogether from the body of sin, and from the infirmities of the flesh." The flesh, the old man, the sinful nature, the body of sin, or the body of death is the corrupt, depraved, fallen nature of man, which remains with saints throughout their whole lives (Rom. 6:6; 7:24; Gal. 5:17). The Canons will develop this idea in article 3.

Article 1, therefore, refutes two fundamental errors.

First, it refutes antinomianism, which is the denial of sanctification. Although antinomians come in different forms, the basic error of antinomianism is the denial that saints are delivered *from the dominion of sin.* An antinomian confesses that he is delivered from the guilt of sin, but he either denies, is reluctant to confess, or downplays the truth of deliverance from the pollution, power, and dominion of sin. Many antinomians, therefore, expect to go to heaven, confessing (they say) salvation by grace alone, while they continue to live in wickedness, in carnality, and in rebellion against God. The Reformed faith has always sharply repudiated antinomianism (Heidelberg Catechism Q&A 43, 64, 70, 86–87).

Second, article 1 refutes perfectionism, which is the denial that the Christian after regeneration retains a sinful flesh or that he must struggle against the flesh. Usually, the perfectionist claims a special work of God's grace in which the Holy Spirit suddenly grants complete deliverance from sin in this life. John Wesley, the aforementioned founder of Methodism, taught the error of perfectionism, and some of his followers even claimed to be perfect. Today, certain charismatic groups, often with the name holiness in their titles, teach perfectionism, which they claim to attain through a "second blessing" experience. The Reformed confessions vehemently repudiate perfectionism (Heidelberg Catechism Q&A 88–91, 114–15, 127; Belgic Confession 15, 24), as does the word of God in 1 John 1:8–10.

It is not the antinomian or the perfectionist who is the subject of preservation in sanctification, but it is the biblical Christian, the imperfect saint. It is for this reason that the grace of God is necessary.

ARTICLE 2: THE SAINT'S DAILY SINS OF INFIRMITY

> Hence spring daily sins of infirmity, and hence spots adhere to the best works of the saints, which furnish them with constant matter for humiliation before God and flying for refuge to Christ crucified; for mortifying the flesh more and more by the spirit of prayer and by holy exercises of piety; and for pressing forward to the goal of perfection, till being at length delivered from this body of death they are brought to reign with the Lamb of God in heaven.

The presence of the flesh or the old man in the Christian explains his sins and imperfections. The Canons highlight two kinds of sins that issue from the corruption of the Christian's flesh: "Hence spring daily sins of infirmity, and hence spots adhere to the best works of the saints." These daily sins and spots are contrasted with the "great and heinous sins" described in article 4, for such great and heinous sins do not "spring daily" from God's children. Christians do not daily commit murder, adultery, and armed robbery, for example. Such sins are great and heinous. Nevertheless, Christians commit many sins, which the Canons classify as "infirmit[ies]." This does not excuse those sins, of course, for all sins are serious in the sight of God. In addition, the Christian performs genuine good works, which, however, are never perfect works. "Spots" or stains or imperfections adhere to "the best works of the saints." Pride, selfishness, lack of love for God and the neighbor, envy, and vanity spoil the holiest activities of Christians. The fathers at Dordt understood by experience what the Christian life is like. They were not ivory-tower theologians, but conscientious Christians and compassionate pastors who desired to comfort and instruct the struggling people of God.

Infirmities and spots are a reality in the Christian life. What, then, is the attitude of God's saints to indwelling sin and corruption? It is not carnal security or a love of sin. The saint has a very different attitude to sin from that of the ungodly world. The reality of indwelling sin gives God's saints good reason for certain spiritual activities: for humiliation before God; for flying for refuge to Christ crucified; for mortifying the flesh more and more by the spirit of prayer and holy exercises of piety; and for pressing forward to the goal of perfection. This is the genuine Christian life—sorrow over sin, humility, gratitude for grace, faith in Jesus Christ, prayer, the use of the ordinary means of grace, and holy struggles with the flesh.

The synod simply restated the teaching of the Belgic Confession:

> Sin always issues forth from this woeful source, as water from a fountain; notwithstanding, it is not imputed to the children of God unto condemnation, but by His grace and mercy is forgiven them. Not that they should rest securely in sin, but that *a sense of this corruption should make believers often to sigh*, desiring to be delivered from this body of death.[4]

Notice where godly sorrow leads the saint, the one who struggles with infirmities and "spots." Godly sorrow does not lead the

4 Belgic Confession 15, in ibid., 41 (emphasis added).

saints to despair, but to the cross of Christ: "Which [infirmities and spots] furnish them with constant matter for...flying for refuge to Christ crucified." Happy is the man whom sin leads to the cross, for at the cross he will find pardon for all of his transgressions.

This struggle will continue until the saints are at last delivered from this body of death (Rom. 7:24–25) and until they are at last brought to reign with the Lamb of God in heaven (2 Tim. 2:11–13). There are here no empty promises of an easy life, but the prospect of "daily" struggles against sin and "constant matter for humiliation." Nevertheless, there is also set before the saints the assurance of final victory and salvation.

Do you know such struggles, believing reader? Take courage: these are the struggles of the Spirit against the flesh within you. Are you a stranger to these things? There is every reason to fear that you are still dead in your sins.

ARTICLE 3: PERSEVERANCE IMPOSSIBLE IN THE SINNER'S STRENGTH

> By reason of these remains of indwelling sin, and the temptations of sin and of the world, those who are converted could not persevere in a state of grace if left to their own strength. But God is faithful, who, having conferred grace, mercifully confirms and powerfully preserves them therein, even to the end.

Having carefully explained from the scriptures the reality of the condition of the converted saint, the Canons draw a conclusion. If the Christian is still imperfect, still struggling with sins and infirmities, and still plagued with his sinful flesh, is salvation possible? Is it possible for such an imperfect saint to persevere in godliness and to reach the final victory? The answer is no: "Those who are converted *could not persevere* in a state of grace" (emphasis added).

From the viewpoint of the Christian, salvation is impossible and perseverance is impossible. The enemies of the believer, the remains of indwelling sin, the temptations of sin and of the world (and we could add the devil) are very powerful (Heidelberg Catechism Q&A 127). Sin is very strong in us, which we know from experience (Heb. 12:15; James 1:14); the sin of the world is very alluring (1 John 2:15–16); and the devil is very dangerous (Eph. 6:10–13; 1 Pet. 5:8–9). Therefore, we could not persevere if God left us to our own strength. However, Arminianism teaches that the saints *could* persevere if they wanted to, if they exerted appropriate effort, and if they used the help that God offers to everyone.

It, therefore, seems hopeless, does it not? "Those who are converted could not persevere in a state of grace if left to their own strength." That is the key, of course: "If left to their own strength." Woe to us if God should leave us to our own strength. What sins we are capable of and what follies we commit when we are left to our own strength! "Wherefore let him that thinketh he standeth take heed lest he fall" (1 Cor. 10:12).

Nevertheless, it is not hopeless because of two beautiful words: "But God" But God is faithful. Because he is true to his promises, his people can trust him and rely upon him. From the perspective of God's faithfulness, salvation is certain and guaranteed, for God confers grace in regeneration, and he "mercifully confirms and powerfully preserves" his weak and sinful saints in his grace "even to the end." God does not leave them to their own strength, but he is with them, enabling them to persevere every step of the difficult pilgrimage toward heaven until they arrive at their heavenly home.

ERROR AND REJECTION 1: PERSEVERANCE CONDITIONAL ON MAN'S FREE WILL

> Error 1: Who teach that the perseverance of the true believers is not a fruit of election, or a gift of God gained by the death of Christ, but a condition of the new covenant, which (as they declare) man before his decisive election and justification must fulfill through his free will.

> Rejection: For the Holy Scripture testifies that this follows out of election, and is given the elect in virtue of the death, the resurrection, and intercession of Christ: *But the elect obtained it and the rest were hardened* (Rom. 11:7). Likewise: *He that spared not his own Son, but delivered him up for us all, how shall he not also with him freely give us all things? Who shall lay anything to the charge of God's elect? It is God that justifieth; who is he that condemneth? It is Christ Jesus that died, yea rather, that was raised from the dead, who is at the right hand of God, who also maketh intercession for us. Who shall separate us from the love of Christ?* (Rom. 8:32–35).

The Reformed view is that perseverance is the fruit of election, while Arminianism teaches that perseverance is "a condition of the new covenant" and therefore a condition of election. We need to remember that the elect, according to Arminianism, are those whom God foresees will believe and persevere in true faith until the end. The Bible teaches that perseverance is the gift of God gained by the death of Christ, for eternal life by definition must include perseverance. After all, life that can be lost or in which one does not persevere is *not* eternal life; if anything, it is temporary life.

Arminianism teaches that the death of Christ did not purchase salvation for anyone, but merely the possibility for God to offer salvation on any condition that he might choose. Man must, according to Arminianism, fulfill the condition of persevering in true faith by his own free will before he can be guaranteed salvation, which the Arminians called "decisive election and justification."

The Canons answer the folly of Arminianism by quoting Romans 11:7 and Romans 8:32–35, for the gift of perseverance is the fruit of election, of the cross, of the resurrection, and of the intercession of Christ. Therefore, final perseverance does not depend on the sinner, but on God.

And that, believing reader, is good news, for woe to us if our final perseverance depends on us.

ERROR AND REJECTION 2: GOD READY TO PRESERVE WILLING SAINTS

> Error 2: Who teach that God does indeed provide the believer with sufficient powers to persevere, and is ever ready to preserve these in him, if he will do his duty; but that though all things which are necessary to persevere in faith and which God will use to preserve faith are made use of, it even then ever depends on the pleasure of the will whether it will persevere or not.

> Rejection: For this idea contains an outspoken Pelagianism, and, while it would make men free, it makes them robbers of God's honor, contrary to the prevailing agreement of the evangelical doctrine, which takes from man all cause of boasting, and ascribes all the praise for this favor to the grace of God alone; and contrary to the apostle, who declares: *That it is God, who shall also confirm you unto the end, that ye be unreprovable in the day of our Lord Jesus Christ* (1 Cor. 1:8).

This error is simply a statement of conditional security or conditional perseverance dressed up in pious sounding language in order to disguise the wicked pride of the Arminian doctrine. God, said the Arminians, gives and is ready to give "sufficient powers to persevere"—the tools, the means, the graces, the benefits, and the powers are available, but it depends on man's willingness to accept these divine offers of help by the power of his free will.

The sharp answer of the Canons is that this is "an outspoken Pelagianism" (Notice again the charge of Pelagianism.) The error presupposes that man can persevere of his own power, while it makes the operation of God's grace depend on the will of man. The truth is that we could never persevere except for God's sovereign, efficacious grace. Arminianism pretends to "make men free," but instead it makes men "robbers of God's honor," which is abhorrent, especially when we contrast it with the gospel or "the evangelical doctrine, which takes from man all cause of boasting, and ascribes all the praise of this favor to the grace of God alone." In other words, Arminianism is a denial of the gospel.

ERROR AND REJECTION 9: CHRIST'S INTERCESSION NOT INFALLIBLE

> Error 9: Who teach that Christ has in no place prayed that believers should infallibly continue in faith.
>
> Rejection: For they contradict Christ Himself, who says: *I have prayed for thee* (Simon), *that thy faith fail not* (Luke 22:32); and the evangelist John, who declares that Christ has not prayed for the apostles only, but also for those who through their word would believe: *Holy Father, keep them in thy name,* and: *I pray not that thou shouldest take them out of the world, but that thou shouldest keep them from the evil one* (John 17:11, 15, 20).

This error links perseverance to Christ's intercession. The Arminians did not deny that Christ intercedes for his people, but they denied the *efficacy* of Christ's intercession. They denied that Christ prayed that believers should *infallibly* continue in true faith. One wonders, then, for what Christ prays. Does he merely pray for them that they would *conditionally* continue in true faith?

Arminianism argues that Christ's intercession depends on man's willingness to cooperate with God's grace, which is a truly horrifying thought. Imagine that Christ stopped interceding for his people until they were ready to pray, and imagine that Christ's intercession depended on their faithfulness to him. Where would Peter be if Jesus had prayed for him *only when he was faithful*? But in this the

Arminian is consistent, for in Arminianism election is conditional, redemption is conditional, regeneration is conditional, *and* Christ's intercession is conditional.

The Canons respond to this error by quoting Christ's words in Luke 22:32 and John 17:11, 15, and 20. Christ prayed that Peter's faith should not fail and, although Peter fell into the lamentable sin of denying Christ, his faith ultimately did *not* fail, for by God's grace he was restored to repentance and commissioned to feed Christ's sheep and lambs (John 21:15–17). Christ prayed "also for those who through their [the apostles'] word would believe: *Holy Father...keep them from the evil one*," which prayer God answered. Christ is the advocate of his people. His effectual atonement and intercession secure their salvation (Rom. 8:34; 1 John 2:1–2). None for whom he intercedes can ever perish. Happy is the man whom Christ represents at God's right hand.

ARTICLE 4: THE SAINT'S SINFUL NEGLECT OF GRACE

> Although the weakness of the flesh cannot prevail against the power of God, who confirms and preserves true believers in a state of grace, yet converts are not always so influenced and actuated by the Spirit of God, as not in some particular instances sinfully to deviate from the guidance of divine grace, so as to be seduced by and comply with the lusts of the flesh; they must, therefore, be constant in watching and prayer, that they be not led into temptation. When these are neglected, they are not only liable to be drawn into great and heinous sins by Satan, the world, and the flesh, but sometimes by the righteous permission of God actually fall into these evils. This the lamentable fall of David, Peter, and other saints described in Holy Scripture demonstrates.

We have learned so far that the believer is a saint (holy) and a sinner, for the believer still has a sinful flesh against which he struggles daily. Yet God has graciously promised to preserve the saint so that his sins do not prevail against him and so that he does not perish. We also learned that this perseverance is impossible from our perspective, although it is certain from God's perspective. In the following articles, we will learn that God's work of preserving his saints does not mean that they never fall into terrible transgressions of God's law. Furthermore, article 4 describes the seriousness of sin in the Christian life.

Let these articles be a sobering warning to us of the deceitfulness of sin and of the need for watchfulness.

Article 4 focuses on the power of God's grace. Remember that God's grace is his power working in his people to deliver them from sin (1 Cor. 15:10; Titus 2:12). The power of God's grace overcomes their sins, so that their sinful flesh can never ultimately prevail against them. Yet God's grace works in them in such a way that he makes them active in, and conscious of, their salvation. They are not asleep as God graciously works in them, for they are not "senseless stocks and blocks" (Canons 3–4.16). Moreover, God uses means in their salvation, for he works in them through the preaching of the gospel and the exercise of prayer. By these means God "confirms and preserves true believers in a state of grace." This does not mean that salvation becomes a cooperative effort between God's grace and man's work, for God *produces* their working and even their willing (Phil. 2:13). This also does not mean that God's grace depends on their activity—that would be Arminian *conditional* perseverance or preservation.

The question is, how do we explain the sins of believers? If God's grace is always working, how can believers sin? The Arminians accused the Reformed fathers of teaching that believers' sins are the fault of God's grace—a monstrous slander. Articles 4–5 are an answer to that false charge. Two things must be borne in mind. First, God's grace always "confirms and preserves true believers in a state of grace"; and second, believers are "not always so influenced and actuated by the Spirit" as not to fall into sin.

Whose fault, then, is it that believers "in some particular instances" fall into sin? Is it God's grace? God forbid. It is the fault of believers. Notice the explanation: first, they "*sinfully*...deviate from the guidance of divine grace"; second, they are (therefore) "*seduced by*...the lusts of the flesh"; third, being seduced, they (therefore) "*comply with* the lusts of the flesh"; fourth they *neglect* the means of grace; and finally God *righteously permits* such negligent believers to fall into evil (emphasis added).

We should notice, then, the pattern. First, the Christian neglects the means of grace. He is not constant in prayer, especially in offering the petition, "Lead us not into temptation, but deliver us from evil." He neglects attendance at public worship and fellowship with God's people. Foolishly, the negligent Christian becomes self-confident, thinking that he does not need to watch and pray, and that he does not need to read scripture or to attend the preaching of the gospel. Because he does not watch, he is not spiritually alert to the dangers to his soul. Having failed to watch, he becomes spiritually drowsy and careless. Second, the Christian without prayer is open to the alluring temptations of Satan and the world. His actions place him in situations and in places where he is liable to be tempted. Presumptuously, he imagines that he will not fall because he overestimates his own strength and he underestimates the power of the enemy. A Christian without prayer, without watchfulness, and without attendance on the means of grace is easy prey for the devil, for the world, and for the flesh.

Third, God permits such a negligent Christian to fall as a chastisement. The Christian is negligent, while God is righteous. Therefore, the fault for the believer's fall into sin is not God's, but the foolish, negligent, presumptuous saint's. God merely withdraws some of the influence of his grace so that the Christian falls by his own natural depravity (Ps. 19:12–13; Luke 22:31–34; 1 Cor. 10:12; Eph. 6:10–18; James 1:13–15; 1 Pet. 5:8). In this regard the Canons mention the "lamentable fall[s] of David, Peter, and other saints."

David neglected his duties as the king of Israel, idling his time on the palace roof until his straying eyes lighted upon Bathsheba. Peter was self-confident, boasting that he could never fall. He disregarded the warnings of Jesus and fell before the questioning of a servant girl. Many other examples of folly, negligence, and presumption are found in the scriptures. When God withdrew the power of his grace, they fell like stones. What a warning to pray earnestly the sixth petition of the Lord's prayer.

ARTICLE 5: THE MISERABLE EFFECTS OF THE NEGLECT OF GRACE

> By such enormous sins, however, they very highly offend God, incur a deadly guilt, grieve the Holy Spirit, interrupt the exercise of faith, very grievously wound their consciences, and sometimes lose the sense of God's favor for a time, until, on their returning into the right way of serious repentance, the light of God's fatherly countenance again shines upon them.

The sins mentioned in articles 4–5 into which the negligent saint might fall are "great and heinous" or "enormous" sins, not the "daily sins of infirmity" or the "spots" adhering to the good works of the saints of article 2. Such "great and heinous" and "enormous" sins are ordinarily the gross public sins that bring shame upon the Christian, upon the church, and upon Christ. Often such sins bring a man under Christian discipline, especially when he persists in them for a time. In sobering words article 5 lays out the dreadful, spiritual consequences of such sins, so that no one can claim that the Reformed faith does not take sin seriously.

First, "they very highly offend God." The sins of God's people displease him greatly. His love for his children does not make him an indulgent father, for he is holy. All sin is detestable to him, especially the sins of his children who bear his name in the world. Second, "they...incur a deadly guilt" (literally, the guilt of death). This is not a loss of justification, but a sense of guilt: the fallen saint feels guilty, knows that he is guilty, and feels the need to be forgiven of that guilt. As long as he lives in that sin without confessing and forsaking it, the deadly guilt weighs heavily upon him. David described this guilt in Psalm 32:3–4: "When I kept silence, my bones waxed old through my roaring all the day long. For day and night thy hand was heavy upon me: my moisture is turned into the drought of summer."

Third, these sins "grieve the Holy Spirit." Because the Spirit is holy, sin grieves him, which shows us that the Holy Spirit is a person whom we can offend. (Only a person, not an impersonal force, power or influence, can be *grieved*.) When the saints grieve the Holy Spirit, he withdraws from them and makes them feel the absence of his gracious presence: when saints grieve the Holy Spirit, he grieves them. Since the Spirit makes them partakers (conscious partakers) of Christ, when they sin he makes them aware of his displeasure by removing from them the consciousness of Christ. The ordinary ministry of the Spirit is to bear witness with their spirits that they the children of God, but when they deliberately commit sin the Spirit no longer does that, or he does it to a lesser degree. The result is that their assurance is shaken, the joy of their salvation disappears or is weakened, their prayer lives seems lifeless and barren, and they cannot cry "Abba Father" as they once did. When the saints experience such spiritual distress, the Spirit is showing them that they have grieved him (Ps. 32:3–4; 51:12), so that they search their hearts and in repentance seek God again.

In Ephesians 4:30 the Spirit whom we must not grieve is the same one who seals us unto the day of redemption. A seal is a mark of ownership, authenticity, or protection. When we fall into sin, the seal is not broken, but our consciousness of the seal is gone. A defiant and disobedient child, although still truly a child and still dearly loved by his parents, simply does not experience the smile of his parents until he turns from his sinful ways. A disobedient Christian simply does not enjoy the smile of his Father's countenance until he repents and seeks forgiveness in the blood of the cross.

Fourth, these sins "interrupt the exercise of faith." Faith is both a spiritual bond with Christ and an activity of the believer. Sin does not break the bond, for believers are eternally united to Christ and can never be separated from him, but the activity or exercise of faith is interrupted. The sinning and impenitent Christian cannot look in confidence to Jesus Christ, for he has taken his eye off Christ and is filled with fears and doubts, which is a dreadful experience for a Christian. Like Peter, he begins to sink until he cries out from a penitent heart, "Lord, save me" (Matt. 14:30).

Fifth, these sins "very grievously wound their consciences." The conscience, which is informed by the word of God, is a person's inner judge either accusing or excusing him (Rom. 2:15). By God's grace, the Christian has a good conscience (1 Pet. 3:16) sprinkled with the blood of Christ (Heb. 9:14), but a Christian who falls into sin has an evil, tormenting, accusing conscience. Perhaps such a Christian cannot sleep or eat until he finally confesses and forsakes his sin.

Sixth, the sinning children of God "sometimes lose the sense of God's favor for a time," so that God's fatherly countenance no longer shines upon them. God always loves and favors his people, but when they displease him, he hides his favor behind a dark cloud, so that they do not enjoy God's fellowship as they once did because they have sinned. When they are walking in the darkness, they cannot walk with God, for he is of the light and in him is no darkness at all (Isa. 59:2; 1 John 1:6–7).

This experience is bitter, but good. God does not allow his children to be happy in sin. It is God's practice to make sin bitter to his children so that they will fear him and avoid sin. In this way God brings them to repentance and to a renewed sense of his love: "Until on their returning into the right way of serious repentance, the light of God's fatherly countenance again shines upon them."

Are you tempted to trifle with sin? Take heed to the warning of article 5, for better to read about these things than to experience the bitterness of the backslider!

ARTICLE 6: GOD'S MERCIFUL PRESERVATION OF THE NEGLECTFUL SAINT

> But God, who is rich in mercy, according to His unchangeable purpose of election, does not wholly withdraw the Holy Spirit from His own people, even in their melancholy falls; nor suffers them to proceed so far as to lose the grace of adoption and forfeit the state of justification, or to commit the sin unto death; nor does He permit them to be totally deserted, and to plunge themselves into everlasting destruction.

How far can God's people fall? Can they fall *beyond all recovery*? In 1610 the Arminians' answer was that they were not sure. In 1618 when the Arminians submitted their Opinions to the synod, their answer was yes. The answer of the Reformed fathers at Dordt was no. When a Christian goes through the experiences described in the previous articles (when he backslides), he deserves to perish, but God is rich in mercy. God pities his child who plunges himself foolishly into misery. Therefore, the chastisement described in the previous article serves his salvation.

God chastises his people, but he does not destroy them. Although they offend God, incur guilt, grieve the Spirit, interrupt the exercise of faith, wound their consciences, and lose the sense of God's favor for a time, God remains faithful to his promises.

First, God's "unchangeable purpose of election" stands, according to which purpose God does not withdraw his grace entirely. Second, God does not withdraw his Holy Spirit wholly from his people, for regeneration is irreversible. Therefore, although the Spirit might be grieved, he does not wholly depart; and while he withdraws the comfortable sense of his favorable presence, he does not forsake the child of God. Third, God does not revoke the grace of adoption, for he does not disown his children so that they are no longer his children. He does not cast them out of the household of faith, but he faithfully and lovingly chastises them *as children* (Heb. 12:5–11). Fourth, they do not "forfeit the state of justification" so that the Judge re-imputes their sins to them and removes the imputed righteousness of Christ from them. Their legal status is that of justified, although they are disobedient children in need of correction. (A father might administer the rod, but he does not cast his naughty children into prison, nor does he sentence them to death.) Fifth, God's children do not "commit the sin unto death," for God does not permit them to be "totally deserted" or to perish in "everlasting destruction."

The fall, therefore, of the backsliding Christian is "melancholy" (sad), but it is not fatal. Salvation is not lost, although the enjoyment of salvation is interrupted and marred for a time (Ps. 37:23–24; John 10:27–30; 1 Pet. 1:5). Consider the example and warning of Samson. He fell grievously in the boudoir of Delilah the Philistine seductress. He was chastised severely with blindness and hard labor in Gaza's prison, but he died in faith and with a contrite heart.

Nevertheless, it is better and far less painful to avoid sin in the first place than to endure the painful chastisements of God's rod administered in love.

ERROR AND REJECTION 3: BELIEVERS CAN AND DO FALL FROM GRACE AND PERISH

> Error 3: Who teach that the true believers and regenerate not only can fall from justifying faith and likewise from grace and salvation wholly and to the end, but indeed often do fall from this and are lost forever.
>
> Rejection: For this conception makes powerless the grace, justification, regeneration, and continued keeping by Christ, contrary to the express words of the apostle Paul: *That, while we were yet sinners, Christ died for us. Much more then, being*

> *justified by his blood, shall we be saved from the wrath of God through him* (Rom. 5:8–9). And contrary to the apostle John: *Whosoever is begotten of God doeth no sin, because his seed abideth in him; and he can not sin, because he is begotten of God* (1 John 3:9). And also contrary to the words of Jesus Christ: *I give unto them eternal life; and they shall never perish, and no one shall snatch them out of my hand. My Father, who hath given them to me, is greater than all; and no one is able to snatch them out of the Father's hand* (John 10:28–29).

The Arminians made two assertions about true believers. First, true regenerated believers *can* fall from justifying faith and from grace and salvation. Second, true regenerated believers *do* fall from justifying faith and from grace and salvation and are lost forever. Moreover, the Arminians asserted that this happens *often*. Do not miss the implication of this: if true regenerated believers can fall away, any Christian could perish. Therefore, I could perish and you could perish. In fact, according to Arminianism there are people in hell today who were once regenerated, who once believed in Jesus Christ, and who once were justified, but who fell away from grace and salvation, and perished. In other words, it is not true that "whom he justified, them he also glorified" (Rom. 8:30). Truly, Arminianism is a terrifying doctrine.

The synod responded that this is an outrageous attack on the power of God's grace, justification, regeneration, and preservation (continued keeping) of Christ and it makes God's salvation dependent on man. Notice the texts quoted in the article: Romans 5:8–9; 1 John 3:9; John 10:28–29.

ERROR AND REJECTION 4: THE TRULY REGENERATE CAN SIN THE SIN UNTO DEATH

> Error 4: Who teach that true believers and regenerate can sin the sin unto death or against the Holy Spirit.

> Rejection: Since the same apostle John, after having spoken in the fifth chapter of his first epistle, verses 16 and 17, of those who sin unto death, and having forbidden to pray for them, immediately adds to this in verse 18: *We know that whosoever is begotten of God sinneth not* (meaning a sin of that character), *but he that is begotten of God keepeth himself, and the evil one toucheth him not* (1 John 5:18).

The Arminians taught that true regenerate believers can—and sometimes do—commit "the sin unto death" or "the sin…against the Holy Spirit," often called the unforgivable or unpardonable sin or blasphemy against the Holy Spirit. In other words, the Arminians taught that true believers can and do apostatize from Christ.

Some conscientious believers are troubled about the unpardonable sin because they think that perhaps they have committed it. Such distressed saints will call the pastor, worried that they have sinned beyond the possibility of forgiveness. Therefore, a few words about this sin are in order. Jesus described this sin in Matthew 12:31–32: "Wherefore I say unto you, All manner of sin and blasphemy shall be forgiven unto men: but the blasphemy against the Holy Ghost shall not be forgiven unto men. And whosoever speaketh a word against the Son of man, it shall be forgiven him: but whosoever speaketh against the Holy Ghost, it shall not be forgiven him, neither in this world, neither in the world to come."

Blasphemy against the Holy Spirit is deliberate, persistent, final apostasy. One who commits such a sin does so without any sense of compunction, conviction, or shame. Such a person never calls the pastor, worried that he might be guilty of such a sin. He does not care—his conscience does not bother him. The Pharisees were such—they had committed or they were in danger of committing that sin. Instead of repenting and believing in Jesus, they attributed his saving works *to the devil.* They said, "This fellow doth not cast out devils, but by Beelzebub the prince of devils" (v. 24). One who commits this sin is hardened in his sin so that he cannot repent and so that he has no desire to repent. If you are sorry for your sins, even if you think that you have committed the unpardonable sin, I can state categorically that you have *not* committed the unpardonable sin. No matter how vile your sins are, come to Jesus, and he will cleanse you: "Though your sins be as scarlet, they shall be white as snow; though they be red like crimson, they shall be as wool" (Isa. 1:18). "If we confess our sins, he is faithful and just to forgive us our sins, and to cleanse us from all unrighteousness" (1 John 1:9).

The Canons respond with masterful exegesis of 1 John 5:16–18. Verse 18 teaches that "We know that whosoever is begotten of God sinneth not." This does not mean that God's regenerated children do not sin, for scripture and the creeds teach that true believers do indeed commit sin (1:8–10). This means that the regenerate do not commit the sin *unto death*, the sin "of that character." God keeps his children and does not permit the evil one to touch them, with the result that they do not commit the sin unto death. Believers have the capacity to commit all kinds of sins, but God mercifully preserves them from committing that particular sin.

Another passage to consider is the "apostasy passage": "It is impossible for those who were once enlightened, and have tasted of the heavenly gift, and were made partakers of the Holy Ghost, and have tasted the good word of God, and the powers of the world to come, if they shall fall away, to renew them again unto repentance; seeing they crucify to themselves the Son of God afresh, and put him to an open shame" (Heb. 6:4–6)

Arminians appeal to this passage because it seems to teach the apostasy of true believers. If true believers can apostatize, true believers can perish, which is the teaching of the Arminians with respect to perseverance. Notice a few points about this passage: nowhere does it unambiguously refer to salvation. Instead, the language is of being "enlightened," of having "tasted," and having been "made partakers" of certain benefits. Such people have come very close to salvation, therefore, but they have not received salvation. They have been enlightened, but not regenerated or converted; they have tasted—and rejected—the heavenly gift, the good word of God, and the powers of the world to come, but they have not been justified and their sins have not been forgiven. Such persons "fall away" from the benefits that they have tasted—they spit them out. They crucify the Son of God afresh. They put Christ to open shame. Such apostates become open and avowed enemies of Jesus Christ.

The passage warns that it is impossible to restore such apostates to repentance. As it stands the passage proves too much for Arminians—they want a passage where a saint can fall away and be restored, perhaps multiple times in a lifetime, but this passage teaches that the apostate is irretrievably lost. In addition, the passage contrasts such apostates, who tasted but never truly partook of salvation, with true believers in Hebrews 6:9: "Beloved, we are persuaded better things of you, and *things that accompany salvation*, though we thus speak" (emphasis added). The readers of the epistle had something that the apostates did not have, the things that accompany salvation. Whatever the apostates had it was not those things that accompany salvation. They came very close to salvation—they were under the preaching of the word; they partook of the sacraments; and they had religious experiences, but they were never converted. They show this by departing from the truth: "They went out from us, but they were not of us; for if they had been of us, they would no doubt have continued with us: but they went out, that it might be made manifest that they were not all of us" (1 John 2:19).

Believers can and do commit sin ("daily sins of infirmity"). Believers can be and sometimes are drawn into "great and heinous sins" or "enormous sins" (from which God always restores them to repentance), but believers cannot and do not commit the sin unto death, for God graciously preserves them from *that* sin.

ERROR AND REJECTION 7: TEMPORARY FAITH INDISTINGUISHABLE FROM JUSTIFYING FAITH

> Error 7: Who teach that the faith of those who believe for a time does not differ from justifying and saving faith except only in duration.
>
> Rejection: For Christ Himself, in Matt. 13:20, Luke 8:13, and in other places, evidently notes, besides this duration, a threefold difference between those who believe only for a time and true believers, when He declares that the former receive the seed in stony ground, but the latter in the good ground or heart; that the former are without root, but the latter have a firm root; that the former are without fruit, but that the latter bring forth their fruit in various measure with constancy and steadfastness.

The Bible speaks of different kinds of faith. Apart from true, saving faith, there are historical faith, miraculous faith, and temporary faith. These latter species of faith are described in Christ's parable of the sower. The Arminians taught that the only essential difference between true, saving faith and temporary faith is its duration; for in true, saving faith, the believer perseveres, while in the case of temporary faith, the believer does not persevere.

This was another attempt by the Arminians to make salvation dependent on the free will of man, for whether his faith is temporary ("the faith of those who believe for a time") or saving ("justifying and saving faith") depends on the continued exercise of his free will.

Historical faith is mere assent to historical propositions. One with historical faith might hold for truth that God created Adam on the sixth day (Gen. 1) and that David slew Goliath with a slingshot and five stones (1 Sam. 17). However, he does not trust in Jesus Christ for salvation and he has no vital, spiritual union with the Savior. Miraculous faith is the belief in the possibility of miracles, either the belief that he can perform them or the belief that another can perform them on him. Many of the Israelites in Jesus' day had miraculous faith, but they did not truly trust in Christ, which is something that he perceived (John 2:23–25). Temporary faith is a sudden but shallow, emotional reaction to Jesus based on a religious experience that does not last, especially when it is tried through persecution. It is to be feared that many "converts" at large evangelistic rallies are of this nature, which is not surprising because the preaching is usually Arminianism.

The Canons respond with a brief explanation of the parable. Christ notes "a threefold difference between those who believe only for a time and true believers." There was a reason they believed only for a time. The main difference is that three kinds of soil (the path, the stony ground, and the thorny ground) bear no fruit, while the fourth kind of soil bears fruit in various measures. The reason they bear no fruit is that the faith of the hearers is not genuine. The Belgic Confession speaks of this in article 24: "It is impossible that this holy faith can be unfruitful in man; for we do not speak of a vain faith, but of such a faith which is called in Scripture *a faith that worketh by love*, which excites man to the practice of those works which God has commanded in His Word."[5]

The first three kinds of hearers in the parable were unbelievers, for their faith was not real. They did not fall away from saving or justifying faith, for they never possessed saving faith and they were never justified. They fell away merely from counterfeit faith or from the appearance of faith. Only the fourth kind of hearer who produced fruit to various degrees possessed true, saving faith. Only he enjoys salvation that he can never lose.

ARTICLE 7: THE CERTAINTY OF FINAL PERSEVERANCE

> For, in the first place, in these falls He preserves in them the incorruptible seed of regeneration from perishing, or being

5 Belgic Confession 24, in ibid., 53.

> totally lost; and again, by His Word and Spirit, certainly and effectually renews them to repentance, to a sincere and godly sorrow for their sins, that they may seek and obtain remission in the blood of the Mediator, may again experience the favor of a reconciled God, through faith adore His mercies, and henceforward more diligently work out their own salvation with fear and trembling.

This article gives the reasons the backslidden saint even in his lamentable falls does not finally perish. We see that in the word "for" or because, which refers back to article 6.

First, God preserves in his people "the incorruptible seed of regeneration" (1 John 3:9; 5:18; 1 Pet. 1:23). The seed of regeneration cannot perish, for the flesh cannot extinguish the Spirit. Second, God renews his people to repentance, which is "a sincere and godly sorrow for their sins" (Ps. 32:5; 2 Cor. 7:10). In the way of repentance the Christian seeks and finds forgiveness in the blood of Christ (1 John 1:9). The result is that the Christian thus restored experiences again God's favor ("the favor of a reconciled God"), the cloud of gloom disappears, and darkness becomes light (Ps. 43:5).

Consequently, the Christian adores God's mercies through faith. What a debtor to divine mercy is the child of God who not only was delivered from sin and death but was also forgiven *again* even after he foolishly plunged into sin. With what wonder did David write after God forgave his sins, "I acknowledged my sin unto thee, and mine iniquity have I not hid. I said, I will confess my transgressions unto the LORD; *and thou forgavest the iniquity of my sin*" (Ps. 32:5, emphasis added). Moreover, having experienced the bitter consequences of sin, the formerly backslidden and now restored saint is more diligent and watchful in the future (Phil. 2:13). David, too, was doubly careful after his sin with Bathsheba:

> 8. I will instruct thee and teach thee in the way which thou shalt go: I will guide thee with mine eye.

9. Be ye not as the horse, or as the mule, which have no understanding: whose mouth must be held in with bit and bridle, lest they come near unto thee.
10. Many sorrows shall be to the wicked: but he that trusteth in the Lord, mercy shall compass him about. (Ps. 32:8–10)

Let us be careful lest we sin against such great mercy.

ERROR AND REJECTION 8: THE PERISHABILITY OF THE SEED OF REGENERATION

Error 8: Who teach that it is not absurd that one having lost his first regeneration is again and even often born anew.

Rejection: For these deny by this doctrine the incorruptibleness of the seed of God, whereby we are born again, contrary to the testimony of the apostle Peter: *Having been begotten again, not of corruptible seed, but of incorruptible* (1 Pet. 1:23).

The Arminians taught that a man might be born again repeatedly. The idea is that a person is regenerated, loses his regeneration, and is restored to regeneration, which process continues repeatedly in a cycle throughout the life of the Christian. The Arminians insisted that it was "not absurd" that this should happen and, therefore, it was not absurd to teach it.

The response of the Reformed fathers was to charge the Arminians with denying the "incorruptibleness of the seed of God." This seed of God is planted into the heart of an elect at regeneration. That seed is the new life of Christ received in principle into the heart of the child of God, which is the source in the Christian of his spiritual life and of his ability to do good works. The Heidelberg Catechism refers to this seed as "the new man," which "new man" the believer "quickens" in conversion.[6] The apostle John referred to this seed as

6 Heidelberg Catechism A 90, in ibid., 121.

impeccable, that is, the seed of God cannot sin. This does not mean that the believer cannot sin, for his sins proceed from his sinful flesh. His sins do not proceed from the impeccable seed of God, but from the corrupt flesh of man, for which he is responsible before God and against which he struggles. John wrote, "Whosoever is born of God doth not commit sin; for his seed remaineth in him: and he cannot sin, because he is born of God" (1 John 3:9).

The Arminian scheme would mean that God plants his seed in a person, which then dies when he commits a serious sin (similar to the Roman Catholic view of mortal sins, which kill grace in the soul). When he repents God plants his seed in him again, which then perishes when he commits another serious sin. This cycle continues with many aborted attempts at regeneration until finally either the seed is preserved or the seed finally perishes. Not only does this mean that the seed is always in a precarious position between life and death, but also that one can never know whether the seed in him is alive or dead.

Such a doctrine is certainly absurd and contrary to the holy scriptures.

ARTICLE 8: THE REASON FOR THE CERTAINTY OF FINAL PERSEVERANCE

> Thus, it is not in consequence of their own merits or strength, but of God's free mercy, that they do not totally fall from faith and grace, nor continue and perish finally in their backslidings; which with respect to themselves is not only possible, but would undoubtedly happen; but with respect to God, it is utterly impossible, since His counsel cannot be changed, nor His promise fail, neither can the call according to His purpose be revoked, nor the merit, intercession, and preservation of Christ be rendered ineffectual, nor the sealing of the Holy Spirit be frustrated or obliterated.

We have seen thus far that the Reformed and Arminians have two different conceptions of perseverance. The Arminian view is that the saint *can* persevere *if he is willing*. The power to persevere is found in man's free will. God is willing to help, but the issue is whether the Christian is willing to cooperate with God's grace. The Reformed view is that the power of sin is so great that the saint could never persevere by his own power. God preserves the saint, for salvation never depends on man.

Article 8 explains why it is impossible for the true believer to perish. Although it is possible for the believer to fall into sin, God always restores his true children to repentance. Negatively, the reason for perseverance is not "in consequence of their own merits or strength." They do not deserve to persevere; in fact, they deserve that God should give them over to their sins when they wickedly give occasion to their flesh. They deserve to experience the bitter chastisement of David, Samson, or Peter. In fact, they deserve much worse punishment, for they deserve to perish in hell. They do not have the strength to persevere, but so often they play with fire while they boast that because they are theologically Reformed they could never fall into serious sins. God must only remove his hand for one moment and they will fall by their natural depravity into humiliating sins. Instead, the reason for perseverance is "God's free mercy," which guarantees two things.

First, God's free mercy guarantees that true saints "do not totally fall from faith and grace." Note well—temporary, bitter, and very serious falls and backslidings *are* possible, but final apostasy is impossible. Painful, life-changing, even devastating, blows with the Father's rod of discipline are possible, but the final disinheritance of God's children is impossible. Therefore, saints must not trifle with sin. Let the Canons of Dordt serve as urgent pastoral warnings.

Second, God's free mercy guarantees that true saints do not "continue and perish finally in their backslidings." God's mercy guaranteed that Samson did not die in Delilah's bosom, but it did not spare him hard labor, blinding, imprisonment, and finally being crushed to death under the rubble of the temple of Dagon after God restored him to broken-hearted repentance over his sin (Judges 16). God's mercy guaranteed that David did not die in bed with Bathsheba, but it did not spare him the loss of several of his sons and Absalom's rebellion, for the sword never departed from his house (2 Sam. 12:10). The Canons warn that from our perspective final apostasy, a total fall from faith and grace, and continuance and perishing in backsliding "[are] not only possible, but would undoubtedly happen." The possibility of perseverance without the grace of God is *precisely zero* (1 Cor. 10:12–13; 1 Pet. 1:5; Jude 24).

The Canons move from the possibilities and infirmities of man to God—"but…God" (Eph. 2:4) or "but with respect to God." What follows is the golden chain of perseverance, for all of the perfections, powers, and purposes of God combine to preserve the saint in salvation because of which "it is utterly impossible" that any true saint could fall from salvation and perish.

First, God's "counsel cannot be changed." God's eternal purpose of unconditional election, the subject of head one, cannot be changed. Therefore, God cannot revoke the election of his children. For God's counsel to change, God himself would have to change, which can never be.

Second, "nor [can God's] promise fail." Since God has promised with a sure and certain word in which he swears an oath by his own name to save his elect, he cannot go back on his word (Rom. 4:16; 9:6; Gal. 3:16; Titus 1:2). This statement in the Canons proves that God makes promises only to the elect—God never (even conditionally) promises to save the reprobate.

Third, God's "call according to His purpose cannot be revoked" (Rom. 8:30; 11:29; 2 Tim. 1:9). Those who are called cannot be uncalled.

Fourth, "the merit, intercession, and preservation of Christ [cannot be] rendered ineffectual." Christ's merit is the righteousness that he has wrought for his people in his lifelong obedience, sufferings, and death on the cross. It is a merit so precious that it cannot fail to save—to the uttermost—all those for whom it was purchased and to whom it is applied. If even one for whom Christ made atonement perished, the merits of his death would fail. Moreover, Christ intercedes for his elect people, for he is their advocate. Therefore, it is impossible for Christ *not* to obtain the blessings for which he makes intercession for his people. If even one for whom Christ prayed perished, his intercession would fail.

Furthermore, Christ preserves his people, for it is impossible for anyone to pluck them out of his hand (John 10:28). If even one whom Christ keeps was plucked from his hand or if even one of the elect was separated from the love of Christ, Christ's preservation would fail.

Fifth, "the sealing of the Holy Spirit [cannot be] frustrated or obliterated." For elect souls to perish, the seal of the Spirit would have to be erased, which cannot happen because they are sealed "with that holy Spirit of promise, which is the earnest of [their] inheritance until the redemption of the purchased possession, unto the praise of his glory" (Eph. 1:13–14). By the Holy Spirit, even him whom we sometimes grieve, "we are sealed unto the day of redemption" (4:30). If even one of the sealed children of God perished, the sealing of the Spirit would fail.

Therefore, the power of the triune God, Father, Son, and Holy Spirit, is the reason the saints are preserved in true faith and persevere in it unto the end. There is no greater assurance than this.

ARTICLE 9: THE CERTAIN ASSURANCE OF FINAL PERSEVERANCE

> Of this preservation of the elect to salvation, and of their perseverance in the faith, true believers for themselves may and do obtain assurance according to the measure of

> their faith, whereby they arrive at the certain persuasion that they ever will continue true and living members of the church, and that they experience forgiveness of sins, and will at last inherit eternal life.

Having taught in the first head that the elect attain the assurance of their eternal and unchangeable election (12–13), in this article the fathers at Dordt taught concerning the assurance of "this preservation of the elect to salvation" and "their perseverance in the faith." This naturally follows, for if the elect are assured of their eternal salvation, they must also be assured of their continuance in the faith and of their final salvation on the last day. Remember that the Arminians taught an assurance of *present salvation* (a person might know that he is saved and in Christ today), but denied the possibility of the assurance of eternal and unchangeable election (Canons 1.12–13, error and rejection 7). Moreover, they denied the assurance of final preservation or perseverance in salvation. No Christian, they insisted, could know that he or she will finally be saved, neither is it necessary or useful to know.

The Canons in a beautiful and pastoral way affirm that the elect children of God *can* and *do* possess assurance of eternal and unchangeable election, of present salvation, and crucially, of final perseverance. Notice the wording of the Canons. "True believers *may*... obtain assurance," and "true believers...*do* obtain assurance" (emphasis added). Assurance is not only a possibility, but also a reality, for all believers. It is not the normal Christian experience to doubt, but to believe and to be assured of one's final perseverance and salvation.

First, this assurance is "the certain persuasion that they ever will continue true and living members of the church." Those words "ever will continue" (an echo of Heidelberg Catechism A 54)[7] are crucial.

---

7 Answer 54 of the Heidelberg Catechism reads: "That the Son of God, from the beginning to the end of the world, gathers, defends, and preserves to Himself by His Spirit and Word, out of the whole human race, a church chosen to everlasting

It is not assurance to believe that I am a true and living member of the church today if I live in constant fear and terror that I will fall away later in life, or if I even entertain the possibility in my mind that I *could* apostatize from Christ and his truth. This is not faith; it is doubt—or unbelief. This is not humility; it is pride, the prideful refusal to believe the promises of God.

Second, this assurance is "the certain persuasion that they… experience forgiveness of sins." This is an echo of the Heidelberg Catechism where the comforted believer confesses, "God, for the sake of Christ's satisfaction, will no more remember my sins…that I may never be condemned before the tribunal of God."[8]

Third, this assurance is "the certain persuasion that they...will at last inherit eternal life." Listen to the echo of Heidelberg Catechism: "[Christ]…shall translate me with all His chosen ones to Himself, into heavenly joys and glory."[9] And remember Heidelberg Catechism answer 58: "After this life I shall inherit perfect salvation."[10] For the believer salvation and eternal life are never abstract concepts: they belong *to me*. "Not only to others, but to me also, remission of sin, everlasting righteousness, and salvation, are freely given by God, merely of grace, only for the sake of Christ's merits."[11] Drink deeply from these passages of the word of God: Romans 8:38–39, 1 Corinthians 1:8, Philippians 1:6, Colossians 1:5, and 2 Timothy 4:7–8.

The Canons add a qualifier, which in no way dilutes the assurance of the Reformed faith. "True believers…obtain assurance *according to the measure of their faith*" (emphasis added). Since assurance is of the essence of faith, the stronger a believer's faith is the stronger his assurance shall be. The weaker a believer's faith is the more he or she shall

---

life, agreeing in true faith; and that I am, and for ever shall remain, a living member thereof" (Ibid., 104).

8 Heidelberg Catechism A 56, in ibid., 105.

9 Heidelberg Catechism A 52, in ibid., 103.

10 Heidelberg Catechism A 58, in ibid., 105–6.

11 Heidelberg Catechism A 21, in ibid., 90–91.

struggle with carnal doubts, as we shall see in article 11. Nevertheless, while the Canons encourage the struggling, doubting saint, they never encourage him to doubt; they never justify his doubt; and they never present doubt as anything other than unhealthy, abnormal, and sinful. Faith and assurance are not the exception, but the norm, for we are to *expect* the people of God to be assured. To lack assurance is a serious spiritual affliction caused by unbelief. Assurance must be encouraged and promoted in the church through the preaching of the gospel of grace (1 Thess. 1:5; Titus 1:1–2).

ARTICLE 10: THE SOURCE OF ASSURANCE OF FINAL PERSEVERANCE

> This assurance, however, is not produced by any peculiar revelation contrary to, or independent of the Word of God, but springs from faith in God's promises, which He has most abundantly revealed in His Word for our comfort; from the testimony of the Holy Spirit, witnessing with our spirit, that we are children and heirs of God (Rom. 8:16); and lastly, from a serious and holy desire to preserve a good conscience and to perform good works. And if the elect of God were deprived of this solid comfort, that they shall finally obtain the victory, and of this infallible pledge or earnest of eternal glory, they would be of all men the most miserable.

Having explained the blessedness of the assurance of perseverance in salvation, this article explains the source of this assurance both negatively and positively. It is vital to look for and to find assurance in the right places, for false assurance or presumption is spiritually hazardous.

Negatively, "this assurance…is not produced by any peculiar revelation contrary to, or independent of the Word of God." This is the condemnation of mysticism, both the mysticism of Roman

Catholicism and the mysticism of certain branches of Protestantism. Rome's position is that assurance of salvation is almost always impossible. In rare occasions God might favor someone with special revelation. However, such revelation is rare—not even popes are favored with it—and often those who claim that they have received such revelation are persecuted and accused of the sin of presumption, for who can test the genuineness of such revelation? Mystical Protestants labor under similar misconceptions: if you enjoy a mysterious, spiritual experience, you can know that you are saved, but the majority of Christians never enjoy such experiences. Therefore, many Christians, according to this pernicious theology, have no assurance and languish in miserable, soul-distressing doubt. Where such theology prevails, it is not uncommon to find that many (even most) in the congregation are reluctant to come to the Lord's supper. This should not be and is contrary to the Reformed faith.

> *But this is not designed (dearly beloved brethren and sisters in the Lord) to deject the contrite hearts of the faithful*, as if none might come to the Supper of the Lord but those who are without sin; for we do not come to this Supper to testify thereby that we are perfect and righteous in ourselves; but on the contrary, considering that we seek our life out of ourselves in Jesus Christ, we acknowledge that we lie in the midst of death; therefore, notwithstanding we feel many infirmities and miseries in ourselves, as namely, that we have not perfect faith, and that we do not give ourselves to serve God with that zeal as we are bound, but have daily to strive with the weakness of our faith, and the evil lusts of our flesh; yet, since we are (by the grace of the Holy Spirit) sorry for these weaknesses, and earnestly desirous to fight against our unbelief and to live according to all the commandments of God; *therefore we rest assured that no sin or infirmity, which still remaineth against our will in us can hinder us from being*

> *received of God in mercy*, and from being made worthy partakers of this heavenly meat and drink.[12]

Positively, first, this assurance "springs from faith." Assurance is of the essence of faith. The object of our faith is "God's promises, which He has most abundantly revealed in his Word for our comfort." The word of God is replete with precious promises, for God knows the weakness of our faith and he is determined to buttress that faith with "exceeding great and precious promises" (2 Pet. 1:4). He even swears an oath in his own name to give us "strong consolation" (Heb. 6:17–18). Therefore, to doubt God's promises is to call God a liar. It is to respond with ingratitude to the merciful God who has revealed his promises "for our comfort." If a father makes abundant promises to his children, but they do not believe, he is offended. If we can trust the promises of our fickle, sinful, earthly fathers, shall we not believe the promises of God our heavenly Father?

Second, the Holy Spirit works in us to enable us to embrace God's promises by faith, for he is the one "witnessing with our spirit that we are children and heirs of God" (Rom. 8:16–17). We are children (now) and we are heirs (forever).

Third, the infallible fruit of this faith is "a serious and holy desire to preserve a good conscience and to perform good works." This third point flows from the first two. We do not find our assurance in introspection, by asking ourselves, "Do I have a good conscience? Do I desire to perform good works?" Instead, assurance springs from faith, which then produces good works. In fact, without true faith it is impossible to perform good works, for "whatsoever is not of faith is sin" (Rom. 14:23).

The article ends with a description of the effect of the lack or the loss of assurance. What would our experience be if we were "deprived of this solid comfort"? Where would we be if we listened

---

12 Form for the Administration of the Lord's Supper, in ibid., 269–70 (emphasis added).

to and believed the hawkers of doubt? What would happen if we did *not* believe that we "shall finally obtain the final victory"? Where would we be without "this infallible pledge or earnest of eternal glory"? Notice the beautiful turns of phrase: final victory; infallible pledge; infallible earnest; and eternal glory. Without this assurance or deprived of it, we would be "of all men the most miserable" (1 Cor. 15:19).

If you love your soul, and if you love the comfort of the gospel, avoid the preachers of doubt. They will make you and your family miserable.

ERROR AND REJECTION 5: THE IMPOSSIBILITY OF ASSURANCE OF FINAL PERSEVERANCE

> Error 5: Who teach that without a special revelation we can have no certainty of future perseverance in this life.
>
> Rejection: For by this doctrine the sure comfort of the true believers is taken away in this life, and the doubts of the papist are again introduced into the church, while the Holy Scriptures constantly deduce this assurance, not from a special and extraordinary revelation, but from the marks proper to the children of God and from the constant promises of God. So especially the apostle Paul: *No creature shall be able to separate us from the love of God, which is in Christ Jesus our Lord* (Rom. 8:39). And John declares: *And he that keepeth his commandments abideth in him, and he in him. And hereby we know that he abideth in us, by the Spirit which he gave us* (1 John 3:24).

The Arminians denied the possibility of the assurance of final perseverance: "We can have no certainty of future perseverance in this life." The only exception to that rule is in the case of "special revelation."

The Canons charge the Arminians with taking away "the sure

comfort of the true believers." For a Reformed believer, this means that the Arminians (and modern purveyors of doubt in Reformed churches) cannot confess this beautiful truth of the Heidelberg Catechism:

> That I with body and soul, both in life and death, am not my own, but belong unto my faithful Savior Jesus Christ; who, with His precious blood, hath fully satisfied for all my sins, and delivered me from all the power of the devil; and so preserves me that without the will of my heavenly Father, not a hair can fall from my head; yea, that all things must be subservient to my salvation.[13]

The fathers of Dordt rightly labeled the Arminian error "the doubts of the papist." The Reformation delivered God's people from the doubts of the papist, but the Arminians sought to introduce these doubts again into the church. John Calvin would have rebuked them sharply:

> Lastly, there was another *most pestilential error*, which not only occupied the minds of men, but was regarded as one of the principal articles of faith, of which it was impious to doubt, viz., that *believers ought to be perpetually in suspense and uncertainty as to their interest in the divine favor. By this suggestion of the devil, the power of faith was completely extinguished*, the benefits of Christ's purchase destroyed, and the salvation of men overthrown. For, as Paul declares, *that faith only is Christian faith which inspires our hearts with confidence, and emboldens us to appear in the presence of God*, (Rom. 5:2.) On no other view could his doctrine in another passage be maintained, viz., that "we have received the Spirit of adoption, whereby we cry, Abba, Father" (Rom.

13 Heidelberg Catechism A 1, in ibid., 83.

> 8:15.) But what is the effect of that hesitancy which our enemies require in their disciples, save *to annihilate all confidence in the promises of God*? Paul argues, that "If they which are of the law be heirs, faith is made void, and the promise made of none effect" (Rom. 4:14.) Why so? Just because the law keeps a man in doubt, and does not permit him to entertain a sure and firm confidence. *But they, on the other hand, dream of a faith, which, excluding and repelling man from that confidence which Paul requires, throws him back upon conjecture, to be tossed like a reed shaken by the wind.*[14]

Besides this, the scriptures "constantly deduce" assurance from a different source, namely "the marks proper to the children of God" and "the constant promises of God." This is so obviously the teaching of the Bible that the Canons quote only a sample of texts to prove it (Rom. 8:39; 1 John 3:24).

ARTICLE 11: BELIEVERS' STRUGGLES WITH CARNAL DOUBTS

> The Scripture moreover testifies that believers in this life have to struggle with various carnal doubts, and that under grievous temptations they are not always sensible of this full assurance of faith and certainty of persevering. But God, who is the Father of all consolation, does not suffer them to be tempted above that they are able, but will with the temptation also make a way to escape, that they may be able to bear it (1 Cor. 10:13), and by the Holy Spirit again inspires them with the comfortable assurance of persevering.

The Canons are realistic and experiential, in that they reflect the *real experiences* of God's children in this world. While assurance of

14 John Calvin, "*The Necessity of Reforming the Church*," in *Tracts and Letters* (Edinburgh, Scotland: Banner of Truth, repr. 2009), 1:136 (emphasis added).

final perseverance is the fruit of true faith, there are times when the Christian's assurance is weak. The source of this trouble is the sinful flesh. As I have repeatedly emphasized, the Canons never praise doubt, which they view as sin, but they still reckon with it as a sad reality, which requires a pastoral approach.

Believers "struggle with various carnal doubts." A *carnal* doubt is a doubt of the flesh—there are no *spiritual* doubts. (The fruit of the Spirit is not doubt, which is unbelief, but faith [Gal. 5:22].) This does not mean that believers lose their assurance, and it certainly does not mean that they fall from the faith, nor that the Christian's faith is obliterated or extinguished. Instead, "they are not always sensible of this full assurance of faith and certainty of persevering." The word "sensible" would be better rendered as "sensitive," for it refers to sense or experience, not to intellect or intelligence. There are times when we do not *feel* assured because of the attacks of the devil, the fears of the flesh, and the workings of unbelief. The Canons describe this as happening "under grievous temptations." When we experience afflictions, our faith falters; or when we fall into sin, our faith is assailed. The Bible calls this being "cast down" or "disquieted" (Ps. 42:9–11; 43:5) and warns us against the "fiery darts of the wicked" against which we take "the shield of faith" (Eph. 6:16).

Nevertheless, God does not leave us to be tormented with such doubts, nor does he leave his children to languish in such misery for prolonged periods. Hear the triumphant note from the Canons—"But God"! God is "the Father of all consolation" (2 Cor. 1:3) who sustains his children in several ways.

First, he does not allow them to be tempted above that they are able, for God who is sovereign over trials and temptations does not allow them to plunge into despair: "There hath no temptation taken you but such as is common to man: but God is faithful, who will not suffer you to be tempted above that ye are able; but will with the temptation also make a way to escape, that ye may be able to bear it" (1 Cor. 10:13).

Second, God will always make a way to escape from every temptation, including the temptation to doubt.

Third, by God's grace his children will be able to bear the temptations. The result of this is that "the Holy Spirit again inspires [believers] with the comfortable assurance of persevering."

Fear not, therefore, believing reader. While you might struggle for a time, doubts are not the norm, and they are temporary. God will deliver you from your doubts and fears and give you the comfort of assurance.

ARTICLE 12: THE SWEET FRUIT OF ASSURANCE OF FINAL PERSEVERANCE

> This certainty of perseverance, however, is so far from exciting in believers a spirit of pride, or of rendering them carnally secure, that, on the contrary, it is the real source of humility, filial reverence, true piety, patience in every tribulation, fervent prayers, constancy in suffering and in confessing the truth, and of solid rejoicing in God; so that the consideration of this benefit should serve as an incentive to the serious and constant practice of gratitude and good works, as appears from the testimonies of Scripture and the examples of the saints.

The Arminians rejected the Reformed doctrine of assurance because they claimed that it would make people careless about their lives and behavior. If you know that you will infallibly be saved and persevere unto the end, they reasoned, there is no incentive to avoid sin, to lead a new and holy life, and to resist temptation. This, you will recognize, is the tired, old objection to salvation by grace alone that is still taught today in Roman Catholicism, Arminianism, and even in Reformed and Presbyterian churches under the auspices of the federal vision.[15] The Canons defend the Reformed faith against this charge of the Arminians.

Negatively, this certainty of perseverance does not excite in believers a "spirit of pride." To be proud of gracious salvation and gracious preservation in salvation is surely abominable. This also does not render believers "carnally secure." Carnal security is the security of the flesh—it has nothing to do with true, Christian security. The carnal man wants an assurance that there are no negative consequences for sin, because he wants license to indulge in his lusts with impunity. This certainty of perseverance is very far from such carnal security, so far that it has the opposite effect on the child of God.

Positively, this certainty of perseverance is "the real source" of the following spiritual graces: humility; filial reverence (the reverence that children have for a father); true piety (or personal and practical godliness); patience in every tribulation; fervency in prayer; constancy in suffering and in confessing the truth (doubters make poor martyrs); and solid rejoicing in God. These are similar to the fruits that believers have regarding their assurance of eternal and unchangeable election listed in head one, article 13. Moreover, the truth that believers are assured of perseverance is "an incentive to the serious and constant practice of gratitude and good works." This is evident from the testimony of the saints recorded in the sacred scriptures.

If you are assured of perseverance in salvation, you will exhibit these spiritual graces and grow in them by the power of God's grace until you are received into heavenly glory on the last day.

ARTICLE 13: THE EFFECT OF ASSURANCE ON THE FORMER BACKSLIDER

> Neither does renewed confidence of persevering produce licentiousness or a disregard to piety in those who are

15 For a guide to the federal vision, see David J. Engelsma, *Federal Vision: Heresy At the Root* (Grandville, MI: Reformed Free Publishing Association, 2012).

> recovering from backsliding; but it renders them much more careful and solicitous to continue in the ways of the Lord, which He hath ordained, that they who walk therein may maintain an assurance of persevering; lest, by abusing His fatherly kindness, God should turn away His gracious countenance from them, to behold which is to the godly dearer than life, the withdrawing whereof is more bitter than death, and they in consequence hereof should fall into more grievous torments of conscience.

If article 12 describes generally the good fruit of assurance in believers, article 13 applies the truth to the specific case of the saint described in articles 4–5, who for a time fell into sin and was graciously restored by the grace of God. After the child of God is restored to repentance and walks again with the Lord, he has "renewed confidence in persevering." What is the effect of this renewed confidence on the restored backslider? He does not say, "I prospered in sin before. Since God is merciful, I will commit sin again." That is what the Arminians thought was the implication of the Reformed teaching on perseverance. That is not at all the effect of the grace of God.

This renewed confidence of persevering does not produce "licentiousness," which is a lack of discipline in moral conduct or a deliberate walking in sin; nor a "disregard to piety," which is the neglect of prayer, of meditation on the scriptures, of worship, and of good works. The opposite is the case: it makes the child of God "much more careful and solicitous [or extremely concerned] to continue in the ways of the Lord."

Therefore, such a restored backslider will not abuse God's fatherly kindness, for the effects of such abuse would be to repeat the awful downward spiral of article 5. No child of God wants to experience that. No child of God who has experienced that once wants to repeat the experience. The fear of restored backsliders is to come under renewed chastisement: "Lest…God should turn away

His gracious countenance from them...and they in consequence hereof should fall into more grievous torments of conscience." Loss of salvation is impossible; final falling away from the faith is impossible—but grievous torments of conscience are possible for the foolish backslider, especially for the backslider who persists in backsliding even after he has been restored.

The godly man has a certain attitude to these things. First, he loves God: to behold God's countenance is "dearer than life" to him. Second, above all things he fears to lose the gracious countenance of God, for the withdrawing of it is "more bitter than death" to him.

Are we careless or carnally secure? God forbid. "If thou, LORD, shouldest mark iniquities, O Lord, who shall stand? But there is forgiveness with thee, *that thou mayest be feared*" (Ps. 130:3–4, emphasis added).

ERROR AND REJECTION 6: THE ALLEGED EVIL FRUIT OF THE ASSURANCE OF FINAL PERSEVERANCE

> Error 6: Who teach that the doctrine of the certainty of perseverance and of salvation, from its own character and nature, is a cause of indolence and is injurious to godliness, good morals, prayers, and other holy exercises, but that on the contrary it is praiseworthy to doubt.
>
> Rejection: For these show that they do not know the power of divine grace and the working of the indwelling Holy Spirit. And they contradict the apostle John, who teaches the opposite with express words in his first epistle: *Beloved, now are we the children of God, and it is not yet made manifest what we shall be. We know that, if he shall be manifested, we shall be like him; for we shall see him even as he is. And every one that hath this hope set on him purifieth himself, even as he is pure* (1 John 3:2–3). Furthermore, these are contradicted by the example of the saints, both of the Old and the New Testament, who though they were assured of

> their perseverance and salvation were nevertheless constant in prayers and other exercises of godliness.

Arminianism slanders the Reformed faith's teaching on "the certainty of perseverance and of salvation." The Arminians alleged that instead of producing good fruit, certainty is the source of indolence (laziness); and is injurious (harmful) to godliness, good morals, prayers, and other holy exercises. On the contrary, argued the Arminians, "It is praiseworthy to doubt." For the Arminian, doubt is virtuous, but the Bible views doubt as *sin*. If it were "praiseworthy to doubt," why did Jesus consistently rebuke unbelief and doubt? "O ye of little faith" (Matt. 6:30); "Why are ye fearful, O ye of little faith?" (8:26); "O thou of little faith, wherefore didst thou doubt?" (14:31).

The Canons answer that such "show that they do not know the power of divine grace and the working of the indwelling Holy Spirit." Shall the Holy Spirit work faith, which is confidence in, and appropriation of, the divine promises, with the result that believers live carelessly in sin? Shall the Holy Spirit produce unholy believers? Shall the blood of Christ that was shed for the remission of sins produce people who wallow in their sins, as pigs wallow in the mud? Shall the Holy Spirit call us with a holy calling and then permit us to live *without holiness*? Of course not. "For this is the will of God, even your sanctification... For God hath not called us unto uncleanness, but unto holiness" (1 Thess. 4:3, 7). Moreover, the Canons appeal to the testimonies of the saints in the holy scriptures: "Though they were assured of their perseverance and salvation were nevertheless constant in prayers and other exercises of godliness" (1 John 3:2–3). Thus the scriptures and the examples of the saints contradict the Arminian teaching.

ARTICLE 14: GOD'S USE OF MEANS IN THE PRESERVATION OF HIS SAINTS

> And as it hath pleased God, by the preaching of the gospel, to begin this work of grace in us, so He preserves, continues, and perfects it by the hearing and reading of His Word,

> by meditation thereon, and by the exhortations, threatenings, and promises thereof, as well as by the use of the sacraments

Moving from the assurance of the certainty of final perseverance, the Canons address the means by which God preserves his people to the end, namely, "the preaching of the gospel." This is according to the good pleasure of God: "As it hath pleased God." By the same means God "preserves, continues, and perfects" his grace in the hearts and lives of his people. The means are stated in this article: first, the hearing of his word; second, the reading of his word; third, meditation on his word; fourth, the exhortations, threatenings, and promises of his word; and lastly, the use of the sacraments.

That fourth point is important, for it sheds light upon one of the purposes of scripture. Why does God include warnings, exhortations, promises, and even threatenings in the Bible? Take warnings—"Let no man deceive you with vain words: for because of these things cometh the wrath of God upon the children of disobedience. Be not ye therefore partakers with them" (Eph. 5:6–7). Why does God include such warnings if God's children *cannot* fall away and perish? He does so because it is exactly *by means of such warnings* that God preserves his people. When they hear such warnings, they—as opposed to the ungodly who scoff at such warnings—turn from their sins. Such warnings are made effectual through the Spirit either to prevent sin or to turn God's people away from sin into the path of true repentance.

The Reformed faith has always taught that God uses means in salvation. He uses means to bring his people to salvation, hence the need for the preaching of the gospel on the mission field. He also uses means to preserve them in salvation, hence their need regularly to hear the word of God in the church. They neglect those means to their spiritual detriment.

ARTICLE 15: THE CHURCH'S TENDER LOVE FOR AND CONSTANT DEFENSE OF THIS INESTIMABLE TREASURE

> The carnal mind is unable to comprehend this doctrine of the perseverance of the saints and the certainty thereof, which God hath most abundantly revealed in His Word, for the glory of His name and the consolation of pious souls, and which He impresses upon the hearts of the faithful. Satan abhors it; the world ridicules it; the ignorant and hypocrite abuse, and heretics oppose it; but the spouse of Christ hath always most tenderly loved and constantly defended it, as an inestimable treasure; and God, against whom neither counsel nor strength can prevail, will dispose her to continue this conduct to the end. Now, to this one God, Father, Son, and Holy Spirit be honor and glory forever. AMEN.

This final article summarizes the truth and concludes head five and the Canons with a high note of doxology. Two main attitudes to the doctrine of the perseverance of the saints are found in the world. Negatively, the carnal mind cannot comprehend or understand it, for carnal "wisdom" concludes that if a believer enjoys the assurance of perseverance, he will be careless and profane. Moreover, Satan "abhors" it, for it is testimony to his defeat. Try as he might, with all of his cruelty and cunning, he cannot snatch one of the elect, redeemed, regenerated children of God from the hand of the Father and of Christ (John 10:28–30). How that must gall him. Furthermore, the world ridicules this truth, for the world views the hope of God's children as pie-in-the-sky foolishness. In addition, the ignorant and the hypocrite abuse this truth, for they use it as an excuse to commit sin, which is never the effect of this doctrine on true saints. Finally, heretics oppose it, heretics such as the Remonstrants of the sixteenth century, as well as Arminians, Roman Catholics, and the men of the federal vision in our day.

Positively, God has "abundantly revealed" this truth in his word. Not merely in a handful of places, but throughout the scriptures, this truth is set forth. Therefore, they are inexcusable who deny it and subvert it by their heresies. This truth is revealed "for the glory of His name," for it makes salvation, from beginning to end, to depend upon God alone. This truth is also revealed for "the consolation of pious souls," for there is no greater comfort than "that I with body and soul, both in life and death, am not my own, but belong unto my faithful Savior Jesus Christ...*who so preserves me* that without the will of my heavenly Father, not a hair can fall from my head; yea, that all things must be subservient to my salvation, and therefore, by His Holy Spirit, He also assures me of eternal life, and makes me sincerely willing and ready, henceforth, to live unto Him."[16]

Furthermore, God "impresses [this truth] upon the hearts of the faithful," both the truth of it, and the assurance that they possess it.

While the enemies of God hate this truth, "the spouse of Christ hath always most tenderly loved...it." The church, which is the spouse of Christ, has "constantly defended it." The true church of Christ has always esteemed it as "an inestimable treasure," a treasure whose value cannot be calculated. God will preserve the church in the love of the truth—and in this truth in particular—"to the end." The true church shall believe the truth of the perseverance of the saints to the end. The true church shall defend the truth of the perseverance of the saints to the end. The true church shall esteem the truth of the perseverance of the saints as an inestimable treasure to the end. The true church with all her members shall persevere in the faith to the end.

The Canons end with a doxology to the God "against whom neither counsel nor strength can prevail:" "Now, to this one God, Father, Son, and Holy Spirit be honor and glory forever. AMEN."

---

16 Heidelberg Catechism A 1, in *Confessions and Church Order*, 83–84 (emphasis added).

Discussion questions on the fifth head

1. Why is the perseverance of the saints the preferred name for the fifth head of doctrine?

2. What is conditional perseverance? How does this fit with the other doctrines of Arminianism?

3. The fifth head does not begin with a discussion of perseverance or with a text such as John 10:28: "I give unto them eternal life; and they shall never perish, neither shall any man pluck them out of my hand." Why is this?

4. In the regenerate believer sin is *present*, but it does not *rule*. What are the implications of this truth? Study Romans 6. Which lessons does the apostle draw from this truth?

5. What is antinomianism? What do the Reformed creeds teach about antinomianism?

6. What is the attitude of the true Christian to his indwelling sin? How does this attitude differ from that of the hypocrite?

7. Show how Dordt in Canons 5.1–3 was experiential and realistic, while giving real hope to the struggling saint.

8. If through impenitence believers can lose a sense of God's favor for a time, does assurance *depend* on the maintenance of good works as a condition? Explain.

9. From the Christian's perspective, perseverance is impossible. Why?

10. From God's perspective, perseverance is not only possible, but also certain. Why?

11. How are Canons 5.4–5 a warning about the deceitfulness of sin and a call to watchfulness? Discuss how you could heed the warning. How should your behavior change?

12. If a member of the church comes to you worried that he has committed the unpardonable sin, how should you respond?

13. Name the different kinds of non-saving faith and explain how these differ from true faith.

14. What is the effect of the mercy of God on one who was backslidden, but is now restored?

15. Explain what the Canons mean by the "incorruptibleness of the seed of God" in regeneration (Canons 5, rejection 8).

16. Reflect upon the reasons that it is impossible for the believer to perish (Canons 5.8). How do these reasons assure *you* of your perseverance in the grace of God?

17. Why is it not praiseworthy to doubt one's own personal perseverance in grace (Canons 5, rejection 6)?

18. Why are those who lack assurance "of all men the most miserable" (Canons 5.10)?

19. Why do the Canons call a lack of assurance "the doubts of the papist" (Canons 5, rejection 5)?

20. Which truths of the word of God should you bring to one who struggles with carnal doubts?

21. If God unconditionally preserves his people, why are "exhortations, threatenings, and promises" necessary (Canons 5.14)?

22. Why does the spouse of Christ tenderly love the truth of the perseverance of the saints (Canons 5.15)? Do *you*?

Proof texts for the fifth head

Psalm 37:23–24, 28
Psalm 121:3–7
John 6:38–40
John 10:27–30
John 17:11–12
Romans 8:33–39
1 Corinthians 1:8–9
Philippians 1:6
1 Peter 1:5
Jude 24

The Conclusion to the Canons

At the end of the Canons the fathers appended a conclusion in which they underlined the importance of the doctrines of the gospel and answered the various slanders of the Arminians.

The conclusion of the Canons begins with an explanation of the context in which they were written. Five articles of doctrine had been "controverted in the Belgic churches." To controvert is to deny or to contradict. The Remonstrants or Arminians had denied five cardinal truths of the Christian faith: eternal, unconditional election; the efficacy of Christ's particular atonement for his elect church; the total depravity of man; the irresistibility, efficacy, and particularity of grace; and the certain perseverance of the saints in holiness by the preserving grace of God. In turn the synod addressed itself to those five controverted articles of faith. Not only do the Canons set forth positively the truth concerning those five articles, but they also refute the errors of the Arminians in the errors and rejections.

The conclusion refers to "the errors, with which they [the Belgic churches] have for some time been troubled." False doctrine always troubles the church, for it subverts the truth of God and it distresses the saints (2 Thess. 2:1–2). The synod was not convened because the fathers at Dordt loved controversy, but because they loved the truth and they were determined to "earnestly contend for the faith which was once delivered unto the saints" (Jude 3). This must be the motivation for our conduct in the church.

After explaining the context and thus the need for the Canons, the Reformed fathers defended the creed as a clear setting forth of the doctrine of God's word for the benefit of God's people. The Canons of Dordt do not constitute highbrow theology suitable only for the learned men of the halls of academia, but they were written for the comfort and edification of all God's people. It is good that we are familiar with the creeds. We should make sure that we are familiar with this creed in particular, and we should not neglect to teach these doctrines to our children. "This doctrine the synod judges to be drawn from the Word of God." This is crucial, which is why the Canons in almost every article either refer to the Bible or quote explicit texts from it. "This doctrine the synod judges to be...agreeable to the confessions of the Reformed churches." The Canons do not contradict the Heidelberg Catechism or the Belgic Confession which preceded it, but they are a development of some of the doctrines contained in the earlier confessions. The Formula of Subscription adopted by the same synod explains the relationship between the earlier confessions and the Canons:

> We, the undersigned...do hereby sincerely and in good conscience before the Lord declare by this, our subscription, that we heartily believe and are persuaded that all the articles and points of doctrine contained in the Confession and Catechism of the Reformed Churches, together with *the explanation of some points of the aforesaid doctrine made by the National Synod of Dordrecht, 1618-'19*, do fully agree with the Word of God.[1]

1 Formula of Subscription, in *Confessions and Church Order*, 326 (emphasis added).

This doctrine is perspicuous, or clearly expressed; simple; and ingenuous, or openly straightforward, frank, and candid. Unlike the Arminians who resorted to subterfuge, the Reformed fathers were open and honest about what they believed and taught, for the truth does not fear scrutiny.

The conclusion of the Canons also condemns the behavior of the Arminians. The Remonstrant heretics "have violated all truth, equity [justice], and charity [Christian love]." They have done so by "wishing to persuade the public" of a whole list of lies and slanderous charges against the Reformed faith. There follows a list of wicked lies propagated by the Arminians, which, declare the fathers at Dordt, "the Reformed churches not only do not acknowledge, but even detest with their whole soul."

We should briefly take note of the slanderous accusations of the Remonstrants, for many of them are still propagated by the enemies of the Reformed faith today. The Arminians, as noted before, began with an attack on the doctrine of predestination, which they detested. They believed that if they attacked the Reformed faith on that point, they could succeed in poisoning men's minds against it: "The doctrine of the Reformed churches concerning predestination, and the points annexed to it, by its own genius and necessary tendency." Following this opening salvo against the truth, the Arminians listed their charges against the Reformed faith and especially against the Reformed doctrine of predestination.

First, the Reformed faith is destructive of Christian piety and morality: it "leads off the minds of men from all piety and religion" (See, however, Canons 1.9, 13; 2.12–13). "It is an opiate administered by the flesh and the devil." An opiate (think of opium) is a drug that makes a man drunk, stupid, insensible, and sleepy. The dispensing pharmacists of this drug, the doctrine of predestination, are the flesh, the sinful nature of man, and the devil. Moreover, the Reformed faith is "the stronghold of Satan, where he lies in wait for all, and from which he wounds multitudes and mortally strikes through many with the darts both of despair and security." A stronghold is a fortress from which an enemy can safely launch an attack. Satan's weapon, alleged the Arminians, which he shoots from the stronghold, is the doctrine of predestination, which is a fiery dart (Eph. 6:16), which produces despair on the one hand and carnal security on the other hand. "They [men] are persuaded by it [the doctrine of predestination] that nothing can hinder the salvation of the elect, let them live as they please; and, therefore, that they may safely perpetuate every species of the most atrocious crimes." Thus the doctrine of predestination supposedly encourages men to be murderers, rapists, adulterers, drunkards and the like, while promising them salvation because they are eternally and unchangeably elect. "If the reprobate should even perform truly all the works of the saints, their obedience would not in the least contribute to their salvation." This is another straw man, for no such reprobate person exists or has ever existed. Ungodly men do not do good works, for they cannot do them, and they do not desire to perform them.

Second, the Reformed faith makes God unjust and presents him as a monster rather than as the God of righteousness, holiness, and truth: "It makes God the author of sin, unjust, tyrannical, hypocritical" (Canons 1.15). "It is nothing more than interpolated Stoicism, Manicheism, Libertinism, Turcism." Here the Arminians attempted to slander the Reformed with guilt by association. "Interpolated" means that the doctrine of predestination is the way in which these errors are introduced into the church of Christ.

Stoicism is an ancient Greek philosophy the teaching of which was that man should strive to be free from passion, unmoved by joy and sorrow, and should submit without complaint to unavoidable affliction. The motto of the Stoic is *Que sera, sera* (Whatever will be, will be). Since all things happen by necessity, and since there is nothing you can do to change anything, you should seek to be unaffected by physical or emotional pain. The more a Stoic subdues or suppresses his feelings and passions, the more freedom he believes he can enjoy. Paul encountered certain Stoics in Athens (Acts 17).

Manicheism is an ancient heresy embraced by Augustine during his unconverted years and founded on the teachings of Mani (AD 216–76). It was a dualistic religion in which two principles of good and evil vied for supremacy in an eternal struggle. Manicheism included the teaching of a good, spiritual world and an evil, material world. Manicheism also alleged that the creation is evil from the beginning, thus denying the fall, and thus teaching that man is evil by necessity (the Belgic Confession condemns the Manicheans in article 12).

Libertinism is named after the Libertines, who were enemies of John Calvin in Geneva. The Libertines, whose name is derived from *liberty*, used their liberty "for an occasion to the flesh" (Gal. 5:13) or "for a cloke of maliciousness" (1 Pet. 2:16) or turned the grace of God "into lasciviousness" (Jude 4). Calvin preached and wrote against such men and insisted on their discipline and excommunication from the church, although often without the support of the civil authorities in Geneva.

Turcism is another name for Islam, for the Turks were the Muslims of that day. Islam has a doctrine of predestination, but it is not the gracious election as outlined in the Canons of Dordt. It is more akin to Stoicism or determinism.

"The same doctrine teaches that God, by a mere arbitrary act of His will, without the least respect or view to any sin, has predestinated the greatest part of the world to eternal damnation, and has created them for this very purpose." The charges here are arbitrariness and cruelty. This is an exaggerated view of predestination, especially of reprobation, which ignores God's purposes in predestination and denies that reprobation serves election. It also ignores the truth that God reprobates men in the way of their sins and that their ultimate damnation is on account of their sins. No one is cast into hell *merely* because God reprobated him, and no one perishes who is not guilty. "That in the same manner in which the election is the fountain and the cause of faith and good works, reprobation is the cause of unbelief and impiety." The emphasis is on the words "in the same manner." While faith and good works flow from the fountain of election, having God as their author, it is not true to say that unbelief and impiety (and evil works) flow from the fountain of reprobation, having God as their author. The Canons strongly repudiate any notion that God is the author of sin (Canons 1.15).

Third, the Arminians appealed to emotion: "That many children of the faithful are torn, guiltless from their mothers' breasts and tyrannically plunged into hell, so that neither baptism, nor the prayers of the church at their baptism can at all profit them." These words are designed to strike terror into the hearts especially of the daughters of the church, to rob them of all comfort at the graves of their little ones, and to turn the merciful and gracious God and Father of our Lord Jesus Christ into the bloodthirsty Molech of the Ammonites (Lev. 20:1–5). Head one, article 17, was penned in response to this attack on the truth of God's word.

I repeat, these errors are things "which the Reformed churches not only do not acknowledge, but even detest with their whole soul."

Having dealt with the Arminian errors, the conclusion to the Canons contains an appeal, a warning, an admonition, and a prayer. The synod "conjures"—the archaic meaning of "conjure" is not the same as the modern meaning. We think of a "conjuror" as a magician. Here, the verb "conjure" means to implore with solemnity or to give a solemn or serious charge. (The emphasis is on the second syllable.) This charge is made to "as many as piously call upon the name of our Savior Jesus Christ." The conjuration (appeal or charge) concerns the way in which pious saints judge "the faith of the Reformed churches."

Negatively, do not judge the Reformed faith "from the calumnies which on every side are heaped upon it." A calumny is a false and malicious statement designed to harm the reputation of another.

The Arminians heaped calumnies upon the Reformed faith—a number of those calumnies have already been quoted and refuted in the conclusion. Do not allow the Arminian slanders to turn you from the truth of the Reformed faith. Do not judge the Reformed faith "from the private expressions of a few among ancient and modern teachers." It is very easy to find a quotation from someone to make him and his doctrine look bad in the sight of men. Heretics have been misquoting Calvin and others for centuries in order to attack Calvin's doctrine. The synod reminded us that many of the writings are "often dishonestly quoted or corrupted and wrested [twisted] to a meaning quite foreign to their intention." Such behavior is a wicked transgression of the ninth commandment: "That I bear false witness against no man, nor falsify any man's words; that I be no backbiter, nor slanderer, that I do not judge, nor join in condemning any man rashly or unheard."[2]

Positively, we must judge the Reformed faith "from the public confessions of the churches themselves, and from the declaration of the orthodox doctrine, confirmed by the unanimous consent of all and each of the members of the whole synod." You do not judge a church or a denomination from a stray statement in a sermon, book, pamphlet, or article, or from a comment from a church member online, but from the official creeds and the decisions of ecclesiastical assemblies. These creeds for the Reformed churches, especially of the Dutch Reformed tradition, are the Heidelberg Catechism, the Belgic Confession, and the Canons of Dordt, as well as the minor confessions of the Church Order, such as the forms used in baptism and the Lord's supper. In these documents a person who sincerely desires to know what a church teaches, assuming, of course, that the church is faithful to its creed, will find what he needs to know.

Echoing the words of answer 112 of the Heidelberg Catechism regarding the ninth commandment, the synod warned the

2 Heidelberg Catechism A 112, in ibid., 133.

"calumniators themselves." A calumniator is one guilty of calumny: he is a slanderer or a false accuser. Obviously, the synod had the Remonstrants in mind: "Moreover, the synod warns calumniators themselves to consider the terrible judgment of God which awaits them for bearing false witness against the confessions of so many churches, for distressing the consciences of the weak, and for laboring to render suspected the society of the truly faithful." God will punish those who malign his people and the truth of his word. The synod had found the Arminians to be guilty and called them to repent before God.

With admirable wisdom the synod appended an admonition to the teachers, preachers, and witnesses of the truth. An admonition to which we should earnestly take heed if we want to glorify God in our teaching, preaching, and witnessing. The conduct of all teachers, preachers, and witnesses must be pious and religious. This, of course, is fundamental to the Christian witness, for one who lives wickedly *cannot* be an effective witness to Jesus Christ. In fact, it was because of the wickedness of the Jews and of professing Christians that the name of God was blasphemed among the nations (Rom. 2:24). Therefore, a rude, crude, needlessly fanatical "Christian witness" does harm to the reputation of the church of Christ and would serve the church better *if he kept his mouth shut.* As Reformed believers we are called to pray that "we may so order and direct our whole lives, our thoughts, words, and actions, that [God's] name may never be blasphemed, but rather honored and praised on our account."[3]

This conduct includes the "handling [of] this doctrine." The doctrine of God is a precious treasure that we must handle "piously and religiously." For example, we must not cast our pearls before swine (Matt. 7:6). We must not make the precious doctrines of God's word the butt of jokes or bumper sticker slogans. This pious

3 Heidelberg Catechism A 122, in ibid., 137.

and religious handling of the truth must occur "in the universities and churches." Clearly, the fathers had theological professors, pastors, and authors in mind. Had the synod met in our day, the fathers undoubtedly would have added "and on social media, such as Facebook posts, online discussions, YouTube videos, blog posts, and Twitter." How much nonsense, foolish questions, strivings about theological differences, accusations and counter-accusations, and unprofitable debating, masquerading itself as "witnessing to the truth" is propagated on the internet today. God has deposited his truth with us not so that we can endlessly argue about it, not so that we can debate and prove ourselves to be right against our theological adversaries, and not even so that we can pursue the truth in a merely intellectual manner, but "to the glory of the divine name, to holiness of life, and to the consolation of afflicted souls." If your belief, discussion, and defense of the truth do not have those aims, there is something very wrong, and you need to repent and seek the truth rightly.

Moreover, the synod urged preachers, theologians, professors, authors, and witnesses to "regulate" their sentiments and their language: "Regulate, by the Scripture, according to the analogy of faith, not only their sentiments, but also their language, and to abstain from all those phrases which exceed the limits necessary to be observed in ascertaining the genuine sense of the Holy Scriptures." Sentiments are feelings—the synod warned against theological hotheads! Language is important; therefore, a theologian must choose his words carefully, not exceeding what the Bible teaches, not exaggerating one doctrine, such as reprobation, at the expense of other doctrines. There ought to be no riding of theological hobbyhorses, but a balanced presentation of the whole counsel of God. How often is this rule not violated in sermons, speeches, books, pamphlets, articles, and especially in online forums. The synod gave good reason for this exhortation: exaggerated sentiments and expressions "may furnish insolent sophists with a just pretext for violently assailing, or even vilifying, the doctrine of the Reformed churches." A sophist is one skilled in elaborate and devious argumentation. An insolent sophist is such an arguer who is insultingly contemptuous in speech, writing, or conduct. To behave foolishly by means of exaggerated expressions of doctrine is to place ammunition into the hands of such insolent sophists (the fathers had the Remonstrants in mind, of course), which they will then use against the doctrine of the Reformed churches.

The synod ended with a threefold petition: first, to cause the truth to prosper by bringing those who err to a knowledge of the truth; second, to shut the mouths of the heretics; and third, to give wisdom to the faithful ministers of God's word to glorify God in their speech and to edify their hearers. This prayer is directed to "Jesus Christ, the Son of God, who, seated at the Father's right hand, gives gifts to men."

Appended to the conclusion are the names of the officers and delegates of synod: "That this is our faith and decision, we certify by subscribing our names."

It is my prayer that the readers of this book wholeheartedly agree with the doctrines confessed by the great Synod of Dordt, that they confess them, and that they adorn such a confession with lives of good works to the glory of God.

Discussion questions on the conclusion to the Canons

1. Which accusations are made against the Arminians in the conclusion to the Canons?
2. The Canons are written in a style that is accessible to all the members of the church; therefore, they are not only for professional theologians. True or false?
3. What is the relationship between the Canons and the Belgic Confession and Heidelberg Catechism?
4. Read the accusations of the Arminians against the doctrine of the Reformed churches as refuted in the conclusion. How many of these accusations are still leveled against the Reformed faith today?
5. How does the Reformed faith differ from Stoicism, Manicheism, Libertinism, and Turcism?
6. God's decree of reprobation is arbitrary and cruel. True or false? Discuss.
7. How should we regulate our language with respect to the doctrines of the Reformed faith without compromising our witness through cowardice or excessive timidity?
8. A bad witness is worse than no witness. True or false? Discuss.
9. How can we adorn the gospel of our salvation with lives of good works?
10. Recall an earlier question: How would you describe your attitude toward the creeds in general and toward the Canons of Dordt in particular? (a) I have never heard of them; (b) I am opposed to them; (c) They are a mere historical curiosity to me;

(d) I accept them as authoritative in the church, but they mean nothing to me personally; (e) I find them a useful summary of the teachings of my church; (f) they express what I believe; (g) I love the creeds and I strive to know them more, preserve them in the church, and teach them to my children.

11. After reading this exposition of the Canons, have you changed in your attitude? Why or why not?

Appendices

Appendix One

The Remonstrance of 1610

(The Five Arminian Articles are quoted from Schaff, *Creeds of Christendom*, 3:545–49.)

Article 1: That God, by an eternal, unchangeable purpose in Jesus Christ his Son, before the foundation of the world, hath determined, out of the fallen, sinful race of men, to save in Christ, for Christ's sake, and through Christ, those who, through the grace of the Holy Ghost, shall believe on this his Son Jesus, and shall persevere in this faith and obedience of faith, through this grace, even to the end; and, on the other hand, to leave the incorrigible and unbelieving in sin and under wrath, and to condemn them as alienate from Christ, according to the word of the Gospel in John iii. 36: "He that believeth on the Son hath everlasting life; and he that believeth not the Son shall not see life; but the wrath of God abideth on him," and according to other passages of Scripture also.

Article 2: That, agreeably thereto, Jesus Christ, the Savior of the world, died for all men and for every man, so that he has obtained for them all, by his death on the cross, redemption, and the forgiveness of sins; yet that no one actually enjoys this forgiveness of sins, except the believer, according to the word of the Gospel of John iii. 16: "God so loved the world that he gave his only-begotten Son, that whosoever believeth in him should not perish, but have everlasting life"; and in the First Epistle of John ii. 2: "And he is the propitiation for our sins; and not for ours only, but also for the sins of the whole world."

Article 3: That man has not saving grace of himself, nor of the energy of his free will, inasmuch as he, in the state of apostasy and sin, can of and by himself neither think, will, nor do anything that is truly good (such as having Faith eminently is); but that it is needful that he be born again of God in Christ, through his Holy Spirit, and renewed in understanding, inclination, or will, and all his powers, in order that he may rightly understand, think, will, and effect what is truly good, according to the word of Christ, John xv. 5: "Without me ye can do nothing."

Article 4: That this grace of God is the beginning, continuance, and accomplishment of any good, even to this extent, that the regenerate man himself, without that prevenient or assisting, awakening, following, and co-operative grace, can neither think, will, nor do good, nor withstand any temptations to evil; so that all good deeds or movements that can be conceived must be ascribed to the grace of God in Christ. But as respects the mode of the operation of this grace, it is not irresistible, inasmuch as it is written concerning many that they have resisted the Holy Ghost, Acts vii, and elsewhere in many places.

Article 5: That those who an incorporated into Christ by a true faith, and have thereby become partakers of his life-giving spirit, have thereby full power to strive against Satan, sin, the world, and their own flesh, and to win the victory; it being well understood that it is ever through the assisting grace of the Holy Ghost; and that Jesus Christ assists them through his Spirit in all temptations, extends to them his hand, and if only they are ready for the conflict and desire his help, and are not inactive, keeps them from falling, so that they, by no craft or power of Satan, can be misled, nor plucked out of Christ's hands, according to the Word of Christ, John x. 28: "Neither shall any man pluck them out of my hand." But whether they are capable through negligence, of forsaking again the first beginnings of their life in Christ, of again returning to this present evil world, of turning away from the holy doctrine which was delivered them, of losing a good conscience, of becoming devoid of grace, that must be more particularly determined out of the Holy Scripture, before we ourselves can teach it with the full persuasion of our minds.

Appendix Two

The Opinions of the Remonstrants 1618

(The Opinions of the Remonstrants are quoted from De Jong, *Crisis in the Reformed Churches,* 220–29 with permission from the Reformed Fellowship.)

A. The Opinion of the Remonstrants regarding the first article, dealing with the decree of Predestination.
   1. God has not decided to elect anyone to eternal life, or to reject anyone from the same, prior to the decree to create him, without any consideration of preceding obedience or disobedience, according to His good pleasure, for the demonstration of the glory of His mercy and justice, or of His absolute power and dominion.
   2. Since the decree of God concerning both the salvation and perdition of each man is not a decree of the end absolutely intended, it follows that neither are such means subordinated to that same decree by which the elect and the reprobate are efficaciously and inevitably led to their final destination.
   3. Therefore God has not with this plan created in the one Adam all men in a state of rectitude, has not ordained the fall and the permission of it, has not withdrawn from Adam the grace which was necessary and sufficient, has not brought it about that the Gospel is preached and that men are externally called, does not confer on them any gifts of the Holy Spirit by means of which he leads some of them to life, but deprives others of the benefit

of life. Christ, the Mediator, is not solely the executor of election, but also the foundation of that same decree of election: the reason why some are efficaciously called, justified, persevere in faith, and are glorified is not that they have been absolutely elected to eternal life. That others are left in the fall, that Christ is not given to them, that they are either not called at all or not efficaciously called—these are not the reasons why they are absolutely rejected from eternal salvation.

4. God has not decreed to leave the greatest part of men in the fall, excluded from every hope of salvation, apart from intervening actual sins.
5. God has ordained that Christ should be a propitiation for the sins of the whole world, and by virtue of that decree He has determined to justify and to save those who believe in Him, and to provide for men means necessary and sufficient for faith in such a way as He knows to be in harmony with His wisdom and justice. But He has by no means determined, by virtue of an absolute decree, to give Christ the Mediator solely to the elect, and through an efficacious calling to bestow faith upon, justify, preserve in the faith and glorify them alone.
6. No one is rejected from life eternal nor from the means sufficient for it by an absolute antecedent decree, so that the merit of Christ, calling, and all the gifts of the Spirit can be profitable to salvation for all, and truly are, unless they themselves by the abuse of these gifts pervert them to their own perdition; but to unbelief, to impiety, and to sins, a means and causes of damnation, no one is predestined.
7. The election of particular persons is decisive, out of consideration of faith in Jesus Christ and of perseverance; not, however, apart from a consideration of faith and

perseverance in the true faith, as a condition prerequisite for electing.

8. Rejection from eternal life is made on the basis of a consideration of antecedent unbelief and perseverance in unbelief; not, however, apart from a consideration of antecedent unbelief and perseverance in unbelief.
9. All the children of believers are sanctified in Christ, so that no one of them who leaves this life before the use of reason will perish. By no means, however, are to be considered among the number of the reprobate certain children of believers who leave this life in infancy before they have committed any actual sin in their own persons, so that neither the holy bath of baptism nor the prayers of the church for them in any way be profitable for their salvation.
10. No children of believers who have been baptized in the name of the Father, the Son, and the Holy Spirit, living in the state of infancy, are reckoned among the reprobate by an absolute decree.

B. The Opinion of the Remonstrants regarding the second article, which deals with the universality of the merit of the death of Christ.

1. The price of redemption which Christ offered to God the Father is not only in itself and by itself sufficient for the redemption of the whole human race but has also been paid for all men and for every man, according to the decree, will, and the grace of God the Father; therefore no one is absolutely excluded from participation in the fruits of Christ's death by an absolute and antecedent decree of God.
2. Christ has, by the merit of his death, so reconciled God the Father to the whole human race that the Father, on

account of that merit, without giving up His righteousness and truth, has been able and has willed to make and confirm a new covenant of grace with sinners and men liable to damnation.

3. Though Christ has merited reconciliation with God and remission of sins for all men and for every man, yet no one, according to the pact of the new and gracious covenant, becomes a true partaker of the benefits obtained by the death of Christ in any other way than by faith; nor are sins forgiven to sinning men before they actually and truly believe in Christ.
4. Only those are obliged to believe that Christ died for them for whom Christ has died. The reprobates, however, as they are called, for whom Christ has not died, are not obligated to such faith, nor can they be justly condemned on account of the contrary refusal to believe this. In fact, if there should be such reprobates, they would be obliged to believe that Christ has not died for them.

C. The Opinion of the Remonstrants regarding the third and fourth articles, concerning the grace of God and the conversion of man.
   1. Man does not have saving faith of himself, nor out of the powers of his free will, since in the state of sin he is able of himself and by himself neither to think, will or do any good (which would indeed to be saving good, the most prominent of which is saving faith). It is necessary therefore that by God in Christ through His Holy Spirit he be regenerated and renewed in intellect, affections, will and in all his powers, so that he might be able to understand, reflect upon, will and carry out the good things which pertain to salvation.
   2. We hold, however, that the grace of God is not only the beginning but also the progression and the completion

of every good, so much so that even the regenerate himself is unable to think, will, or do the good, or to resist any temptations to evil, apart from that preceding or prevenient, awakening, following and cooperating grace. Hence all good works and actions which anyone by cogitation is able to comprehend are to be ascribed to the grace of God.

3. Yet we do not believe that all zeal, care, and diligence applied to the obtaining of salvation before faith itself and the Spirit of renewal are vain and ineffectual—indeed, rather harmful to man than useful and fruitful. On the contrary, we hold that to hear the Word of God, to be sorry for sins committed, to desire saving grace and the Spirit of renewal (none of which things man is able to do without grace) are not only not harmful and useless, but rather most useful and most necessary for the obtaining of faith and of the Spirit of renewal.
4. The will in the fallen state, before calling, does not have the power and the freedom to will any saving good. And therefore we deny that the freedom to will saving good as well as evil is present to the will in every state.
5. The efficacious grace by which anyone is converted is not irresistible; and though God so influences the will by the Word and the internal operation of His Spirit that he both confers the strength to believe or supernatural powers, and actually causes man to believe—yet man is able of himself to despise that grace and not to believe, and therefore to perish through his own fault.
6. Although according to the most free will of God the disparity of divine grace is very great, nevertheless, the Holy Spirit confers, or is ready to confer, as much grace to all men and to each man to whom the Word of God is preached as is sufficient for promoting the conversion

of men in its steps. Therefore sufficient grace for faith and conversion falls to the lot not only of those whom God is said to will to save according to the decree of absolute election, but also of those who are not actually converted.

7. Man is able through the grace of the Holy Spirit to do more good than he actually does, and to avoid more evil than he actually avoids; and we do not believe that God simply does not will that man should do more good than he does and avoid more evil than he does avoid, and that God has decreed precisely from eternity that both should so happen.
8. Whomever God calls to salvation, he calls seriously, that is, with a sincere and completely unhypocritical intention and will to save; nor do we assent to the opinion of those who hold that God calls certain ones externally whom He does not will to call internally, that is, as truly converted, even before the grace of calling has been rejected.
9. There is not in God a secret will which so contradicts the will of the same revealed in the Word that according to it (that is, the secret will) He does not will the conversion and salvation of the greatest part of those whom He seriously calls and invites by the Word of the Gospel and by His revealed will; and we do not here, as some say, acknowledge in God a holy simulation, or a double person.
10. Nor do we believe that God calls the reprobate, as they are called, to these ends: that He should the more harden them, or take away excuse, or punish them the more severely, or display their inability; nor, however, that they should be converted, should believe, and should be saved.
11. It is not true that all things, not only good but also bad, necessarily occur, from the power and efficacy of the secret will or decree of God, and that indeed those who

sin, out of consideration of the decree of God, are not able to sin; that God wills to determine and to bring about the sins of men, their insane, foolish, and cruel works, and the sacrilegious blasphemy of His name—in fact, to move the tongues of men to blasphemy, and so on.

12. To us the following is false and horrible: that God impels men to sins which He openly prohibits; that those who sin do not act contrary to the will of God properly named; that what is unrighteous (that is, what is contrary to His precept) is in agreement with the will of God; indeed, that it is truly a capital crime to do the will of God.

D. The Opinion of the Remonstrants with respect to the fifth article, which concerns Perseverance.

1. The perseverance of believers in the faith is not an effect of the absolute decree by which God is said to have chosen singular persons defined by no condition of obedience.
2. God provides true believers with as much grace and supernatural powers as He judges, according to His infinite wisdom, to be sufficient for persevering and for overcoming the temptations of the devil, the flesh, and the world; it is never to be charged to God's account that they do not persevere.
3. True believers can fall from true faith and can fall into such sins as cannot be consistent with true and justifying faith; not only is it possible for this to happen, but it even happens frequently.
4. True believers are able to fall through their own fault into shameful and atrocious deeds, to persevere and to die in them; and therefore finally to fall and to perish.
5. Nevertheless we do not believe that true believers, though they may sometimes fall into grave sins which are vexing

to their consciences, immediately fall out of every hope of repentance; but we acknowledge that it can happen that God, according to the multitude of His mercies, may recall them through His grace to repentance; in fact, we believe that this happens not infrequently, although we cannot be persuaded that this will certainly and indubitably happen.

6. The following dogmas, therefore, which by public writings are being scattered among the people, we reject with our whole mind and heart as harmful to piety and good morals: namely, (1) True believers are not able to sin deliberately, but only out of ignorance and weakness. (2) True believers through no sins can fall out of the grace of God. (3) A thousand sins, even all the sins of the whole world, are not able to render election invalid. (4) To believers and to the elect no sins, however great and grave they can be, are imputed; but all present and future sins have already been remitted. (5) True believers, having fallen into destructive heresies, into grave and most atrocious sins, like adultery and homicide, on account of which the church, after the justification of Christ, is compelled to testify that it is not able to tolerate them in its external communion and that they will have no part in the kingdom of Christ unless they are converted, nevertheless are not able to fall from faith totally and finally.
7. A true believer, as for the present time he can be certain about his faith and the integrity of his conscience, and thus also concerning his salvation and the saving benevolence of God toward him, for that time can be and ought to be certain; and on this point we reject the pontifical opinion.

A true believer can and ought indeed to be certain for the future that he is able, by diligent watchfulness, through prayers, and through other holy exercises, to persevere in true faith, and he ought also to be certain that divine grace for persevering will never be lacking; but we do not see how he can be certain that he will never afterwards be remiss in his duty but that he will persevere in faith and in those works of piety and love which are fitting for a believer in this school of Christian warfare; neither do we deem it necessary that concerning this thing a believer should be certain.

Appendix Three

The Judgment of the Synod of Dort Concerning the Five Articles of the Arminians

Behold, I am against them that prophesy false dreams, saith the LORD...yet I sent them not, nor commanded them: therefore they shall not profit this people at all, saith the LORD.—Jeremiah 23:32

(The Judgment of the Synod of Dort Concerning the Five Articles of the Arminians is quoted from *The True Covenanter*, accessed June 18, 2018, http://www.truecovenanter.com/gospel/synod_of_dort.html.)

THE JUDGMENT OF THE SYNOD HOLDEN AT DORT
Concerning the five Articles: As also their sentence
touching Conrad Vorstius

Acts 15:25: It seemed good unto us, being assembled with one accord...

LONDON
PRINTED BY JOHN BILL
M.DC.XIX

THE JUDGMENT OF THE NATIONAL SYNOD OF THE REFORMED BELGIQUE CHURCHES
Assembled at Dort, 1618 and 1619.

In which Synod were admitted many Divines of note,
being of the Reformed Churches.
Of Great Britaine,
Of the Countie of Palatine of Rhene,
Of Hassia,
Of Helvetia,
Of the Correspondance of Weterav,
Of Geneva,
Of Breme, and
Of Embden,
Concerning the five Articles controverted in the Belgique Churches:
Published (by reading in Latin in the great Church at Dort)
May 6, 1619. *Stilo Novo.*
Englished out of the Latine copie.

THE PREFACE
IN THE NAME OF OUR LORD AND SAVIOUR JESUS CHRIST. AMEN.

Amongst the manifold comforts, which our Lord and Saviour Jesus Christ hath imparted to his Church militant in this troublesome pilgrimage, that is deservedly extolled which he left unto her at his departure to his Father into the heavenly Sanctuary, saying, I am with you always unto the end of the world. The truth of this comfortable promise is manifested from time to time in all ages of the Church, which having from the beginning been oppugned, not only by the open violence of enemies, and impiety of hereticks, but further by the underhand cunning of seducers, certainly, if at any time the Lord should have left her destitute of the guard of his saving presence, she had now long since been either oppressed by the power of tyrants, or, to her utter overthrow, seduced by the fraud of imposters.

But that good shepherd, who loves his flock to the end, for

whom he hath laid down his life, hath always opportunity, and many times miraculously, with an outstretched arm, repressed the rage of persecutors, and discovered the winding by-paths of seducers, and scattered their fraudulent purposes; by each of which he hath evidently shewed himself to be present in his Church. Fair evidence hereof is given in the histories concerning godly Emperors, Kings, and Princes, whom the Son of God hath so often raised up for the safeguard of his Church, and inflamed with a holy zeal of his house; and by their means hath not only curbed the fury of tyrants, but also, in his Church's behalf, when it grappled with false teachers, diversly corrupting religion, hath procured the remedy of sacred Synods: wherein the faithful servants of Christ have jointly with their prayers, counsels, and labours courageously stood for God's Church, and his truth, fearlessly opposed the instruments of Satan, howsoever changing themselves into Angels of light, rooted up the weeds of errours, and dissension, preserved the Church in agreement of the pure religion, and left unto posterity the sincere worship of God uncorrupted.

With like favour our faithful Saviour hath given a testimony of his gracious presence at this time to the long distressed Church of the Low-Countries. For this Church being by God's mighty hand set free from the tyranny of the Romish Antichrist, and from the fearful idolatry of Popery, so often wonderfully preserved amidst the dangers of a long-continuing war, and flourishing in the concord of true doctrine, and of discipline to the praise of her God, the admirable increase of the weal-publick, and joy of all other reformed Churches, hath first covertly, afterwards openly, with manifold both old and new errors been assaulted by one James Harmans, alias Arminius, and his followers, assuming the title of Remonstrants, and brought into so great hazard through the ceaseless turmoils of scandalous dissentions, and schisms, that, had not our Saviour's merciful hand in time been interposed, these flourishing Churches had been utterly consumed with the horrible flames of discord and schism.

But blessed for ever be the Lord, who, after he had for a while hidden his countenance from us (who had many ways provoked his wrath and indignation) hath witnessed to the whole world, that he is not forgetful of his covenant, and despiseth not the sighs of his people.

For when in man's understanding scarce any hope of remedy appeared, God did put into the minds of the most illustrious and mighty LL. the States General of the united Provinces, by the counsel and direction of the most renowned, and valiant Prince of Orange, to determine to meet with these outrageous mischiefs by such lawful means as have been long time approved by the example of the Apostles themselves, and of the Christian Church following them; and also heretofore with great benefit used even in the Belgic Church itself: and by their authority to call together a Synod out of all the Provinces subject to their government, to be assembled at Dort: many most grave Divines being entreated thereto, and obtained by the favour of the most high and mighty JAMES, King of Great Britain, and of most illustrious and potent Princes, Landgraves, and Commonwealths, that by the common judgment of so many Divines of the reformed Churches, those opinions of Arminius, and his followers might accurately be examined, and determined of by the rule of God's word only, the true doctrine established, and the false rejected, and concord, peace, and tranquility (by God's blessing) restored to the Church of the Low-Countries. This is that good gift of God, wherein the Belgic Churches triumph, and both humbly confess, and thankfully profess the never-failing mercies of their Saviour.

Wherefore (a fast, and publick prayers being formerly enjoined and performed in all the Belgic Churches by the authority of the chief Magistrate, for the deprecation of God's anger, and imploring his gracious aid) this venerable Synod, assembled together at Dort in the name of the Lord, inflamed with the love of God's honour, and salvation of his Church, and upon the invocation of God's holy name bound by oath, that they would hold the sacred Scripture as the only rule of their verdict, and demean themselves in the hearing and determining of this cause with a good and upright conscience, hath diligently and with great patience labored herein, to persuade the chief patrons of these assertions, cited to appear before them, more largely to unfold their opinion concerning the five notorious controverted Articles, as also the reasons of such their opinion. But they rejecting the judgment of the Synod, and refusing to answer to interrogatories in such manner as was fitting: when as neither the admonitions of the Synod, nor instance of the generous and worthy Deputies of the States General, nay nor the command of the most illustrious and mighty Lords the States General themselves, could prevail any thing at all with them; the Synod, by the commandment of the said Lords, the States General, was fain to take another course, heretofore used and received in ancient Synods. And so the search of their Tenets concerning the five Articles was undertaken out of their own Books, Confessions, and Declarations partly heretofore set forth, partly now exhibited to this Synod.

Which search, and examination being now by God's singular mercy dispatched, and finished with all diligence, conscience, and faithfulness, and with the joint consent of all and every one; this Synod for the advancement of God's glory, for the upholding of that truth which leadeth to salvation, and for the maintaining of peace and tranquility as well in men's consciences, as in the Belgic Churches, determineth to publish this their Judgment; wherein the true doctrine agreeable with God's word, touching the five foresaid heads of doctrine is declared, and the false and disagreeing with God's word, is rejected; as followeth.

THE SENTENCE

Of the Synod concerning the Remontrants

The truth, by God's grace, being hitherto explained, and maintained, errors rejected, and unjust calumnies removed out of the way; this

Synod of Dort, (of whose task this part yet remains) doth seriously, vehemently, and by the authority (which according to God's word, it obtains over all the members of her Churches) in Christ's name entreat, exhort, warn, and enjoin all, and every Pastor of Churches in the united Provinces, all Professors, Doctors, and Rectors of Universities, and Schools, and briefly all in general, to whom either the charge of souls, or instruction of youth is committed, that they abandoning the five known Articles of the *Remonstrants* (which are both erroneous in themselves, and lurking holes for other errours) for their parts, and as much as in them lieth, preserve, clear and untainted, this wholesome doctrine of the saving truth, drawn from the most pure fountain of God's word, that they propound, and expound it discreetly, and faithfully to the people and youth; and diligently declare the use of it, which will be most comfortable, and profitable both in life and in death unto them: that they instruct with mildness, and inform with the evidence of truth, such of the flock as wander, and are of another mind, being carried out of the way with new opinions (if at any time God shall give unto them repentance to acknowledge the truth) that, being restored to a better mind, they may with one spirit, mouth, faith, and love, return again unto the Church of God, and Communion of Saints. That so at the last, the wound of the Church being closed up, and grown together, all the members thereof may have one heart, and one soul in the Lord.

And, forasmuch as there are some gone out from among us under the title of *Remonstrants* (which name of *Remonstrants* as also of *Contra-Remonstrants*, the SYNOD thinks fit henceforth forever to be forgotten and abolished) who, violating the discipline, and order of the Church, and contemning the admonitions, and judgments of their brethren, have by their factious projects, and unlawful means greatly, and very dangerously troubled, about these points of doctrine, the Netherland Churches, heretofore most flourishing, andlinked together in faith, and love: have renewed old and noxious errors, and also forged new; dispersing them among the people both in public, and private, by word, and writing, and most eagerly maintaining them: moreover have, without measure, or ceasing, laid on [a] load of slanders, and reproaches, to disgrace the doctrine hitherto received in these Churches: and filled all places far and near with scandals, dissensions, turmoils, and scruples of conscience: which heinous offences against the faith, against charity, against good manners, and against the unity and peace of the Church, seeing they are not sufferable in any, certainly in Pastors they must of necessity be punished with a very severe censure, such as hath in all ages been inflicted by the Church in such cases.

Hereupon the Synod, having called upon God's most holy name, well knowing their own authority, warranted out of God's word, insisting [*continuing*] in the footsteps of all lawful Synods, as well ancient, as those of later times, and strengthened with the authority of most Illustrious LL. *the States General*, declareth, and judgeth those Pastors, who were leaders of factions, and parties, and teachers of errors, to be held guilty and convict of corrupting religion, rending the unity of the Church, and raising most grievous scandals; and moreover those that were cited to this Synod, to be further guilty of intolerable contumacy against the decrees of the supreme Magistrate published in this Synod, and against this venerable Synod itself.

For which causes the Synod first of all, straitly inhibiteth and debarreth the said cited persons, from all Ecclesiastical function, discharges them of their places, and also holds them unworthy of any office in the Universities, until by serious repentance, fully evidenced by their contrary words, actions, and endeavours, they make satisfaction unto the Church, and be truly and fully reconciled unto her, and re-entertained into the communion thereof. Which we most heartily wish in our Lord and Saviour Christ, for their own good, and the joy of the whole Church.

But as for the rest of whom this National Synod hath not taken notice, we commit them (according to the accustomed order) to the Provincial Synods, Classes, and Presbyteries: which are to provide with all diligence, that the Church may neither receive any hurt for the present, nor have cause to fear it for the time to come: to distinguish, with the spirit of discretion, between the followers of those errours, namely to deprive with all speed the stubborn, clamorous, factious, and turbulent, of their Ecclesiastical and Scholastical Offices, which belong to the cognizance of those Synods: for which purpose we warn them presently, and without delay, upon the receipt of the Judgment of this National Synod (the license and authority of the Magistrate being obtained thereto) to assemble and meet together, lest by lingering and slackness, the mischief gather strength, and get further ground. But as for those, that have fallen off through weakness, being transported by the storm of the times, and happily waver, yea or dissent in matters of lesser moment, yet are modest, peaceable, of blameless conversation, and willing to be better instructed, they are to provoke and stir up such, with all gentleness, charity, and patience, to true and perfect concord with the Church: yet with this *proviso*, that they be very cautelous [*cautious*], that they admit none into the sacred Ministry, who shall refuse to subscribe unto, and teach the Doctrine declared in these Synodical Constitutions: and further, that they retain none in the Ministry, by whose manifest dissention, the Doctrine, with so universal a consent, approved in this Synod, may be impeached, and the concord of Pastors, and tranquility of the Church again disturbed.

Moreover, this venerable Synod, earnestly adviseth all Ecclesiastical assemblies to be careful and watchful, over the flocks committed [to] their charge, in time to meet withall innovations, covertly springing up in the Church, and to pluck up such tares out of the Lord's field: likewise, that they have a special eye and care over Schools, and the Governours of Schools, lest by private and crooked opinions instilled into youth, the like mischief hereafter grow again upon the Church, and Commonwealth.

Finally, as this Synod yieldeth humble thanks to the most

Illustrious, and mighty L.L. the States General of the united Provinces, for that in so needful and seasonable a time, they have relieved the afflicted and decayed estate of this Church, by affording the remedy of a Synod, received into their protection the true and faithful servants of God; taken order to have the pledge of all blessings, and of God's presence, namely the truth of his Word, religiously, and holily preserved, in their Dominions, and spared neither cost, nor pains, to advance and perfect so great a work (for which good offices performed by them, the Synod most heartily wisheth of God, a most plentiful both spiritual, and temporal reward, into the bosoms of them all in the public, and of every of them in their particular:) so also it further earnestly, and humbly entreats the said most gracious L.L. that they would be pleased, to will and command this wholesome Doctrine, faithfully expressed by this Synod, according to God's word, and the consent of the Reformed Churches, to be solely and publickly taught in their Dominions; to nip in the head all upstarting heresies, and errors; to curb unquiet and turbulent spirits; still to approve themselves true and loving Foster-Fathers of the Church; to ratify this Synodical Sentence decreed against the forementioned persons, according to the Ecclesiastical authority, confirmed by the laws of the Land: and lastly, by their approbation, and strength of their authority thereto added, to confirm the determinations concluded by this Synod, and make them forever inviolable.

Subscribed in the name, and by the appointment of the Synod.
Sebastianus Damman, Secretary of the Synod.
Festus Hommius, Pastor of the Church of Leyden, and Register of the National Synod.

In witness of the enacting hereof,
DANIEL HEINSIUS

THE APPROBATION

Of the LL. the Estates Generall.

The Estates general of the united Provinces of the Netherlands to all that shall see, or read these presents, GREETING:

Whereas, for the abolishment of those lamentable, and most hurtful controversies, some years since (to the great damage of our Common-weale, and breach of our Church-peace) raised about the notorious *five Articles*, (so called) and the points appendant thereon, We thought fit, according to the good course usually taken both in God's Church generally, and particularly in the Belgique Church itself, to summon a *National* SYNOD of all the Churches of our united Provinces, to be assembled at DORT; and for the better celebrating the said Synod to the especial benefit of these Countries, have, without spare of our labour or charges, requested, and obtained to be sent thither many worthy, learned, and notable Divines of the Reformed Churches in divers foreign Nations, as by their several subscriptions unto the Synodical Judgment doth appear: and have also, for the well ordering of the said Synod, deputed for every several Province our *Delegates*, who by their presence from the beginning to the ending of the Sessions of that Assembly, might take care, that all things might be carried there (according to our sincere intention) in the fear of God, in decent order, and by the rule of God's word only. And whereas the said Synod hath now, by God's singular blessing, with so joint a consent of all and every, as well Strangers as Domestics, given their Judgment concerning the aforesaid Heads of doctrine, and hath moreover passed a Synodical censure upon the Teachers of those erroneous points; and also, with our knowledge, and consent, hath upon the sixth of May last past, published the said decrees and sentence: WE, being desirous, that the Churches of these Countries may fully enjoy the fruit of this great, and holy Work, (being such as the Reformed Churches never saw before) and holding nothing more dear, nor more pertinent to our charge, than the glory of God's most sacred name, the maintaining and spreading of the true Reformed Religion (which is the foundation of our prosperity, and the bond of combination among the confederate Provinces) than the concord, peace, and tranquility of our Churches; as also the preserving of correspondence, and communion between the Churches within these Countries, and all other foreign Reformed Churches, from which we neither may, nor can dissever ourselves, *having viewed*, recognized, and duly examined and weighed the aforesaid *Judgment* and *Sentence* of the Synod, have fully in all points approved, confirmed, and ratified, and by these presents do approve, confirm, and ratify the same.

Hereby *willing* also, and *ordaining*, that no doctrine concerning the aforesaid five doctrinal Heads, other than that, which shall be conformable and agreeing with the forenamed *Judgment*, shall be taught, or spread in the Churches of these Countries. And accordingly, we enjoin and command all Ecclesiastic Assemblies, all Church-Ministers, Professors, and Doctors of Divinity, Rectors of Colleges, and all and every one, whom these things may any way concern, faithfully and sincerely to follow the same, and to conform themselves thereunto in the performance of their Ministry and functions.

And to the end that our good intention may attain full effect on all sides, *we* enjoin, and command, the States Generals, and Deputies of States, the Counsellors, and Deputies of the Provinces of Gelders, Zutphen, Holland, and Westfriesland, Zeland, Utrecht, Friesland, Over-Issel, Gronning, and the Omlands, and all other Officers, Judges, and Justicers, to observe and maintain, and cause to be observed and maintained, the aforesaid Synodical *Judgment*, with the appertenances: so that neither themselves make any immutation of them, nor suffer to be attempted by others in any sort: For that we hold, and judge this course necessary to be taken for the promoting of God's glory, for the welfare and securing of this State, and for the peace and tranquility of this Church.

Given under our Seal, signed by our President, and subscribed by our Secretary, at Gravenhage, *Jul.* 2. 1619. A. PLOOS.

By order from the said States Generall.

C. AARSEN.

The Seal in red wax underneath.

THE SENTENCE

Of the National Synod of Dort,

Concerning the doctrine of

CONRADUS VORSTIUS, Doctor of Divinity.

Whereto is annexed the DECREE of the Illustrious and mighty LL. *the Estates of Holland and West-Friesland,* ensuing upon the said sentence.

Whereas it hath pleased the high and mighty LL. *the States general,* by their nobel and worthy Commissioners, to require this Synod, to deliver summarily their judgment concerning the Divinity, or Doctrine broached by *Conradus Vorstius,* Doctor of Divinity in his writings, and withall to declare, whether such his doctrine be fit to be taught in the reformed Churches or Schools, as wholesome and tending to edification, or might without breach of piety be tolerated in the same: this *venerable Synod,* having in the fear of God duly weighed, and examined the premisses, hath with joint suffrages declared, and by this present sentence doth declare, That the said *Conrad Vorstius* (besides that concerning the five controverted Articles, he defendeth and maintaineth the errors of the *Remonstrants,* rejected by this Synod) doth in his latter writings, but especially in the Tractate, entitled, *Of God, and his attributes,* make bold with, not one or two Articles of the reformed Religion, but most of the fundamental heads of Divinity; namely, such as concern the Trinity of persons in the Godhead, the Simplicity, Infiniteness, Immensity, Essential Omnipresence, Omniscience, Omnipotency, Wisdom, and Immutability of the Essence of God; as also concerning the Creation, the Providence of God, the Hypostatical Union of the two natures in Christ, the full and perfect Satisfaction performed by Christ for our sins, the Justification of man before God by Faith, and many other Articles particularized, as well by the most high and mighty King of *Great Britain*, as by divers professed Divines; the said *Vorstius* in those points, partly calling into question many things, the certain and resolved truth whereof hath long since out of God's word been received, and professed by all reformed Churches: and partly avouching expressly many things contrary to the truth of God, revealed in the holy Scriptures, and to the Confessions of all Reformed Churches, impeaching God's glory, hurtful to piety and man's salvation, and either wholly consorting, or very near bordering upon the blasphemies of the baleful heretic *Socinus*.

And moreover, that he in many passages of his writings, doth most dangerously undermine the chief grounds, founded upon God's word, and thence soundly deduced both by venerable Antiquity, and also by later Reformed Doctors, for the establishing of orthodox Doctrine, especially such as prove the eternal Deity of our Lord Jesus Christ, without substituting in the place of those arguments any other for the further confirmation of true doctrine. Also, that he useth busily to propound, and urge to the utmost such sophisms, as may involve and encumber the Truth; and, as for assoiling [*solving*] them, never to attempt it, but rather to leave them in their full strength, that they may stick in the minds of his readers. So that it manifestly appeareth, that his intent was cunningly to make way for the secret instilling of the impious heresies of *Socinus* and others: and that he, under pretence of inquiring, doth bestir himself to seduce others. And for amends, he hath, though to no purpose, endeavoured for the hiding his said sleights, to daub them over with divers vain distinctions, frivolous excuses, wretched shifts, and juggling dissimulations.

And therefore, that not only this his dissolute license in Skeptical questioning of the principal heads of the Christian religion, his slippery, doubtful, and winding manner of teaching is pernicious to God's Church, ill befitting such high and sacred matter, and in that regard most unworthy an orthodox teacher; but more especially, that his doctrine itself concerning many very weighty points, is in no wise to be tolerated in Reformed Churches and Schools, but to be thence banished and rooted out, with detestation, as being contrary both to the word of God, and to the Confessions of the Reformed Churches, impious, blasphemous, and many ways contumelious against the Majesty and truth of God.

But as for *Conradus Vorstius* himself, who as yet hath abated no whit of his errors, and hath obstinately contemned the admonitions, and judgments of Reformed Princes, Doctors, Universities, and Churches, not caring to make any due reparation of that scandal, which by his Books he hath raised, the *Synod* declareth him to be altogether unworthy the function, and name of an Orthodox Professor, and Doctor.

Lastly, this Synod doth earnestly, and fervently intreat the Illustrious and mighty LL. *the Estates General*, that they would be pleased by their authority, quickly to take away this scandal from the Reformed Churches; and withal to take order that the Belgic Churches be no longer infected with this spot, and with such Heresies, and blasphemous opinions; and that for the effecting hereof the writings of this *Vorstius*, and of other the like, may with all possible caution be suppressed. And withal prayeth unto God, more and more to keep, and establish the Reformed Churches in peace, and in the profession of Orthodox Doctrine, against such profane Heresies, and contentions, and confusions, arising out of them: and mercifully to enlighten, and bring back into the way of truth, the said *Conradus Vorstius*, and all others, that wander with him, that the Church may rejoice, rather for their conversion, than their confusion.

Concluded, and pronounced in the National Synod of Dort,
May 4. 14 1619.

This we testify,

Johannes Bogermannus, President

Jacobus Rolandus, Hermannus Faukelius, Assistants

Sebastianus Damman, Festus Hommius, Scribes

Of the Synod.

THE DECREE

The Illustrius and mighty LL. the Estates of Holland, and West-Friesland, having in their Assembly viewed the Sentence pronounced by the National Synod of Dort, against the person, writings, and books of Conradus Vorstius, Doctour of Divinity, all things duly considered; have upon fore-deliberation judged and determined, that inasmuch as he was after a peculiar manner admitted to the Professorship of the University of Leiden, it therefore belongeth most properly to themselves to determine that which is fit in his case.

Whereupon accordingly they remove the aforenamed Conrad Vorstius from his functions in the said University, and from henceforth call in his stipend there. And forasmuch as it is evident, that his remaining in these parts is hurtful, as well to the common weal, as to the Church, they banish him out of Holland, and West-Freisland, charging him to depart thence within the space of six weeks, and not to return thither upon such arbitrary penalty as shall in that case be inflicted upon him, as a troubler of the public peace; affording him notwithstanding, for the discharge of his journey, the half year's stipend, whereinto he is now entered.

Moreover they command, that special letters be dispatched to him, whereby he may be certified of these particulars, with express charge unto him to address himself to the performance hereof.

Enacted at the Hage June 27. 17 1619.
By the appointment of the Illustrius and mighty LL. the Estates of Holland and West-Friesland
Subscribed,
A. DUYCK.

LONDON
Printed by JOHN BILL.
M.DC.XIX

THE DECLARATION OF THE DECREE
Made by the Generall States of the United Netherland Provinces, Against certain Arminians, or Remonstrants, for their perpetual banishment.
Dated the 15 of July, 1619. *Stilo Novo.*

Translated out of the Dutch copy, printed at the Grauenhage by Hillebrant Jacobsz, ordinary Printer to the States.

LONDON
Printed by *Felix Kingston* for *Nathaniel Newbery*, and are to be sold at the Signe of the Starre, under Saint *Peters* Church in Cornehill, and in Popes-head Alley, 1619.

THE DECLARATION OF THE DECREE
Made by the Generall States of the United *Netherland* Provinces, against *certain Arminians or Remonstrants, for their* perpetual banishment.
Dated the 15 of July, 1619. *Stilo Novo.*

The States General of the United Netherland Provinces, having well, wisely and deliberately considered of, and consulted upon, the several reports as well by the Secular, as the Ecclesiastical Deputies of the National Synod from time to time made unto them, concerning the behaviours and actions of the thirteen persons here under named, as also of the two others that joined with them, during the continuance of the said Synod; and specially upon the two Decrees, bearing date the one, the first, the other, the eighteenth of January last past, made and pronounced against them in the name of the said General States; as also upon the sentence pronounced by the said Synod upon the sixth of May against them, and by the said General States ratified and approved. In like sort having well considered upon their answer made unto certain propositions and interrogatories, which by the said General States upon the 25 of May, in the Town of Dort were propounded unto them: together with their answers by word of mouth upon the third, and again this present 19 day of July, by every one of them severally and apart reiterated, before the assembly of the said General States, touching an Act made for the dismissing of them from their Spiritual functions: and appointing them to live as Secular persons, the contents thereof being, that they should faithfully promise, with upright hearts and consciences, from thenceforth, not to intrude themselves, nor once take upon them to deal in any spiritual affairs, services or ceremonies, as Ministers, Teachers, or Officers of the Church, nor to meddle with the same in any manner whatsoever, openly or secretly, directly or indirectly, neither within nor without the Towns, Villages, and places of the United Provinces, nor the resorts thereof, but to behave themselves civilly, honestly, peaceably and modestly, as particular and Secular subjects ought to do, and to govern themselves orderly according to the commandments and precepts of the superior power, and to be obedient thereunto. To the which Decree and sentence so pronounced, every one of them severally for himself (*Henricus Leo* only excepted, who thereunto willingly subscribed) made answer, that concerning their consciences, they were not bound to be obedient unto the said General States, for that thereby (as they said) they were prohibited and restrained from participating their counsels and opinions concerning their doctrine to and amongst the assemblies of those that are of their opinions in their religion, which might be required of them, ought of the public Churches. Their said answer and declaration being wholly conformable to the hurtful, dangerous and pernicious complot and league made by some of their confederates, in form and manner of an Anti-synod, without the consent and commission of the lawful Magistrates, in the Town of Rotterdam, upon the fifth of March last past: whereunto they (or at the least, the most part of them) upon the 25 of May aforesaid, did confess and acknowledge to be consenting, and acquainted therewithal; in such manner, that by their aforesaid proceedings, as also by all other their actions and comportments, it evidently appeareth, and is most manifest, that they stubbornly and wilfully continue in their insupportable stiff-neckedness, and disobedience against their lawful Magistrates, and that the same their proceedings tend only, to a further disquietness and trouble of the minds and wills of the good and faithful inhabitants and subjects of the said United Provinces, as also to the perturbation not only of politic government, but of the religion which they, by all the means they could devise hitherto have sought, and yet seek to with-draw and separate from the general and upright feeling, and consent of the true Reformed Churches, both within and without the land. Therefore the said General States have declared, and by these presents do declare the said persons and their adherents aforesaid, to be hereby discharged, and wholly dismissed of, and from all Spiritual functions, offices and duties usually performed in the Church, and merely made Secular persons, and that they whose names are hereafter recited, be banished.

The Names of such principal Remonstrants, as are perpetually banished by this Decree

Bernerus Wezekius, Henricus Hollingerus, Simon Episcopius, Iohannes Arnoldi Corinus, Bernardus Dwinglonius, Eduardus Popius, Theophilus Rickwaerdius, Phillippus Pinakerus, Diminicus Sampa,

Isaacus Frederici, Samuel Neranus, Thomas Goswinus, Assuerus Mathisius, and *Carolus Niellius.*

These by certain Officers thereunto appointed, shall be brought forth of prison, and conducted out of the United Provinces, and the Sovereign Resorts of the same, never to come nor return into them again; before, and until such time as it shall sufficiently appear, and be made manifest unto the said General States, that they are ready and willing to be conformable, and to sign unto the aforesaid Act; and shall have obtained the said General States warrant and license so to do, upon pain for doing the contrary, from that time forward (as perturbers of the common peace and quietness of the land) to be punished according to the discretions of the General States.

Given at the Assembly of the said General States in the Graven Hage, the 15 of July, 1619. *Stilo Novo.* Signed, *A. Ploos.* And underneath, by order from the General-States, Signed *C. Aerssen.*